Best-selling
One-story
Home Plans

SUNSET BOOKS

Vice President, General Manager:
  Richard A. Smeby
Vice President, Editorial Director:
  Bob Doyle
Production Director:
  Lory Day
Director of Operations:
  Rosann Sutherland
Art Director:
  Vasken Guiragossian

Cover: Pictured is plan KLF-9710 on page
192. Photograph by Mark Englund.

10 9 8 7 6 5 4 3 2
First printing May 2001
Copyright 2001 Sunset Publishing Corporation,
Menlo Park, CA 94025.
First Edition.
Library of Congress Catalog Card Number:
2001090573
ISBN: 0-376-01196-3
Printed in the United States.

For additional copies of Best-selling One-story Home
Plans or any other Sunset book, call 1-800-526-5111
or visit our web site at **www.sunsetbooks.com**.

CUSTOMIZING YOUR HOME

Custom homes once were the product of a lengthy and often expensive design process requiring numerous meetings between owner, builder and architect.

Now there's an alternative, a faster and less expensive means of acquiring a custom home. Instead of starting from scratch, you can select any stock plan from this book and change it to suit your particular needs and preferences. The stock plans within this book are well-conceived, time tested and are offered at an affordable price.

Before placing your order for blueprints, consider the type and number of changes you plan to make to your selected design. If you wish to make only minor design changes such as moving interior walls, changing window styles, or altering foundation types, we strongly recommend that you purchase reproducible masters. These master drawings, which contain the same information as the blueprints, are easy to modify because they are printed on erasable, reproducible paper. Also, by starting with complete detailed drawings, and planning out your changes, the cost of having a design professional or your builder make the required drawing changes will be considerably less. After the master drawings are altered, multiple blueprint copies can be made from them.

If you anticipate making a lot of changes (such as moving exterior walls and changing the overall appearance of the house) we suggest you discuss your changes with a local architect or design professional. With major design changes, it is always advisable to seek out the assistance of an architect or design professional to review and redraw that portion of the blueprints affected by your changes. Some structural changes may even be necessary to comply with local codes. Your area may have specific requirements for snow loads, energy codes, wind loads, and so forth. Those types of changes are likely to require the services of an architect or engineer.

Typically, having a set of reproducible masters altered by a local designer can cost as little as a couple hundred dollars, whereas redrawing a portion or all of the blueprints can cost considerably more depending on the extent of the changes. Like most projects, the more planning and preparation you can do on your own, the greater the savings to you.

Finally, you'll have the satisfaction of knowing that your custom home is uniquely and exclusively yours.

WHAT'S THE RIGHT PLAN FOR YOU?

As you look through this book, many of the homes will appear to be just what you're looking for. But are they? Consider some of the following questions for determining your dream home.

One way to find out if the home is right for you is to carefully analyze what you want in a home. Though it's not always easy, it's an important first step because of the investment you are about to make and the satisfaction and enjoyment you will receive from building your dream home.

For most people, budget is the most crucial element in narrowing the choices. Generally, the size or square footage of living area in a home establishes the cost of a new home.

After you have determined the size of the home you desire, you must choose a specific style.

So, your next task is to consider the type of home you want. Should it be traditional, contemporary or vacation style? If yours is an infill lot in an existing neighborhood, is the design compatible with the existing architecture? If not, will the subdivision permit you to build the design of your choice.

And what about the site itself? Site topography and size is a consideration of floor plan development. For example, if the lot is shallow in depth, a sprawling ranch may be the ideal design. If the lot is narrow, you may want to consider a narrow lot design allowing you to maximize the site space. Also, slopes (both gentle and steep) will affect the home design you select. If you want the look of a one-story ranch but need a multi-level design, an atrium ranch may be the perfect style in this instance.

Next there is the issue of orientation, that is, the direction you want the house to face. Considering the north-south or east-west orientation of the site itself, will the plan you choose allow you to take advantage of the sun's warmth in winter? Perhaps choosing a plan with many windows will help warm the inside with natural sunlight.

The tough part is choosing the floor plan that will best satisfy your needs and lifestyle. To a large extent, that depends on where you are in life – just starting out, whether you have toddlers or teenagers or if you're an "empty nester" and/or retiree. By categorizing this book into sections, it will be easier to locate specific styles based on your lifestyle needs.

For those just starting out, sections *Up to 1,799 Sq. Ft.* and *1,800 Sq. Ft. And Up* may be most useful. Since square footage is usually based on budget, these two sections offer an array of styles all within specific square footage parameters. An *Atrium Ranch* may be ideal for those with teenagers. This style usually features living areas for recreation and relaxation on the lower level and bedrooms on the main level for more privacy. While, the family with toddlers will need bedrooms near each other for convenience and an enclosed staircase for safety reasons. The *Retirement* plans generally include two bedrooms with the option to convert a third bedroom into an office or den. Some may be looking for a more relaxed, cozier feel to their home, the *Cottage* plans offer this style. *Vacation* homes usually include many windows for sweeping rear views of seaside, lakeside, mountains or wooded backdrops. For those of you with lot restrictions, we offer *Narrow Lot* plans with a maximum width of 50 feet.

Experts in the field suggest that the best way to determine your needs is to begin by listing everything you like and dislike about your current home. Next, think about the components of the home. Do you want, or need, both a living room and family room? How many bedrooms, full baths, and/or storage areas do you need? And don't forget about space for hobbies, an office, workshop or laundry.

When you have completed your wish list, think about how you want your home to function. In architectural terms, think about spatial relationships and circulation. In other words, consider the traffic flow and convenience of rooms to each other. From the entry foyer to living, sleeping and food preparation areas, how well does the home you selected work.

As you can see, deciding what you want in your dream home, where you want it, and how you want it to look is thought provoking and time consuming. Consider all the questions addressed in this article to help determine your needs, as well as referring to the seven sections in this book for direction in correctly matching your lifestyle.

Although we've only scratched the surface, we've tried to present key considerations that will help guide you in selecting the home plan that's right for you.

Dramatic Windowed Dining Room

Total Living Area:	**2,003 sq. ft.**
Blueprint Price Code:	**D**
Garage:	528 sq. ft.
Front porch:	67 sq. ft.
Screened porch:	195 sq. ft.

FEATURES

- Octagonal dining room with tray ceiling and deck overlook

- L-shaped island kitchen serves living and dining rooms

- Master bedroom boasts luxury bath and walk-in closet

- Living room features columns, elegant fireplace and 10' ceiling

- 3 bedrooms, 2 baths, 2-car garage

- Basement foundation

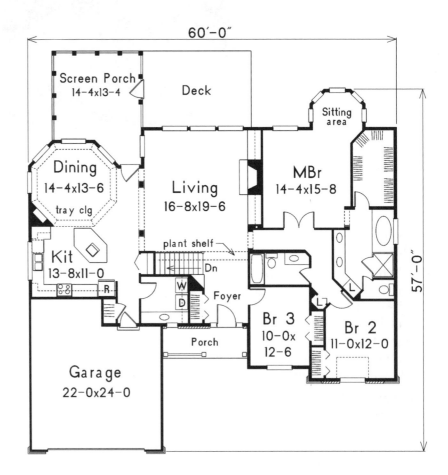

Plan 567-0348

Mark Englund/HomeStyles

Better by Design

- For the family that values an easygoing lifestyle, but also wants to impress friends with a beautiful home, this Southern-style design fits the bill.
- Hanging baskets dripping with vibrant flowers will dress up the front porch.
- Inside, handsome columns lend a look of distinction to the formal dining room, the ideal spot for classy meals. After dinner, guests can drift into the living room to continue their conversation. Plant shelves above display lush florals and greenery for all to admire.
- Casual meals have a place of their own in the kitchen and breakfast nook. While Mom and Dad prepare dinner in the kitchen, they can chat with the kids doing homework in the nook.
- Across the home, the master suite's sitting room provides an oasis of peace and quiet. The handy wet bar there puts you steps closer to that first cup of morning coffee, while a skylight lets sunshine pour in. Two more skylights in the bath brighten this space as well.

Plan 567-J-9320

Bedrooms: 3+	Baths: 2½
Living Area:	
Main floor	2,348 sq. ft.
Total Living Area:	**2,348 sq. ft.**
Future upper floor	860 sq. ft.
Standard basement	2,348 sq. ft.
Garage	579 sq. ft.
Exterior Wall Framing:	2x4

Foundation Options:

Standard basement

Crawlspace

Slab

(Please specify foundation type when ordering.)

BLUEPRINT PRICE CODE:	C

NOTE:
The above photographed home may have been modified by the homeowner. Please refer to floor plan and/or drawn elevation shown for actual blueprint details.

UPPER FLOOR

Future 21-8~12-0

Open to Below

Future 13-5~12-0

Balcony

Future 35-5~11-4

MAIN FLOOR

70-10

65-4

Patio

Garage 24-6~21-2

M.Bath 16-2~16-1 12-0 vaulted clg

Sitting Rm. 12-10~9-8 9-0 clg

Porch 20-2~10-0

Master Bedroom 16-2~15-3 9-0 clg

Living 18-0~17-2 20-0 vaulted clg

Laun

Kitchen 17-0~11-8 9-0 clg

Bedroom 11-3~14-3 9-0 clg

Bedroom 11-7~12-3 10-0 clg

Foyer 10-0 clg

Dining 14-0~12-6 10-0 clg

Breakfast 11-3~10-0 9-0 clg

Porch 36-0~8-2

Plan 567-J-9320

Classic Ranch

- With decorative brick quoins, a columned porch and stylish dormers, the exterior of this classic one-story provides an interesting blend of Early American and European design.
- Just off the foyer, the bayed formal dining room is enhanced by a gorgeous stepped ceiling.
- The spacious Great Room, separated from the dining room by a columned arch, features a stepped ceiling, a handy built-in media center and a striking fireplace. Lovely French doors lead to a big backyard patio.
- The breakfast room, which shares an eating bar with the kitchen, boasts an airy ceiling. French doors access a sunny rear porch.
- The master bedroom has a tray ceiling, a bright bay window and a walk-in closet. The master bath features a whirlpool tub in a bayed nook and a separate shower.
- The front-facing bedroom is enhanced by a vaulted area over an arched transom window.

VIEW INTO GREAT ROOM

Plan 567-HAX-93304

Bedrooms: 3	Baths: 2
Living Area:	
Main floor	1,860 sq. ft.
Total Living Area:	**1,860 sq. ft.**
Standard basement	1,860 sq. ft.
Garage	434 sq. ft.
Exterior Wall Framing:	2x4

Foundation Options:

Standard basement
Crawlspace
Slab
(Please specify foundation type when ordering.)

BLUEPRINT PRICE CODE: B

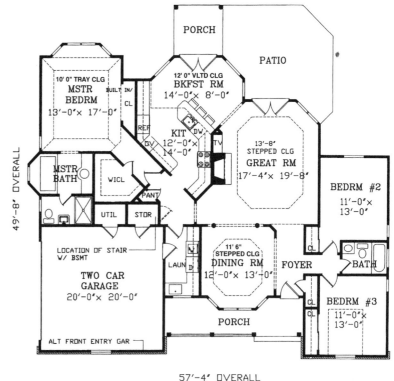

MAIN FLOOR

Plan 567-HAX-93304

Wonderful Detailing

- The wonderfully detailed front porch, with its graceful arches, columns and railings, gives this home a character all its own. Dormer windows and arched transoms further accentuate the porch.
- The floor plan features a central living room with a 10-ft.-high ceiling and a fireplace framed by French doors. These doors open to a covered porch or a sun room, and a sheltered deck beyond.
- Just off the living room, the island kitchen and breakfast area provide a spacious place for family or guests. The nearby formal dining room has arched transom windows and a 10-ft. ceiling, as does the bedroom off the foyer. All of the remaining rooms have 9-ft. ceilings.
- The unusual master suite includes a window alcove, access to the porch and a fantastic bath with a garden tub.
- A huge utility room, a storage area off the garage and a 1,000-sq.-ft. attic space are other bonuses of this design.

Plan 567-J-90019

Bedrooms: 3	Baths: 2½
Living Area:	
Main floor	2,410 sq. ft.
Total Living Area:	**2,410 sq. ft.**
Standard basement	2,410 sq. ft.
Garage	512 sq. ft.
Storage	86 sq. ft.
Exterior Wall Framing:	2x4
Foundation Options:	
Standard basement	
Crawlspace	
Slab	
(Please specify foundation type when ordering.)	
BLUEPRINT PRICE CODE:	C

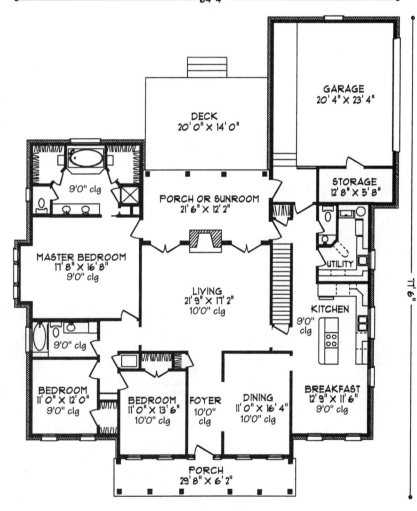

MAIN FLOOR

Plan 567-J-90019

Appealing Ranch Has Attractive Front Dormers

Total Living Area:	1,642 sq. ft.
Blueprint Price Code:	B
Garage:	520 sq. ft.
Front porch:	32 sq. ft.

FEATURES

- Walk-through kitchen boasts vaulted ceiling and corner sink overlooking family room

- Vaulted family room features cozy fireplace and access to rear patio

- Master bedroom includes sloped ceiling, walk-in closet and private bath

- 3 bedrooms, 2 baths, 2-car garage

- Basement foundation, drawings also include slab and crawl space foundations

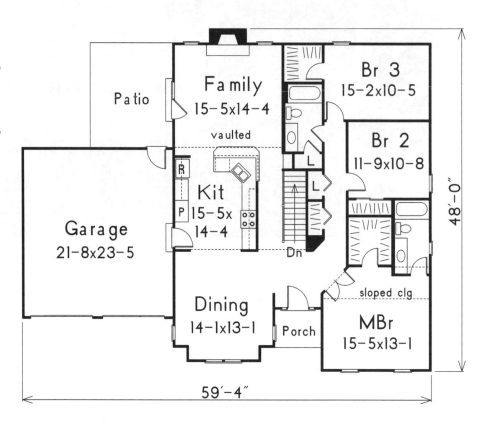

Plan 567-0282

TO ORDER BLUEPRINTS USE THE FORM ON PAGE 256 OR CALL **TOLL-FREE 1-800-367-7667**

Summer Home Or Year-Round

Total Living Area:	1,403 sq. ft.
Blueprint Price Code:	**A**
Drive-under garage:	513 sq. ft.
Front porch:	28 sq. ft.

FEATURES

- Impressive living areas for modest-sized home

- Special master/hall bath linen storage, step-up tub and lots of window light

- Spacious closets everywhere you look

- 3 bedrooms, 2 baths, 2-car drive under garage and second bath on lower floor

- Basement foundation

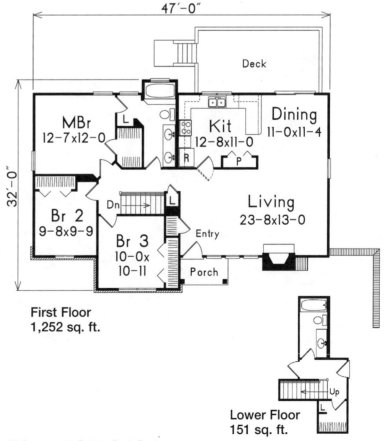

First Floor
1,252 sq. ft.

Lower Floor
151 sq. ft.

Plan 567-0484

Distinctive Ranch Has A Larger Look

Total Living Area: 1,360 sq. ft.
Blueprint Price Code: A
Garage: 430 sq. ft.

FEATURES

- Double-gabled front facade frames large windows

- Entry area is open to vaulted great room, fireplace and rear deck creating an open feel

- Vaulted ceiling and large windows add openness to kitchen/breakfast room

- Convenient den convertible to third bedroom

- Plan easily adapts to crawl space or slab construction, with the utilities replacing the stairs

- 3 bedrooms, 2 baths, 2-car garage

- Basement foundation

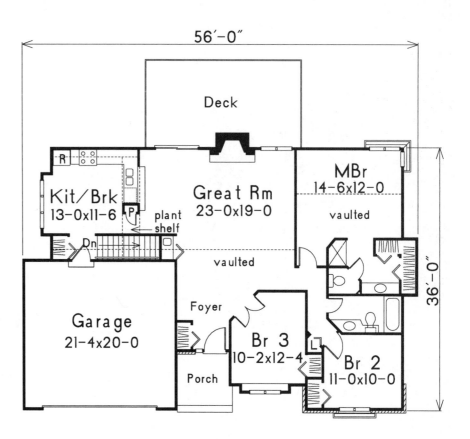

Plan 567-0105

Flexible Design Is Popular

Total Living Area:	**1,440 sq. ft.**
Blueprint Price Code:	**A**
Garage:	550 sq. ft.
Front porch:	90 sq. ft.
Back porch:	144 sq. ft.

FEATURES

- Open floor plan with access to covered porches in front and back
- Lots of linen, pantry and closet space throughout
- Laundry/mud room between kitchen and garage is a convenient feature
- 2 bedrooms, 2 baths
- Basement foundation

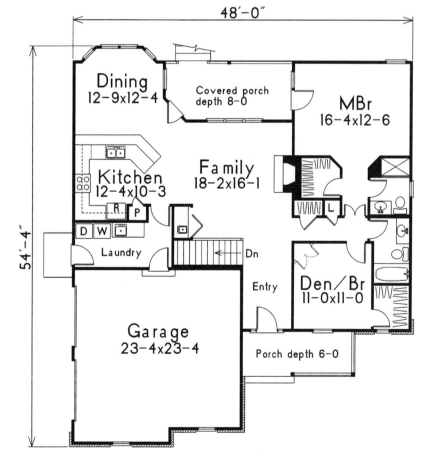

Plan 567-0769

Quality Details Inside and Out

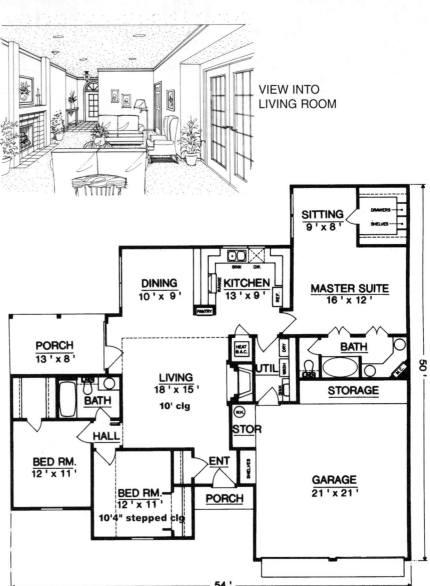

VIEW INTO
LIVING ROOM

- A sparkling stucco finish, an eye-catching roofline and elegant window treatments hint at the quality features found inside this exquisite home.
- The airy entry opens to a large, central living room, which is embellished with a 10-ft. ceiling and a dramatic fireplace.
- The living room flows into a nice-sized dining area. A covered side porch expands the entertaining area.
- A functional eating bar and pantry are featured in the adjoining U-shaped kitchen. The nearby hallway to the garage neatly stores a washer, a dryer and a laundry sink.
- Secluded to the back of the home is a private master suite with a romantic sitting area and a large walk-in closet. The master bath offers dual sinks and an exciting oval tub.
- Two secondary bedrooms and another bath are located on the other side of the living room and entry.

Plan 567-E-1435

Bedrooms: 3	Baths: 2
Living Area:	
Main floor	1,442 sq. ft.
Total Living Area:	**1,442 sq. ft.**
Garage and storage	516 sq. ft.
Exterior Wall Framing:	2x4
Foundation Options:	
Crawlspace	
Slab	
(Please specify foundation type when ordering.)	
BLUEPRINT PRICE CODE:	A

MAIN FLOOR

SITTING
9' x 8'

DINING
10' x 9'

KITCHEN
13' x 9'

MASTER SUITE
16' x 12'

PORCH
13' x 8'

BATH

LIVING
18' x 15'
10' clg

UTIL

BATH

STORAGE

HALL

STOR

BED RM.
12' x 11'

ENT

GARAGE
21' x 21'

BED RM.
12' x 11'
10'4" stepped clg

PORCH

50'

54'

Plan 567-E-1435

Friendly Country Charm

- An inviting front porch welcomes you to this friendly one-story home.
- The porch opens to a spacious central living room with a warm fireplace and functional built-in storage shelves.
- The bay window of the adjoining dining room allows a view of the backyard.

The dining area also enjoys an eating bar provided by the adjacent walk-through kitchen.
- The nice-sized kitchen also has a windowed sink and easy access to the laundry room and carport.
- Three bedrooms and two baths occupy the sleeping wing. The oversized master bedroom features a lovely boxed-out window, two walk-in closets and a private bath. The secondary bedrooms share the second full bath.

Plan 567-J-8692

Bedrooms: 3	Baths: 2
Living Area:	
Main floor	1,633 sq. ft.
Total Living Area:	**1,633 sq. ft.**
Standard basement	1,633 sq. ft.
Carport	380 sq. ft.
Exterior Wall Framing:	2x4

Foundation Options:
Standard basement
Crawlspace
Slab
(Please specify foundation type when ordering.)

BLUEPRINT PRICE CODE:	B

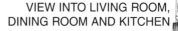

VIEW INTO LIVING ROOM, DINING ROOM AND KITCHEN

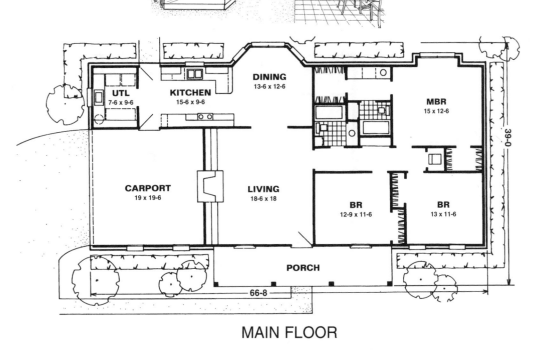

MAIN FLOOR

Plan 567-J-8692

Luxurious Master Suite

- The inviting facade of this gorgeous one-story design boasts a sheltered porch, symmetrical architecture and elegant window treatments.
- Inside, beautiful arched openings frame the living room, which features a dramatic fireplace and a wet bar that is open to the deluxe kitchen.
- The roomy kitchen is highlighted by an island cooktop, a built-in desk and a snack bar that faces the bayed eating area and the covered back porch.
- Isolated to the rear of the home, the master suite is a romantic retreat, offering an intimate sitting area and a luxurious bath. Entered through elegant double doors, the private bath showcases a skylighted corner tub, a separate shower, his-and-hers vanities, and a huge walk-in closet.
- The two remaining bedrooms have walk-in closets and share a hall bath.

Plan 567-E-2106

Bedrooms: 3	Baths: 2
Living Area:	
Main floor	2,177 sq. ft.
Total Living Area:	**2,177 sq. ft.**
Standard basement	2,177 sq. ft.
Garage	484 sq. ft.
Storage	86 sq. ft.
Exterior Wall Framing:	2x4

Foundation Options:

Standard basement

Crawlspace

Slab

(Please specify foundation type when ordering.)

BLUEPRINT PRICE CODE:	C

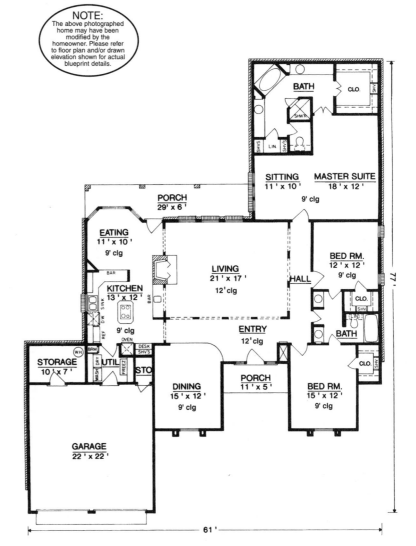

Mark Englund/HomeStyles

MAIN FLOOR

Plan 567-E-2106

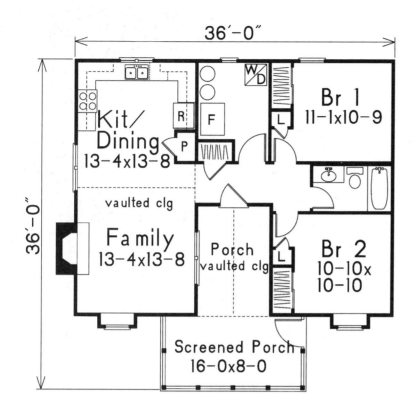

36'-0"

Kit/Dining
13-4x13-8

Br 1
11-1x10-9

vaulted clg

Family
13-4x13-8

Porch
vaulted clg

Br 2
10-10x
10-10

36'-0"

Screened Porch
16-0x8-0

Excellent For Weekend Entertaining

Total Living Area:	924 sq. ft.
Blueprint Price Code:	AA
Screened porch:	224 sq. ft.

FEATURES

- Box bay window seats brighten interior while enhancing front facade

- Spacious kitchen with lots of cabinet space and large pantry

- T-shaped covered porch is screened in for added enjoyment

- Plenty of closet space throughout with linen closets in both bedrooms

- 2 bedrooms, 1 bath

- Slab foundation

Plan 567-0697

Compact Ranch
An Ideal Starter
Home

Total Living Area:	988 sq. ft.
Blueprint Price Code:	**AA**
Garage:	400 sq. ft.
Front entry:	21 sq. ft.

FEATURES

- Great room features corner fire-place

- Vaulted ceiling and corner windows add space and light in great room

- Eat-in kitchen with vaulted ceiling accesses deck for outdoor living

- Master bedroom features separate vanity and private access to the bathroom

- 2 bedrooms, 1 bath, 2-car garage

- Basement foundation

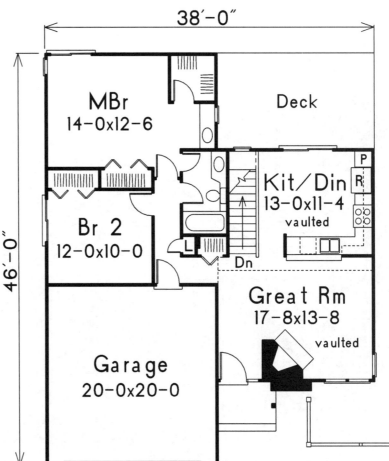

Plan 567-0273

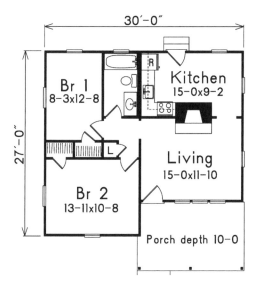

Perfect Outdoor Getaway

Total Living Area:	**733 sq. ft.**
Blueprint Price Code:	**AAA**
Front Porch:	**150 sq. ft.**

FEATURES

- Bedrooms separate from kitchen and living area for privacy
- Centrally located bathroom is easily accessible
- 2 bedrooms, 1 bath
- Pier foundation

Plan 567-N131

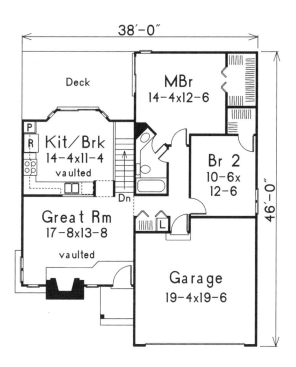

Breakfast Bay Area Opens To Deck

Total Living Area:	**1,020 sq. ft.**
Blueprint Price Code:	**AA**
Garage:	417 sq. ft.
Front porch:	26 sq. ft.

FEATURES

- Kitchen features open stairs, pass-through to great room, pantry and deck access
- Great room with vaulted ceiling and fireplace
- 2 bedrooms, 1 bath, 2-car garage
- Basement foundation

Plan 567-0274

Half-Round Highlights And Gables Unify The Facade

Total Living Area:	1,847 sq. ft.
Blueprint Price Code:	C
Garage:	452 sq. ft.
Front porch:	36 sq. ft.

FEATURES

- Kitchen includes island cooktop and sunny breakfast area

- Master suite features vaulted ceilings and skylighted bath with large tub, separate shower and walk-in closet

- Service bar eases entertaining in vaulted dining and living rooms

- Family room, complete with corner fireplace, accesses outdoor patio

- 3 bedrooms, 2 baths, 2-car garage

- Slab foundation

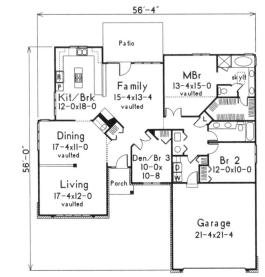

Plan 567-0280

Convenient Center Entry

Total Living Area:	1,134 sq. ft.
Blueprint Price Code:	AA
Garage:	462 sq. ft.
Front entry:	36 sq. ft.

FEATURES

- Kitchen has plenty of counter space, island work top, large pantry and access to the garage

- Living room features vaulted ceiling, fireplace and access to an expansive patio

- Bedroom 1 has large walk-in closet

- Convenient linen closet in the hall

- 2 bedrooms, 1 bath, 2-car garage

- Basement foundation

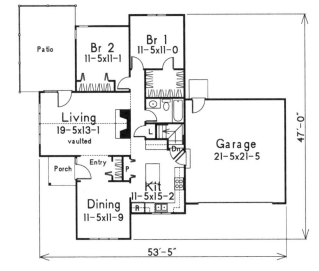

Plan 567-0500

One-Story with Impact

- Striking gables, a brick facade and an elegant sidelighted entry give this one-story plenty of impact.
- The impressive interior spaces begin with a raised ceiling in the foyer. To the left of the foyer, decorative columns and a large picture window grace the formal dining room.
- The wonderful living spaces center around a huge family room, which features a vaulted ceiling and another pair of columns that separate it from the hall. A stunning fireplace is framed by a window and a beautiful French door.
- The open kitchen and breakfast area features a built-in desk, a pantry closet and a pass-through above the sink.
- An elegant tray ceiling is featured in the master suite, which also boasts a vaulted bath with a garden spa tub, a separate shower, a big walk-in closet and an attractive plant shelf.

Plan 567-HFB-1553

Bedrooms: 3	Baths: 2
Living Area:	
Main floor	1,553 sq. ft.
Total Living Area:	**1,553 sq. ft.**
Daylight basement	1,553 sq. ft.
Garage and storage	410 sq. ft.
Exterior Wall Framing:	2x4

Foundation Options:
Daylight basement
Crawlspace
Slab
(Please specify foundation type when ordering.)

BLUEPRINT PRICE CODE:	B

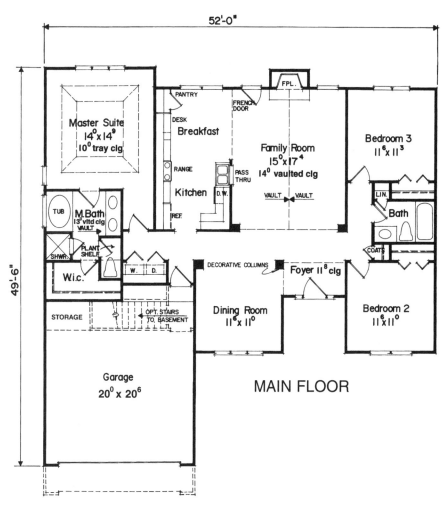

MAIN FLOOR

Plan 567-HFB-1553

Designed For Handicap Access

Total Living Area:	1,578 sq. ft.
Blueprint Price Code:	B
Garage:	390 sq. ft.
Front porch:	70 sq. ft.
Back porch:	100 sq. ft.

FEATURES

- Plenty of closet, linen and storage space
- Covered porches in the front and rear of home add charm to this design
- Open floor plan with unique angled layout
- 3 bedroom, 2 baths, 2-car garage
- Basement foundation

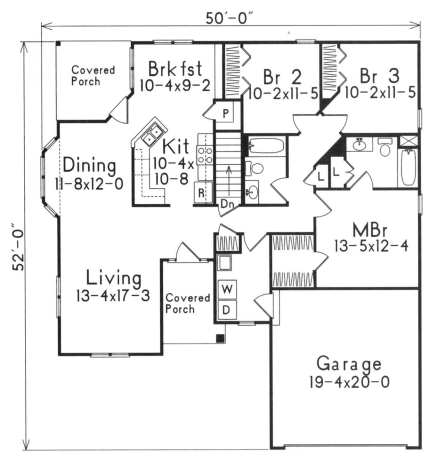

Plan 567-0741

Cozy Ranch Home

Total Living Area:	**950 sq. ft.**
Blueprint Price Code:	**AA**
Garage:	236 sq. ft.
Front entry:	18 sq. ft.

FEATURES

- Deck adjacent to kitchen/breakfast area for outdoor dining

- Great room features vaulted ceiling, open stairway and fireplace

- Secondary bedroom with sloped ceiling and box bay window can convert to den

- Master bedroom with walk-in closet, plant shelf, separate dressing area and private access to bath

- Kitchen has garage access

- 2 bedrooms, 1 bath, 1-car garage

- Basement foundation

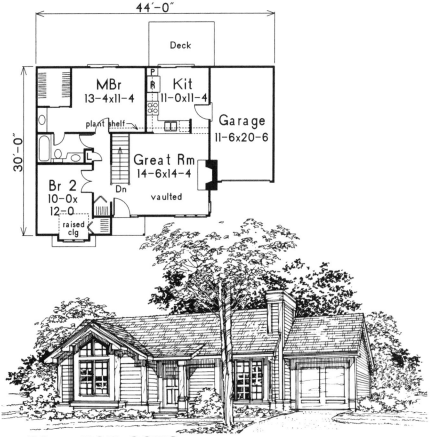

Plan 567-0276

Front Porch And Center Gable Add Style To This Ranch

Total Living Area:	**988 sq. ft.**
Blueprint Price Code:	**AA**
Garage:	306 sq. ft.
Front porch:	56 sq. ft.

FEATURES

- Pleasant covered porch entry

- Living, dining and kitchen areas are combined to maximize space

- Entry has convenient coat closet

- Laundry closet is located adjacent to bedrooms

- 3 bedrooms, 1 bath, 1-car garage

- Basement foundation, drawings also include crawl space foundation

Plan 567-0195

Meant to Be

- One glimpse of the beautiful front view will tempt you, and a good look at the stunning rear view will convince you, that this home was meant to be yours!
- The vaulted, skylighted entry ushers you to the Great Room, which vaults up to 10 feet and features an inspiring fireplace. Sliding glass doors provide speedy access to an incredible wraparound deck.
- Equipped for any sudden culinary inspirations, the well-planned kitchen features its own pantry. You'll also appreciate its close proximity to the garage

when it's time to unload those heavy grocery bags.
- The master suite will take your breath away, with its walk-in closet and a secluded bath with dual sinks and a spa tub. Exquisite French doors create easy access to the deck.
- Imagine magical nights on the deck. With the kids at Grandma's house, put on some soft music and use the deck as your own private dance floor!
- A vast unfinished area in the daylight basement promises excitement. Turn it into a game room for the ultimate in entertainment! A fourth bedroom and a full bath complete the space.

Plan 567-SUN-1310-C

Bedrooms: 3+	Baths: 3½
Living Area:	
Main floor	1,636 sq. ft.
Daylight basement (finished)	315 sq. ft.
Total Living Area:	**1,951 sq. ft.**
Daylight basement (unfinished)	730 sq. ft.
Garage	759 sq. ft.
Exterior Wall Framing:	2x6
Foundation Options:	
Daylight basement	
Crawlspace	
Slab	

(Please specify foundation type when ordering.)

BLUEPRINT PRICE CODE:	B

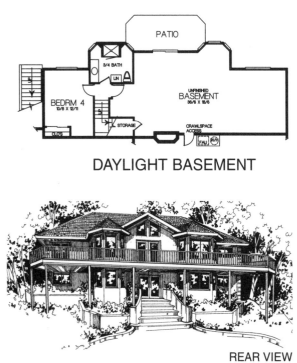

DAYLIGHT BASEMENT

REAR VIEW

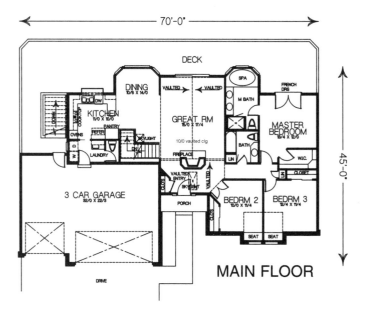

MAIN FLOOR

Plan 567-SUN-1310-C

Spacious Floor Plan

Total Living Area:	**1,558 sq. ft.**
Blueprint Price Code:	**B**
Garage:	440 sq. ft.
Front porch:	42 sq. ft.

FEATURES

- Spacious utility room located conveniently between garage and kitchen/dining area

- Bedrooms separated off main living areas by hallway add privacy

- Living area with fireplace and vaulted ceilings opens to kitchen and dining area

- Master suite enhanced with large bay window, walk-in closet and private bath

- 3 bedrooms, 2 baths, 2-car garage

- Basement foundation

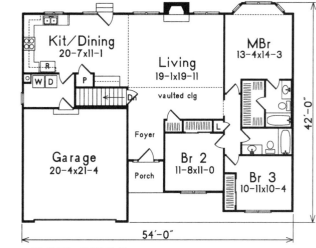

Plan 567-0702

Open Ranch Design

Total Living Area:	**1,630 sq. ft.**
Blueprint Price Code:	**B**
Garage:	450 sq. ft.
Front porch:	14 sq. ft.

FEATURES

- Crisp facade and full windows front and back offer open viewing

- Wrap-around rear deck is accessible from breakfast room, dining room and master bedroom

- Vaulted ceiling in living room and master bedroom

- Sitting area and large walk-in closet complement master bath

- 3 bedrooms, 2 baths, 2-car garage

- Basement foundation

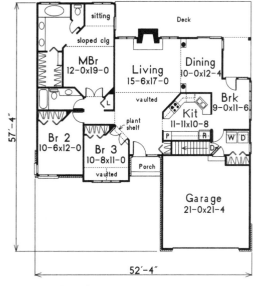

Plan 567-0161

All in One!

- This plan puts today's most luxurious home-design features into one attractive, economical package.
- The covered front porch and the gabled roofline, accented by an arched window and a round louver vent, give the exterior a homey yet stylish appeal.
- Just inside the front door, the raised ceiling offers an impressive greeting. The spacious living room is flooded with light through a central skylight and a pair of French doors that frame the smart fireplace.
- The living room flows into the nice-sized dining room, also with a raised ceiling. The adjoining kitchen offers a handy laundry closet, lots of counter space and a sunny dinette that opens to an expansive backyard terrace.
- The bedroom wing includes a wonderful master suite with a sizable sleeping room and an adjacent dressing area with two closets. Glass blocks above the dual-sink vanity in the master bath let in light yet maintain privacy. A whirlpool tub completes the suite.
- The larger of the two remaining bedrooms boasts a high ceiling and an arched window.

Plan 567-HHFL-1680-FL

Bedrooms: 3	Baths: 2
Living Area:	
Main floor	1,367 sq. ft.
Total Living Area:	**1,367 sq. ft.**
Standard basement	1,367 sq. ft.
Garage	431 sq. ft.
Exterior Wall Framing:	2x6

Foundation Options:

Standard basement
Slab
(Please specify foundation type when ordering.)

BLUEPRINT PRICE CODE:	A

VIEW INTO LIVING ROOM

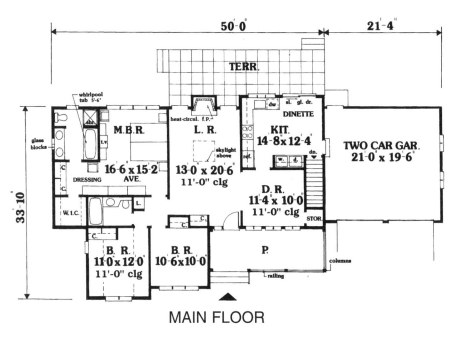

MAIN FLOOR

Plan 567-HHFL-1680-FL

Vaulted Ceiling Adds Spaciousness

Total Living Area:	990 sq. ft.
Blueprint Price Code:	**AA**
Front porch:	378 sq. ft.

FEATURES

- Wrap-around porch on two sides of this home
- Private and efficiently designed
- Space for efficiency washer and dryer unit for convenience
- 2 bedrooms, 1 bath
- Crawl space foundation

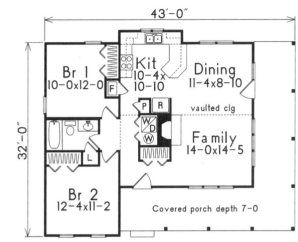

Plan 567-0766

Perfect Home For A Small Family

Total Living Area:	864 sq. ft.
Blueprint Price Code:	**AAA**
Front porch:	56 sq. ft.

FEATURES

- L-shaped kitchen with convenient pantry is adjacent to dining area
- Easy access to laundry area, linen closet and storage closet
- Both bedrooms include ample closet space
- 2 bedrooms, 1 bath
- Crawl space foundation, drawings also include basement and slab foundations

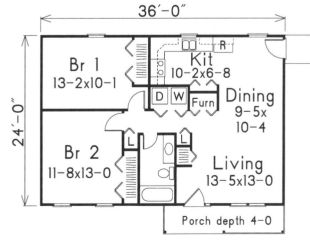

Plan 567-0502

Casual Exterior, Filled With Great Features

Total Living Area:	**1,958 sq. ft.**
Blueprint Price Code:	**C**
Garage:	473 sq. ft.
Front entry:	24 sq. ft.
Rear porch:	174 sq. ft.

FEATURES

- Large wrap-around kitchen opens to a bright cheerful breakfast area with access to large covered deck and open stairway to basement

- Kitchen nestled between the dining and breakfast rooms

- Master suite includes large walk-in closet, double-bowl vanity, garden tub and separate shower

- Foyer features attractive plant shelves and opens into living room that includes attractive central fireplace

- 3 bedrooms, 2 baths, 2-car garage

- Basement foundation

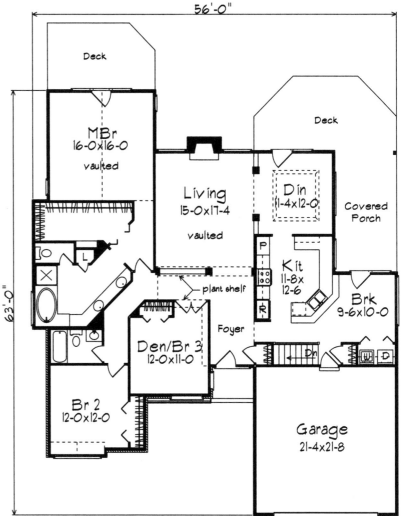

Plan 567-0387

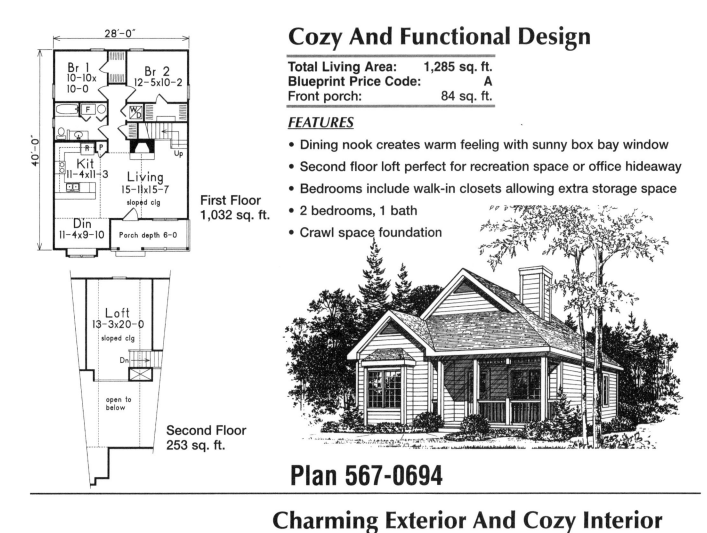

Cozy And Functional Design

Total Living Area:	1,285 sq. ft.
Blueprint Price Code:	A
Front porch:	84 sq. ft.

FEATURES

- Dining nook creates warm feeling with sunny box bay window
- Second floor loft perfect for recreation space or office hideaway
- Bedrooms include walk-in closets allowing extra storage space
- 2 bedrooms, 1 bath
- Crawl space foundation

Br 1 10-10x 10-0

Br 2 12-5x10-2

Kit 11-4x11-3

Living 15-11x15-7 sloped clg

Din 11-4x9-10

Porch depth 6-0

Up

28'-0"
40'-0"

First Floor 1,032 sq. ft.

Loft 13-3x20-0 sloped clg

Dn

open to below

Second Floor 253 sq. ft.

Plan 567-0694

Charming Exterior And Cozy Interior

Total Living Area:	1,127 sq. ft.
Blueprint Price Code:	AA
Garage:	380 sq. ft.
Front entry:	30 sq. ft.
Rear deck:	153 sq. ft.

FEATURES

- Master suite with walk-in closets, deck access and private bath
- Great room with vaulted ceiling, fireplace and sliding doors to deck
- Ideal home for a narrow lot
- 2 bedrooms, 2 baths, 2-car garage
- Basement foundation

34'-8"
52'-0"

Covered Deck

MBr 12-0x14-0 vaulted

Great Rm 14-4x22-6 vaulted

Br 2 11-0x11-6

Dn

Dining plant shelf

Garage 19-4x19-4

Kit 9-0x 12-0

Plan 567-0277

Great Design For Vacation Home Or Year-Round Living

Total Living Area:	**990 sq. ft.**
Blueprint Price Code:	**AA**
Front porch:	154 sq. ft.

FEATURES

- Covered front porch adds charming feel
- Vaulted ceiling in kitchen, family and dining rooms creates a spacious feel
- Large linen, pantry and storage closets throughout
- 2 bedrooms, 1 bath
- Crawl space foundation

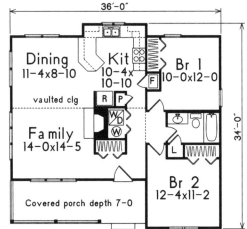

Plan 567-0767

Ideal Home or Retirement Retreat

Total Living Area:	**1,013 sq. ft.**
Blueprint Price Code:	**AA**

FEATURES

- Vaulted ceiling in both family room and kitchen with dining area just beyond breakfast bar
- Plant shelf above kitchen is a special feature
- Oversized utility room has space for full-size washer and dryer
- Hall bath is centrally located with easy access from both bedrooms
- 2 bedrooms, 1 bath
- Slab foundation

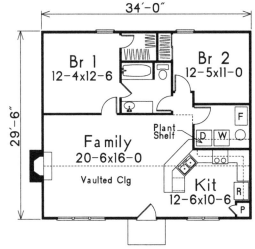

Plan 567-0693

An A-Frame For Every Environment

Total Living Area:	**618 sq. ft.**
Blueprint Price Code:	**AAA**
Covered Deck:	120 sq. ft.

FEATURES

- Memorable family events are certain to be enjoyed on this fabulous partially covered sundeck

- Equally impressive is the living area with its cathedral ceiling and exposed rafters

- A kitchenette, bedroom and bath conclude the first floor with a delightful sleeping loft above bedroom and bath

- 1 bedroom, 1 bath

- Pier foundation

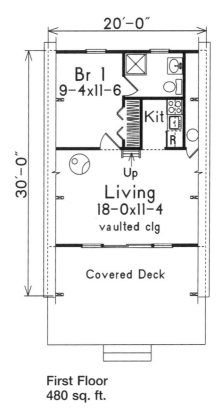

20'-0"

30'-0"

Br 1
9-4x11-6

Kit

R

Up

Living
18-0x11-4
vaulted clg

Covered Deck

First Floor
480 sq. ft.

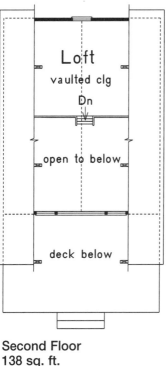

Loft
vaulted clg

Dn

open to below

deck below

Second Floor
138 sq. ft.

Plan 567-N145

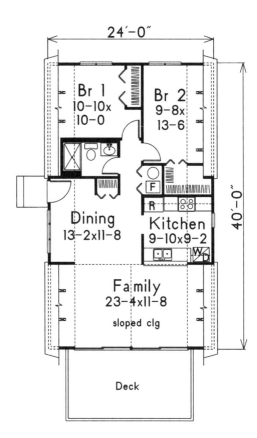

24'-0"

Br 1
10-10x
10-0

Br 2
9-8x
13-6

40'-0"

Dining
13-2x11-8

F
R

Kitchen
9-10x9-2

W/D

Family
23-4x11-8
sloped clg

Deck

Vacation Paradise

Total Living Area:	960 sq. ft.
Blueprint Price Code:	AA

FEATURES

- Interesting roof and wood beams overhang a generous-sized deck
- Family/living area is vaulted and opens to dining and kitchen
- Pullman-style kitchen has been skillfully designed
- Two bedrooms and hall bath are located at the rear of home
- 2 bedrooms, 1 bath
- Crawl space foundation

Plan 567-N005

24'-0"

Br 1
10-6x12-8

Br 2
10-1x10-4

**First Floor
1,080 sq. ft.**

46'-0"

L

Br 3
9-1x11-0

R

Kit
10-6x9-4

Dining
9-5x6-10

vaulted clg

Dn

Living
17-4x14-2

Deck

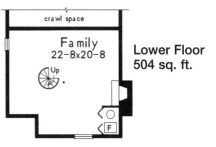

crawl space

Family
22-8x20-8

**Lower Floor
504 sq. ft.**

Up

F

Nestled Oasis Romances The Sun

Total Living Area:	1,584 sq. ft.
Blueprint Price Code:	B

FEATURES

- Vaulted living/dining room features stone fireplace, ascending spiral stair and separate vestibule with guest closet
- Master bedroom adjoins a full bath
- 3 bedrooms, 2 baths
- Basement foundation, drawings also include crawl space and slab foundations

Plan 567-N130

Comfortable Vacation Retreat

Total Living Area:	**1,073 sq. ft.**
Blueprint Price Code:	**AA**
Front porch:	105 sq. ft.
Screened porch:	84 sq. ft.

FEATURES

- Home includes lovely covered front porch and a screened porch off dining area
- Attractive box window brightens kitchen
- Space for efficiency washer and dryer located conveniently between bedrooms
- Family room spotlighted by fireplace with flanking bookshelves and spacious vaulted ceiling
- 2 bedrooms, 1 bath
- Crawl space foundation

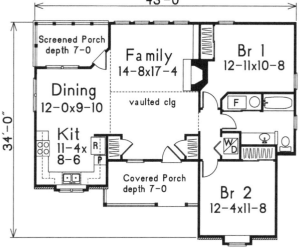

Plan 567-0699

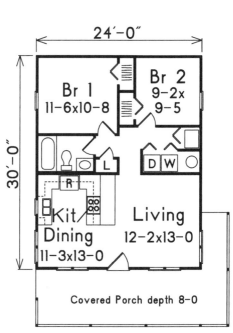

Covered Porch depth 8-0

Designed For Comfort And Utility

Total Living Area:	**720 sq. ft.**
Blueprint Price Code:	**AAA**
Front porch:	124 sq. ft.

FEATURES

- Abundant windows in living and dining rooms provide sunlight
- Secluded laundry area with handy storage closet
- U-shaped kitchen with large breakfast bar opens into living area
- Large covered deck offers plenty of outdoor living space
- 2 bedrooms, 1 bath
- Crawl space foundation, drawings also include slab foundation

Plan 567-0547

Comfortable, Open Plan

- This comfortable home defines function and style, with a sharp window wall to brighten the central living areas.
- In from the broad front deck, the living/family room boasts a fireplace, a cathedral ceiling and soaring views. The fireplace visually sets off the dining room, which extends to the backyard patio through sliding doors.
- The galley-style kitchen offers a bright sink and an abundance of counter space, with a laundry closet and carport access nearby.
- The secluded and spacious master bedroom features private deck access, a walk-in closet and a private bath.
- On the other side of the home, two good-sized secondary bedrooms share another full bath.

Plan 567-C-8160	
Bedrooms: 3	**Baths:** 2
Living Area:	
Main floor	1,669 sq. ft.
Total Living Area:	**1,669 sq. ft.**
Daylight basement	1,660 sq. ft.
Carport	413 sq. ft.
Storage	85 sq. ft.
Exterior Wall Framing:	2x4
Foundation Options:	
Daylight basement	
Crawlspace	
Slab	
(Please specify foundation type when ordering.)	
BLUEPRINT PRICE CODE:	B

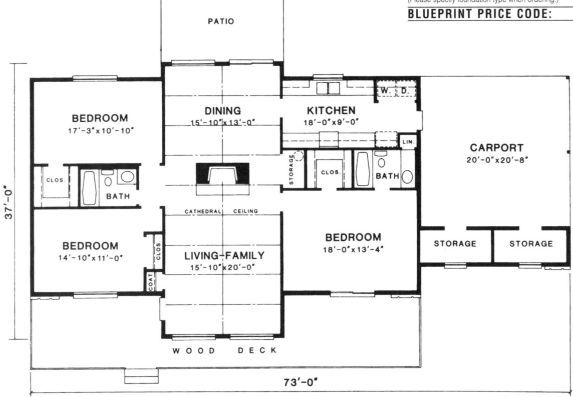

MAIN FLOOR

Plan 567-C-8160

Comfortable Ranch Design

- This affordable ranch design offers numerous amenities and is ideally structured for comfortable living, both indoors and out.
- A tiled reception hall leads into the spacious living and dining rooms, which feature a handsome brick fireplace, an 11-ft. sloped ceiling and two sets of sliding glass doors to access a lovely backyard terrace.
- The adjacent family room, designed for privacy, showcases a large boxed-out window with a built-in seat. The kitchen features an efficient U-shaped counter, an eating bar and a pantry.
- The master suite has its own terrace and private bath with a whirlpool tub.
- Two additional bedrooms share a second full bath.
- The garage has two separate storage areas—one accessible from the interior and the other from the backyard.

Plan 567-K-518-A

Bedrooms: 3	Baths: 2
Living Area:	
Main floor	1,276 sq. ft.
Total Living Area:	**1,276 sq. ft.**
Standard basement	1,247 sq. ft.
Garage and storage	579 sq. ft.
Enclosed storage	12 sq. ft.
Exterior Wall Framing:	2x4 or 2x6

Foundation Options:

Standard basement

Slab
(Please specify foundation type when ordering.)

BLUEPRINT PRICE CODE:	**A**

VIEW INTO LIVING ROOM AND DINING ROOM

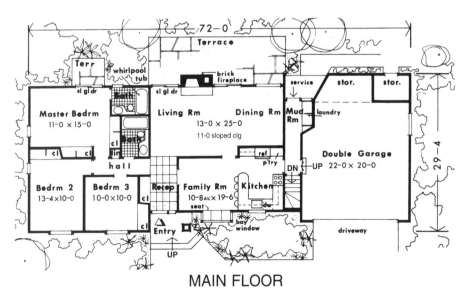

MAIN FLOOR

Plan 567-K-518-A

Corner Window Wall Dominates Design

Total Living Area:	**784 sq. ft.**
Blueprint Price Code:	**AAA**

FEATURES

- Outdoor relaxation will be enjoyed with this home's huge wrap-around wood deck

- Upon entering the spacious living area, a cozy free-standing fireplace, sloped ceiling and corner window wall catch the eye

- Charming pullman-style kitchen features pass-through peninsula to dining area

- 3 bedrooms, 1 bath

- Pier foundation

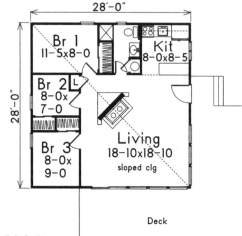

Plan 567-N087

Master Suite Spacious & Private

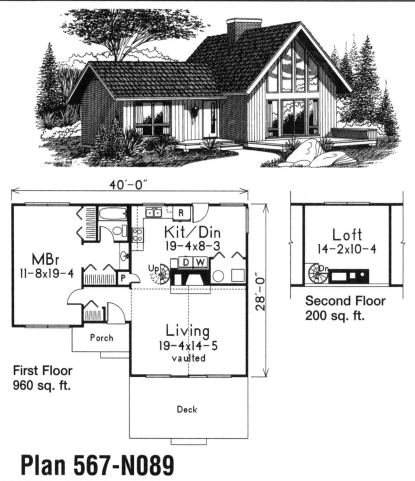

Total Living Area:	**1,160 sq. ft.**
Blueprint Price Code:	**AA**

FEATURES

- Kitchen/dining area combines with laundry area creating a functional organized area

- Spacious vaulted living area has large fireplace and is brightened by glass doors accessing large deck

- Ascend to second floor loft by spiral stairs and find a cozy hideaway

- Master suite brightened by many windows and includes private bath and double closets

- 1 bedroom, 1 bath

- Crawl space foundation

Plan 567-N089

Designed For Seclusion

Total Living Area: 624 sq. ft.
Blueprint Price Code: AAA

FEATURES

- Combine stone, vertical siding, and lots of glass; add low roof line and you have a cozy retreat

- Vaulted living area features free-standing fireplace that heats adjacent stone wall for warmth

- Efficient kitchen includes dining area and view to angular deck

- Two bedrooms share a hall bath with shower

- 2 bedrooms, 1 bath

- Pier foundation

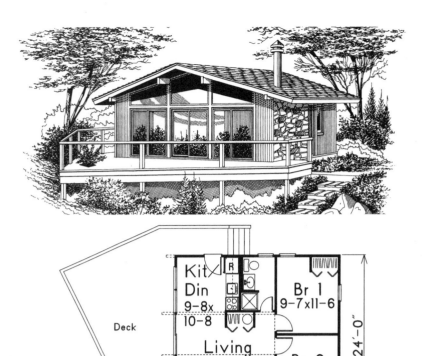

Deck

Kit
Din
9-8x
10-8

Living
15-5x12-8
sloped clg

R

Br 1
9-7x11-6

Br 2
9-7x11-6

24'-0"

26'-0"

Plan 567-N010

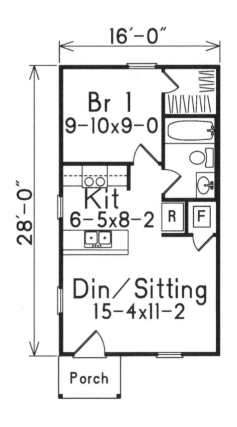

16'-0"

28'-0"

Br 1
9-10x9-0

Kit
6-5x8-2

R   F

Din/Sitting
15-4x11-2

Porch

Irresistible Retreat

Total Living Area: 448 sq. ft.
Blueprint Price Code: AAA
Front porch: 24 sq. ft.

FEATURES

- Bedroom features large walk-in closet ideal for storage

- Combined dining/living area ideal for relaxing

- Galley style kitchen is compact and efficient

- Covered porch adds to front facade

- 1 bedroom, 1 bath

- Slab foundation

Plan 567-0695

Tudor Influences Enhance This Duplex

Total Living Area:	**1,326 sq. ft.**
Blueprint Price Code:	**B**
Front porch:	312 sq. ft.

FEATURES

- See-through fireplace from living room into bedroom makes lasting impression
- Covered front porch perfect for relaxing evenings
- Galley-style kitchen is compact but well-organized for efficiency
- Each unit has 1 bedroom, 1 bath
- Slab foundation
- Duplex has 663 square feet of living space per unit

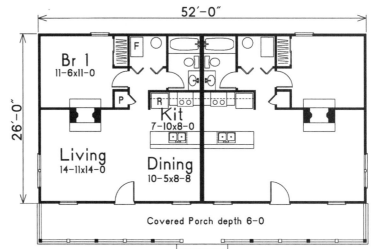

Plan 567-0704

Efficient And Open Duplex Design

Total Living Area:	**896 sq. ft.**
Blueprint Price Code:	**AAA**
Front porch:	186 sq. ft.

FEATURES

- Small cabin duplex well-suited for rental property or permanent residence
- Compact, yet convenient floor plan
- Well-organized for economical construction
- 1 bedroom, 1 bath
- Slab foundation
- Duplex has 448 square feet of living space per unit

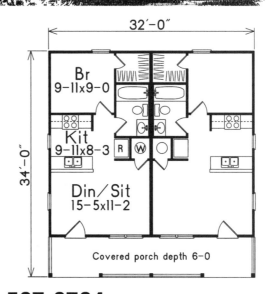

Plan 567-0764

High-Profile Contemporary

- This design does away with wasted space, putting the emphasis on quality rather than on size.
- The angled floor plan minimizes hall space and creates smooth traffic flow while adding architectural appeal. The roof framing is square, however, to allow for economical construction.
- The spectacular living and dining rooms share a 16-ft. cathedral ceiling and a fireplace. Both rooms have lots of glass overlooking an angled rear terrace.
- The dining room includes a glass-filled alcove and sliding patio doors topped by transom windows. Tall windows frame the living room fireplace and trace the slope of the ceiling.
- A pass-through joins the dining room to the combination kitchen and family room, which features a snack bar and a clerestory window.
- The sleeping wing provides a super master suite, which boasts a skylighted dressing area and a luxurious bath. The optional den, or third bedroom, shares a second full bath with another bedroom that offers a 14-ft. sloped ceiling.

Plan 567-K-688-D

Bedrooms: 2+	Baths: 2½
Living Area:	
Main floor	1,340 sq. ft.
Total Living Area:	**1,340 sq. ft.**
Standard basement	1,235 sq. ft.
Garage and storage	500 sq. ft.
Exterior Wall Framing:	2x4 or 2x6
Foundation Options:	
Standard basement	
Slab	
(Please specify foundation type when ordering.)	
BLUEPRINT PRICE CODE:	**A**

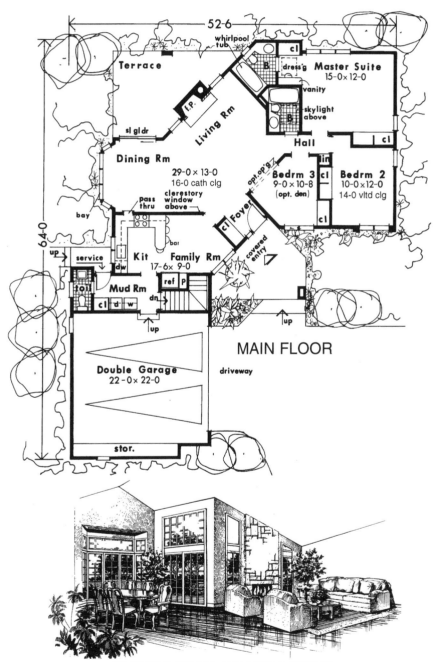

MAIN FLOOR

VIEW INTO DINING AND LIVING ROOMS

Plan 567-K-688-D

Year-Round Hideaway

Total Living Area:	416 sq. ft.
Blueprint Price Code:	AAA
Front porch:	156 sq. ft.

FEATURES

- Open floor plan creates spacious feeling
- Covered porch has rustic appeal
- Plenty of cabinetry and workspace in kitchen
- Large linen closet centrally located and close to bath
- Sleeping area, 1 bath
- Slab foundation

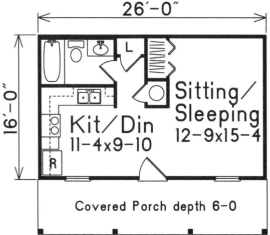

Plan 567-0700

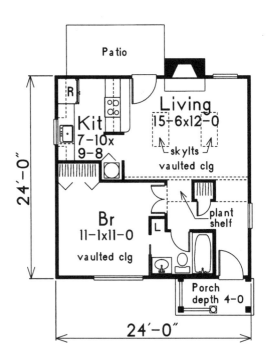

Cottage With Class

Total Living Area:	576 sq. ft.
Blueprint Price Code:	AAA
Front porch:	36 sq. ft.

FEATURES

- Perfect country retreat features vaulted living room and entry with skylights and plant shelf above
- Double-doors enter a vaulted bedroom with bath access
- Kitchen offers generous storage and pass-through breakfast bar
- 1 bedroom, 1 bath
- Crawl space foundation

Plan 567-0476

Cozy Vacation Retreat

Total Living Area: 1,391 sq. ft.
Blueprint Price Code: A

FEATURES

- Large living room with masonry fireplace features soaring vaulted ceiling

- A spiral staircase in hall leads to huge loft area overlooking living room below

- Two first floor bedrooms share a full bath

- 2 bedrooms, 1 bath

- Pier foundation, drawings also include crawl space foundation

First Floor
884 sq. ft.

Second Floor
507 sq. ft.

Plan 567-N049

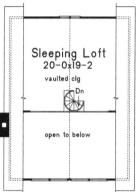

Graciously Designed Refuge

Total Living Area: 527 sq. ft.
Blueprint Price Code: AAA

FEATURES

- Cleverly arranged home has it all

- Foyer spills into the dining nook with side entry access

- An excellent kitchen offers a long breakfast bar and borders the living room with free-standing fireplace

- A cozy bedroom has a full bath just across the hall

- 1 bedroom, 1 bath

- Crawl space foundation

Plan 567-N118

Great Planning

- Great planning gives this home its smart floor plan, sharp looks and affordability.
- The raised entry steps down to a versatile Great Room with a 12-ft. vaulted ceiling and an angled fireplace.
- The galley-style kitchen hosts a breakfast nook overlooking the deck and patio. The kitchen, nook and dining area also have 12-ft. vaulted ceilings.
- The master bedroom features a boxed-out window, a walk-in closet and a 12-ft. vaulted ceiling. The master bath includes a spa tub and separate shower.
- Another full bath serves the two remaining bedrooms.

Plan 567-B-902

Bedrooms: 2+	Baths: 2
Living Area:	
Main floor	1,368 sq. ft.
Total Living Area:	**1,368 sq. ft.**
Standard basement	1,368 sq. ft.
Garage	412 sq. ft.
Exterior Wall Framing:	2x4
Foundation Options:	
Standard basement	
(Please specify foundation type when ordering.)	
BLUEPRINT PRICE CODE:	**A**

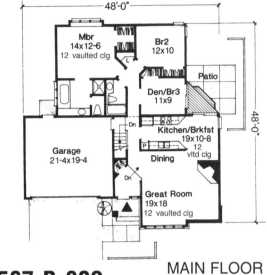

MAIN FLOOR

Plan 567-B-902

Catch the Rays!

- This passive-solar design is angled to capture as much sunlight as possible.
- Double doors at the entry open into the spacious living and dining areas.
- The formal space features a 14-ft. domed ceiling with skylights, a central fireplace and sliding glass doors leading to a glass-enclosed sun room.
- The bright eat-in kitchen merges with the den, where more sliding glass doors open to one of three backyard terraces.
- In the sleeping wing, the master bedroom boasts ample closets, a private terrace and a luxurious whirlpool bath.

Plan 567-K-534-L

Bedrooms: 3	Baths: 2
Living Area:	
Main floor	1,647 sq. ft.
Total Living Area:	**1,647 sq. ft.**
Standard basement	1,505 sq. ft.
Garage	400 sq. ft.
Exterior Wall Framing:	2x4 or 2x6
Foundation Options:	
Standard basement	
Slab	
(Please specify foundation type when ordering.)	
BLUEPRINT PRICE CODE:	**B**

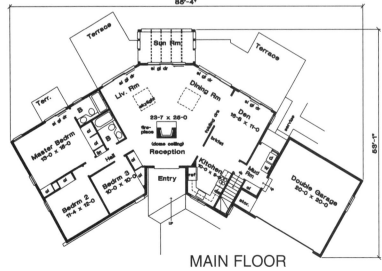

MAIN FLOOR

Plan 567-K-534-L

Trendsetting Contemporary Retreat

Total Living Area: 1,528 sq. ft.
Blueprint Price Code: B

FEATURES

- Large deck complements handsome exterior

- Family room provides a welcome space for family get-togethers and includes a sloped ceiling and access to studio/loft

- Kitchen features dining space and view to deck

- A hall bath is shared by two bedrooms on first floor which have ample closet space

- 2 bedrooms, 1 bath

- Crawl space foundation

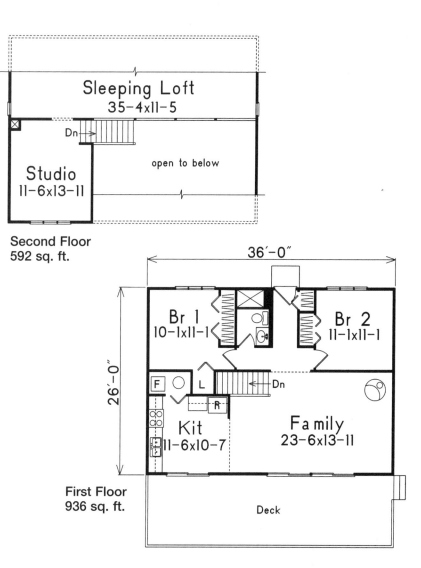

Second Floor
592 sq. ft.

Sleeping Loft
35-4x11-5

Studio
11-6x13-11

Dn   open to below

36'-0"

26'-0"

Br 1
10-1x11-1

Br 2
11-1x11-1

Kit
11-6x10-7

Family
23-6x13-11

Dn

First Floor
936 sq. ft.

Deck

Plan 567-N124

Outstanding One-Story

- This sharp one-story home has an outstanding floor plan, attractively enhanced by a stately brick facade.
- A vestibule introduces the foyer, which flows between the formal living spaces at the front of the home.
- The large living room features a 14-ft., 8-in. sloped ceiling and dramatic, high windows. The spacious dining room has easy access to the kitchen.

- The expansive family room is the focal point of the home, with a 16-ft. beamed cathedral ceiling, a slate-hearth fireplace and sliding glass doors to a backyard terrace.
- The adjoining kitchen has a snack bar and a sunny dinette framed by a curved window wall that overlooks the terrace.
- Included in the sleeping wing is a luxurious master suite with a private bath. A skylighted dressing room and a big walk-in closet are also featured.
- The two secondary bedrooms share a hall bath that has a dual-sink vanity. A half-bath is near the mud/laundry room.

Plan 567-K-278-M

Bedrooms: 3	Baths: 2½
Living Area:	
Main floor	1,803 sq. ft.
Total Living Area:	**1,803 sq. ft.**
Standard basement	1,778 sq. ft.
Garage	493 sq. ft.
Storage	58 sq. ft.
Exterior Wall Framing:	2x4 or 2x6

Foundation Options:

Standard basement
Slab
(Please specify foundation type when ordering.)

BLUEPRINT PRICE CODE:	**B**

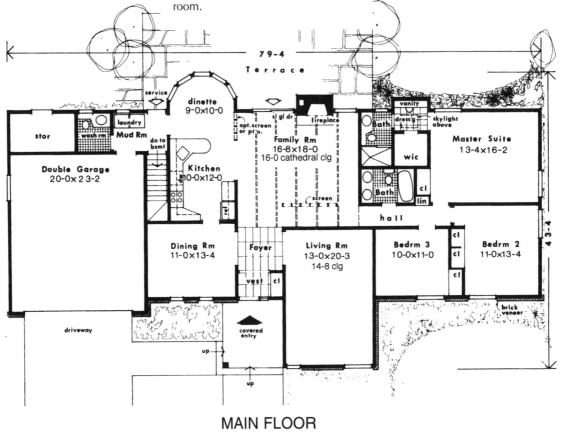

MAIN FLOOR

Plan 567-K-278-M

Small Home Is Remarkably Spacious

Total Living Area:	912 sq. ft.
Blueprint Price Code:	AA
Drive-under garage:	562 sq. ft.
Front porch:	95 sq. ft.

FEATURES

- Front porch for leisure evenings
- Dining area with bay window, open stair and pass-through kitchen creates openness
- Basement includes generous garage space, storage area, finished laundry and mechanical room
- 2 bedrooms, 1 bath, 2-car drive under garage
- Basement foundation

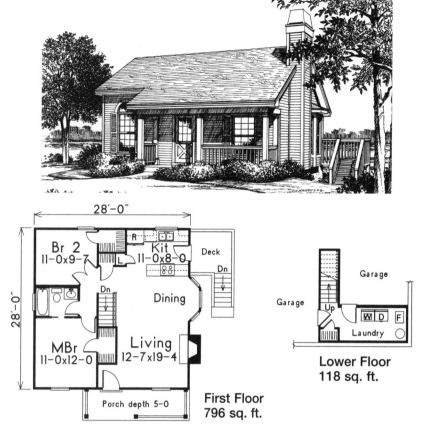

First Floor
796 sq. ft.

Lower Floor
118 sq. ft.

Plan 567-0657

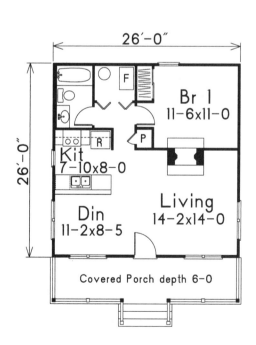

Covered Porch depth 6-0

Small And Cozy Cabin

Total Living Area:	676 sq. ft.
Blueprint Price Code:	AAA
Front porch:	156 sq. ft.

- See-through fireplace between bedroom and living area
- Combined dining/living area creates open feeling
- Full-length front covered porch perfect for enjoying the outdoors
- Additional storage available in utility room
- 1 bedroom, 1 bath
- Crawl space foundation

Plan 567-0696

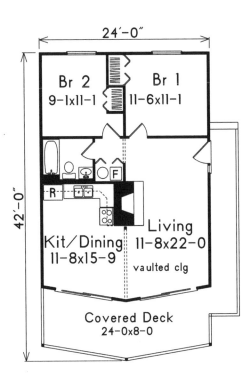

24'-0"

Br 2
9-1x11-1

Br 1
11-6x11-1

42'-0"

R

F

Kit/Dining
11-8x15-9

Living
11-8x22-0
vaulted clg

Covered Deck
24-0x8-0

Riverside Views From Covered Deck

Total Living Area:	792 sq. ft.
Blueprint Price Code:	AAA
Covered deck:	184 sq. ft.

FEATURES

- Attractive exterior features wood posts and beams, wrap-around deck with railing and glass sliding doors with transoms

- Living, dining and kitchen area enjoy sloped ceilings, cozy fireplace and views over deck

- Two bedrooms share a bath just off the hall

- 2 bedrooms, 1 bath

- Crawl space foundation, drawings also include slab foundation

Plan 567-N114

Clerestory Windows Enhance Home's Facade

Total Living Area:	1,176 sq. ft.
Blueprint Price Code:	AA

FEATURES

- Efficient kitchen offers plenty of storage, a dining area and a stylish eating bar

- A gathering space is created by the large central living room

- Closet and storage space throughout helps keep sporting equipment organized and easily accessible

- Each end of home is comprised of two bedrooms and full bath

- 4 bedrooms, 2 baths

- Crawl space foundation, drawings also include slab foundation

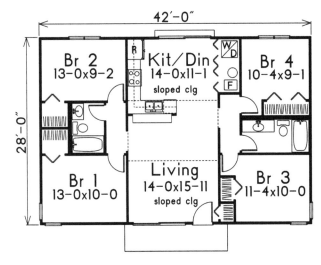

42'-0"

Br 2
13-0x9-2

R

Kit/Din
14-0x11-1
sloped clg

W
D

F

Br 4
10-4x9-1

28'-0"

Br 1
13-0x10-0

Living
14-0x15-11
sloped clg

Br 3
11-4x10-0

Plan 567-N064

Open Format For Easy Living

Total Living Area:	**2,282 sq. ft.**
Blueprint Price Code:	**D**
Detached garage:	576 sq. ft.
Front porch:	273 sq. ft.

- Living and dining rooms combine to create a large, convenient entertaining area that includes a fireplace

- Comfortable veranda allows access from secondary bedrooms

- Second floor game room overlooks foyer and includes a full bath

- Kitchen and breakfast areas are surrounded by mullioned windows

- 3 bedrooms, 3 baths, 2-car detached garage

- Slab foundation, drawings also include crawl space foundation

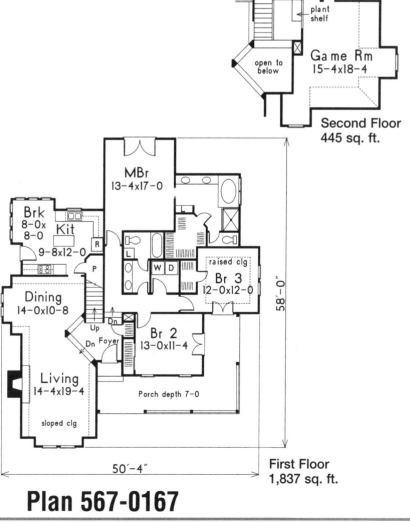

Plan 567-0167

Recessed Stone Entry Provides A Unique Accent

Total Living Area:	717 sq. ft.
Blueprint Price Code:	AAA
Front entry:	24 sq. ft.

FEATURES

- Incline ladder leads up to cozy loft area
- Living room features plenty of windows and vaulted ceiling
- U-shaped kitchen includes a small bay window at the sink
- 1 bedroom, 1 bath
- Slab foundation

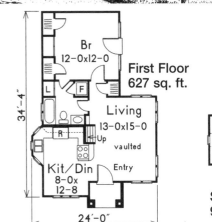

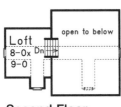

First Floor 627 sq. ft.

Br 12-0x12-0

Living 13-0x15-0 vaulted

Entry

Kit/Din 8-0x 12-8

34'-4"

24'-0"

Loft 8-0x 9-0

open to below

Second Floor 90 sq. ft.

Plan 567-0242

Sensational Cottage Retreat

Total Living Area:	647 sq. ft.
Blueprint Price Code:	AAA
Front porch:	103 sq. ft.

FEATURES

- Large vaulted room for living/sleeping with plant shelves on each end, stone fireplace and wide glass doors
- Roomy kitchen is vaulted and has a bayed dining area and fireplace
- Step down into a sunken and vaulted bath featuring a 6'-0" whirlpool tub-in-a-bay with shelves at each end for storage
- Large palladian windows adorn each end of the cottage giving a cheery atmosphere
- 1 living/sleeping room, 1 bath
- Crawl space foundation

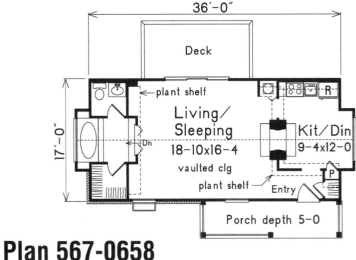

36'-0"

Deck

17'-0"

plant shelf

Living/ Sleeping 18-10x16-4 vaulted clg

plant shelf

Kit/Din 9-4x12-0

Entry

Porch depth 5-0

Plan 567-0658

Room to Spare

- You'll be amazed at the roominess of this livable, space-efficient home.
- The fanciful facade showcases dormers up top, keystones, a bay window and a beautiful wraparound porch.
- Inside, the spacious living room offers a cozy fireplace, as well as a windowed overlook and access to a rear porch.
- Both dining spaces feature bay windows and are bridged by the kitchen, with its corner sink and useful snack bar. A nearby utility room offers a sizable pantry and storage space.

- The posh master suite sits on the opposite end of the home, where it enjoys privacy among other exciting amenities. A boxed-out window and a stepped ceiling mark the bedroom, while a corner tub, a separate shower and dual walk-in closets grace the private bath, accessed by double doors.
- Two additional bedrooms in the home's sleeping wing bask in spaciousness while sharing a full hall bath.
- An attached, two-car garage and storage is located off the utility room and provides passage to the rear porch.

Plan 567-RD-1948	
Bedrooms: 3	**Baths:** 2
Living Area:	
Main floor	1,948 sq. ft.
Total Living Area:	**1,948 sq. ft.**
Garage and storage	581 sq. ft.
Exterior Wall Framing:	2x4
Foundation Options:	
Crawlspace	
Slab	
(Please specify foundation type when ordering.)	
BLUEPRINT PRICE CODE:	B

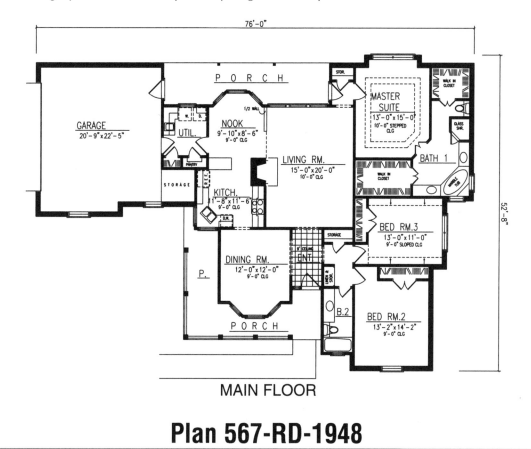

MAIN FLOOR

Plan 567-RD-1948

Flexible Layout For Various Uses

Total Living Area: 1,143 sq. ft.
Blueprint Price Code: AA
Front porch: 164 sq. ft.

FEATURES

- Enormous stone fireplace in family room adds warmth and character

- Spacious kitchen with breakfast bar overlooks family room

- Separate dining area great for entertaining

- Vaulted family room and kitchen create open atmosphere

- 2 bedrooms, 1 bath

- Crawl space foundation

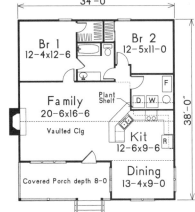

Plan 567-0698

Country Cottage Offers Vaulted Living Space

Total Living Area: 962 sq. ft.
Blueprint Price Code: AA
Front porch: 272 sq. ft.

FEATURES

- Both the kitchen and family rooms share warmth from the fireplace

- Charming facade features covered porch on one side, screened porch on the other and attractive planter boxes

- L-shaped kitchen boasts convenient pantry

- 2 bedrooms, 1 bath

- Crawl space foundation

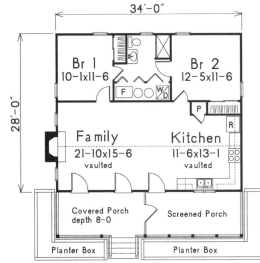

Plan 567-0651

Rural Roots

- Lovely shuttered windows and cozy railed porches show off this home's inviting rural roots.
- Step from the foyer into the vast, welcoming family room. With a high ceiling and a corner fireplace, this room greets guests with comfort.
- Off the well-appointed kitchen, a bayed dining room enjoys ample sunlight, making it the perfect spot for mealtime.
- The secluded master suite boasts a private bath with his-and-hers walk-in closets and a handy dual-sink vanity.
- Two additional bedrooms provide plenty of space for kids or guests. The full hall bath is nearby.

Plan 567-L-1772

Bedrooms: 3	Baths: 2
Living Area:	
Main floor	1,772 sq. ft.
Total Living Area:	**1,772 sq. ft.**
Detached garage	576 sq. ft.
Exterior Wall Framing:	2x4
Foundation Options:	
Slab	
(Please specify foundation type when ordering.)	
BLUEPRINT PRICE CODE:	**B**

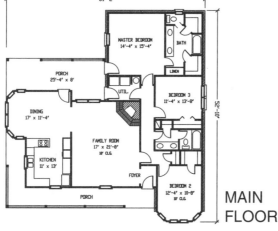

MAIN FLOOR

Plan 567-L-1772

Tried and True

- Time-tested traditional touches abound in this appealing country-style home.
- The central living room anchors the home, with a cozy fireplace flanked by built-in bookshelves serving as the focal-point for family gatherings.
- An octagonal dining room borders the sunny kitchen, where you'll find a handy pantry and plenty of space.
- The master suite includes a private bath with his-and-hers walk-in closets.
- The kids get their space, too—a pair of good-sized bedrooms with ample closet space share a nearby hall bath.

Plan 567-RD-1418

Bedrooms: 3	Baths: 2
Living Area:	
Main floor	1,418 sq. ft.
Total Living Area:	**1,418 sq. ft.**
Garage and storage	464 sq. ft.
Exterior Wall Framing:	2x4
Foundation Options:	
Crawlspace or slab	
(Please specify foundation type when ordering.)	
BLUEPRINT PRICE CODE:	**A**

MAIN FLOOR

Plan 567-RD-1418

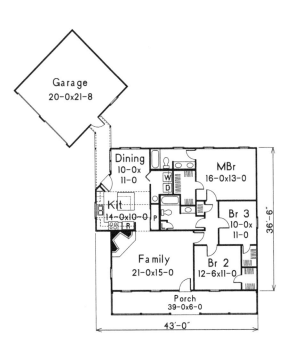

Garage
20-0x21-8

Dining
10-0x
11-0

MBr
16-0x13-0

W
D

Kit
14~0x10~0

Br 3
10-0x
11-0

P

Family
21-0x15-0

Br 2
12-6x11-0

Porch
39-0x6-0

36'-6"

43'-0"

Rambling Country Bungalow

Total Living Area:	1,475 sq. ft.
Blueprint Price Code:	B
Garage:	440 sq. ft.
Front porch:	234 sq. ft.

FEATURES

- Family room features a high ceiling and corner fireplace
- Hallway leads to bedrooms all with large walk-in closets
- Covered breezeway joins main house and garage
- 3 bedrooms, 2 baths, 2-car side entry garage
- Slab foundation, drawings also include crawl space foundation

Plan 567-0203

Rustic Design With Modern Features

Total Living Area:	1,000 sq. ft.
Blueprint Price Code:	AA
Front porch:	168 sq. ft.

FEATURES

- Large mud room with separate covered porch entrance
- Full-length covered front porch
- Bedrooms on opposite sides of the home for privacy
- Vaulted ceiling creates an open and spacious feeling
- 2 bedrooms, 1 bath
- Crawl space foundation

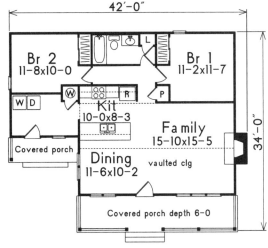

42'-0"

Br 2
11-8x10-0

Br 1
11-2x11-7

W D

W

R

P

Kit
10-0x8-3

Family
15-10x15-5
vaulted clg

Covered porch

Dining
11-6x10-2

34'-0"

Covered porch depth 6-0

Plan 567-0765

Sheltered Entrance Opens To Stylish Features

Total Living Area:	**1,661 sq. ft.**
Blueprint Price Code:	**B**
Garage:	450 sq. ft.
Front porch:	70 sq. ft.
Rear porch:	56 sq. ft.

- Large open foyer with angled wall arrangement and high ceiling adds to spacious living room

- Dining/kitchen area has impressive cathedral ceiling and French door allowing access to the patio

- Utility room conveniently located near kitchen

- Secluded master bedroom has large walk-in closets, unique brick wall arrangement and 10' ceiling

- 3 bedrooms, 2 baths, 2-car garage

- Slab foundation

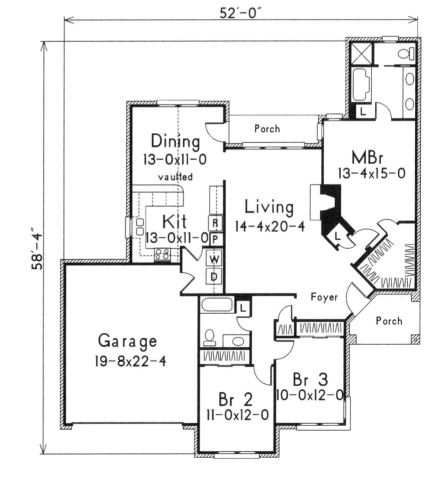

Plan 567-0216

Covered Porch Is Focal Point Of Entry

Total Living Area:	1,595 sq. ft.
Blueprint Price Code:	B
Garage:	441 sq. ft.
Front porch:	264 sq. ft.

FEATURES

- Dining room has convenient built-in desk and provides access to the outdoors

- L-shaped kitchen area features island cooktop

- Family room has high ceiling and a fireplace

- Private master suite includes large walk-in closet and bath with separate tub and shower units

- 3 bedrooms, 2 baths, 2-car side entry garage

- Slab foundation, drawings also include crawl space foundation

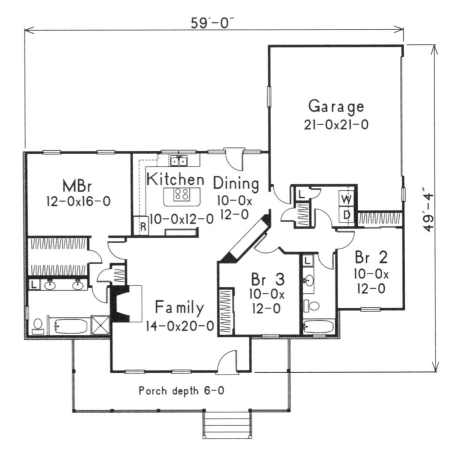

Plan 567-0293

TO ORDER BLUEPRINTS USE THE FORM ON PAGE 256 OR CALL **TOLL-FREE 1-800-367-7667**

Masterful Plan

- This home features a master suite so luxurious it deserves its own wing.
- A large entry hall invites visitors into a spacious, skylighted living room. The adjacent dining room offers a built-in china hutch.
- The kitchen features an angled snack bar and a bayed eating area.
- The kitchen, eating area, living room and dining room are all heightened by 12-ft. ceilings.
- The luxurious master suite is secluded from the two smaller bedrooms at the opposite side of the home.

Plan 567-E-1811

Bedrooms: 3	Baths: 2
Living Area:	
Main floor	1,800 sq. ft.
Total Living Area:	**1,800 sq. ft.**
Garage and storage	634 sq. ft.
Exterior Wall Framing:	2x6
Foundation Options:	
Crawlspace, slab	
(Please specify foundation type when ordering.)	
BLUEPRINT PRICE CODE:	**B**

MAIN FLOOR

Plan 567-E-1811

Great Country Getaway!

- A shady front porch and shuttered windows grace the exterior of this country cottage.
- Natural light illuminates the bayed dining room. A French door accesses the backyard.
- The U-shaped kitchen provides service to the dining room and a pass-through snack counter makes it easy to offer refreshment to guests in the living area.
- Blueprints include plans for two more bedrooms with walk-in closets.

Plan 567-L-186-EXA

Bedrooms: 1+	Baths: 1
Living Area:	
Main floor (1 bedroom)	829 sq. ft.
Main floor (3 bedrooms)	1,184 sq. ft.
Total Living Area:	**1,184 sq. ft.**
Exterior Wall Framing:	2x4
Foundation Options:	
Slab	
(Please specify foundation type when ordering.)	
BLUEPRINT PRICE CODE:	**A**

OPT. ADDITION TO MAIN FLOOR

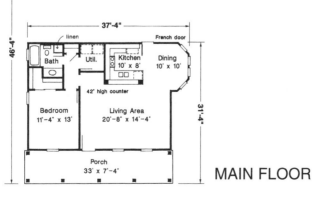

MAIN FLOOR

Plan 567-L-186-EXA

View from the Veranda

- Welcome the new day from the kitchen's cheerful morning room and spend long summer evenings relaxing on the veranda.
- Past the foyer, a living room with a gas fireplace flows into the dining room, which offers sliding glass doors to a covered deck. These spaces will easily fulfill all your entertainment needs.

- The kitchen boasts an island workstation and a large walk-in pantry.
- A conveniently located laundry room is accessible from both the kitchen's morning room and the home's side-entry, two-car garage.
- The bedroom wing features a lavish master suite, where a French door leads out to a private covered deck. The master bath offers a luxurious jetted tub and a separate shower. A walk-in closet adds to the suite's amenities.
- Two additional bedrooms and a full bath complete this wing.

Plan 567-WH-9518	
Bedrooms: 3	Baths: 2
Living Area:	
Main floor	1,463 sq. ft.
Total Living Area:	**1,463 sq. ft.**
Standard basement	1,447 sq. ft.
Garage	407 sq. ft.
Exterior Wall Framing:	2x6
Foundation Options:	
Standard basement	
(Please specify foundation type when ordering.)	
BLUEPRINT PRICE CODE:	A

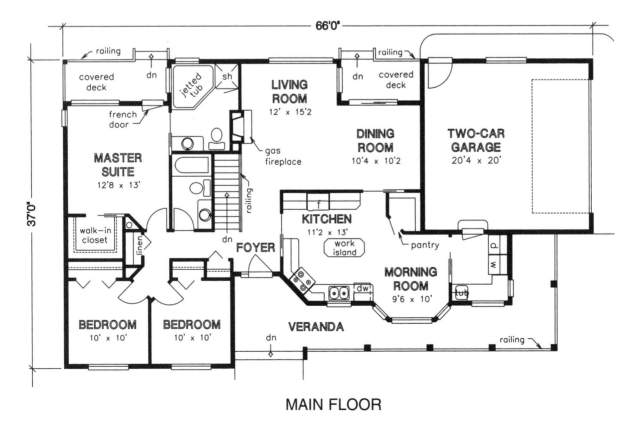

MAIN FLOOR

Plan 567-WH-9518

TO ORDER BLUEPRINTS USE THE FORM ON PAGE 256 OR CALL **TOLL-FREE 1-800-367-7667**

Big on Features

- This charming home puts the emphasis on quality rather than size, providing luxury features at a modest price.
- The detailed front porch leads to the living room, where a railing creates a hallway effect while using very little space. The living room's 10-ft. tray ceiling adds dimension and elegance.
- Straight ahead, the dining room has a 9-ft. stepped ceiling, a convenient laundry closet and access to the patio. The adjoining kitchen offers an island counter and a pantry closet.

Plan 567-HAX-91316

Bedrooms: 3	Baths: 2
Living Area:	
Main floor	1,097 sq. ft.
Total Living Area:	**1,097 sq. ft.**
Basement	1,097 sq. ft.
Garage	461 sq. ft.
Exterior Wall Framing:	2x4
Foundation Options:	

Daylight basement, standard basement, slab
(Please specify foundation type when ordering.)

BLUEPRINT PRICE CODE:	**A**

MAIN FLOOR

Plan 567-HAX-91316

Relax and Enjoy

- The pretty porch that stretches along the front of this traditional home provides plenty of room for relaxation.
- Inside, handsome columns introduce the living room and the dining room, on either side of the foyer.
- The Great Room, the breakfast nook and the kitchen flow together to create a casual spot for family fun.
- A stepped ceiling crowns the master suite, while a bay window serves as a sitting area.

Plan 567-HAX-5374

Bedrooms: 3	Baths: 2
Living Area:	
Main floor	1,902 sq. ft.
Total Living Area:	**1,902 sq. ft.**
Standard basement	1,925 sq. ft.
Garage and storage	534 sq. ft.
Utility room	18 sq. ft.
Exterior Wall Framing:	2x4
Foundation Options:	

Standard basement
Crawlspace
Slab
(Please specify foundation type when ordering.)

BLUEPRINT PRICE CODE:	**B**

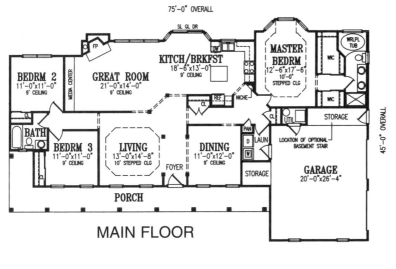

MAIN FLOOR

Plan 567-HAX-5374

Covered Porch Adds Charm To Entrance

Total Living Area:	**1,655 sq. ft.**
Blueprint Price Code:	**B**
Garage:	484 sq. ft.
Front porch:	240 sq. ft.

FEATURES

- Master bedroom features 9' ceiling, walk-in closet and bath with dressing area

- Oversized family room includes 10' ceiling and masonry see-through fireplace

- Island kitchen with convenient access to laundry room

- Handy covered walkway from garage to dining/kitchen area

- 3 bedrooms, 2 baths, 2-car garage

- Crawl space foundation

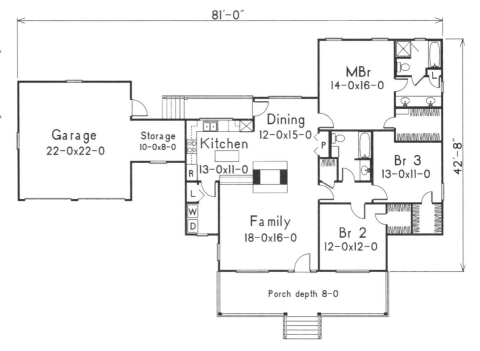

Plan 567-0294

Quaint Cottage With Inviting Front Porch

Total Living Area: 1,020 sq. ft.
Blueprint Price Code: AA
Front porch: 144 sq. ft.

- Living room is warmed by a fireplace
- Dining and living rooms are enhanced by vaulted ceilings and plant shelves
- U-shaped kitchen with large window over the sink
- 2 bedrooms, 1 bath
- Slab foundation

Plan 567-0650

Country-Style With Spacious Rooms

Total Living Area: 1,197 sq. ft.
Blueprint Price Code: AA
Front porch: 91 sq. ft.

- U-shaped kitchen includes ample work space, breakfast bar, laundry area and direct access to outdoors
- Large living room with convenient coat closet
- Master bedroom features large walk-in closet
- 3 bedrooms, 1 bath
- Crawl space foundation, drawings also include basement and slab foundations

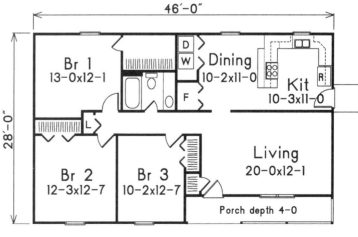

Plan 567-0507

Cozy Vacation Retreat

Total Living Area:	**581 sq. ft.**
Blueprint Price Code:	**AAA**

FEATURES

- Living/dining room features a convenient kitchenette and spiral steps leading to the loft area

- Large loft space easily converted to a bedroom or work area

- Entry space has a unique built-in display niche

- 1 bedroom, 1 bath

- Slab foundation

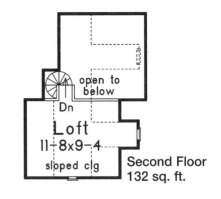

Second Floor
132 sq. ft.

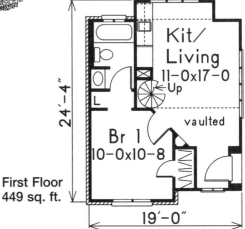

First Floor
449 sq. ft.

Plan 567-0243

Front Porch Welcomes Guests

Total Living Area:	**1,393 sq. ft.**
Blueprint Price Code:	**B**
Detached garage:	505 sq. ft.
Front porch:	96 sq. ft.

FEATURES

- L-shaped kitchen features walk-in pantry, island cooktop and is convenient to laundry room and dining area

- Master bedroom features walk-in closet and private bath

- View to the patio and garage from dining area

- 3 bedrooms, 2 baths, 2-car detached garage

- Crawl space foundation, drawings also include slab foundation

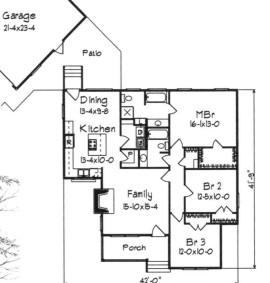

Plan 567-0447

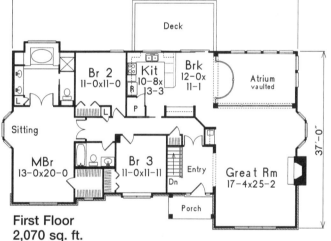

Rear View

Sensational Atrium Generates Excitement

Total Living Area: 2,070 sq. ft.
Blueprint Price Code: C
Drive-under garage: 620 sq. ft.
Front porch: 50 sq. ft.

- Large great room offers masonry fireplace, wet bar and rear views through two-story vaulted atrium

- Informal dining area comprises functional U-shaped kitchen, walk-in pantry, computer center and breakfast balcony with atrium overlook

- Master bath features step-up Roman whirlpool with arched window, TV alcove, separate shower/toilet area and linen closet

- 3 bedrooms, 2 baths, 2-car drive-under garage with storage area

- Walk-out basement foundation

First Floor
2,070 sq. ft.

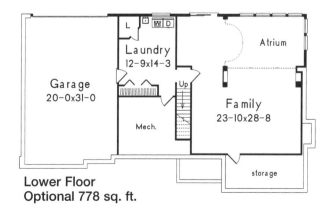

Lower Floor
Optional 778 sq. ft.

Plan 567-0733

Appealing Gabled Front Facade

Total Living Area:	**2,412 sq. ft.**
Blueprint Price Code:	**D**
Garage:	700 sq. ft.
Front porch:	126 sq. ft.

FEATURES

• Coffered ceiling in dining room adds character and spaciousness

• Great room enhanced by vaulted ceiling and atrium window wall

• Spacious well-planned kitchen includes breakfast bar and overlooks breakfast room and beyond to deck

• Luxurious master suite features enormous walk-in closet, private bath and easy access to laundry area

• 4 bedrooms, 2 baths, 3-car side entry garage

• Walk-out basement foundation

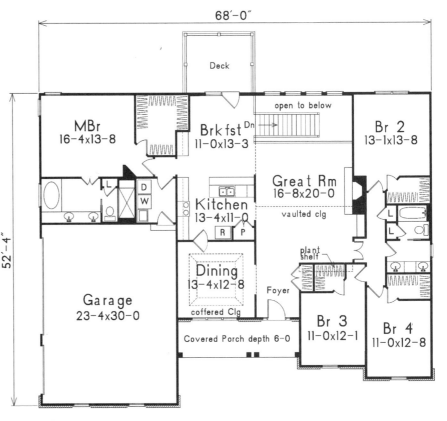

Plan 567-0703

Rear View

Graciously Designed Atrium Ranch

Total Living Area:	2,218 sq. ft.
Blueprint Price Code:	**D**
Garage:	412 sq. ft.
Front porch:	80 sq. ft.

- Vaulted great room features arched colonade from entry, bay windowed atrium with staircase and classically designed fireplace

- Exciting kitchen area enjoys a vaulted ceiling, bay doors to deck, pass-through breakfast bar and walk-in pantry

- Breakfast room offers bay window and snack bar open to kitchen with convenient laundry nearby

- 4 bedroom, 2 baths, 2-car garage

- Walk-out basement foundation

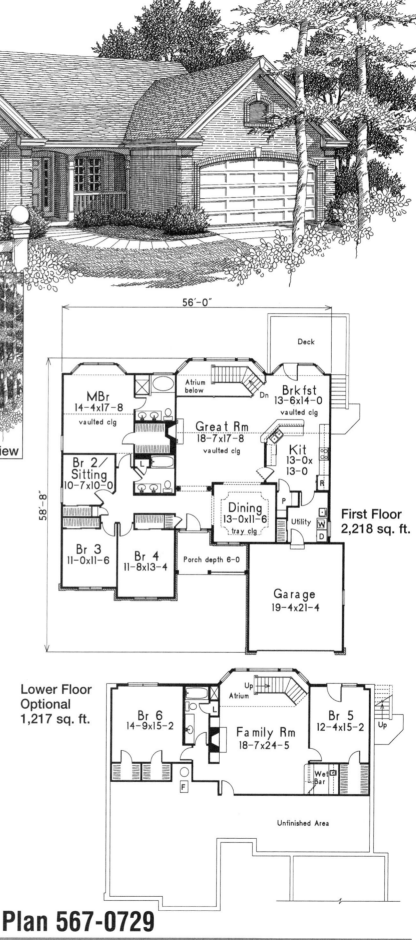

56'-0"

58'-8"

Deck

MBr
14-4x17-8
vaulted clg

Atrium below

Brkfst
13-6x14-0
vaulted clg

Dn

Great Rm
18-7x17-8
vaulted clg

Kit
13-0x
13-0

Br 2/
Sitting
10-7x10-0

Dining
13-0x11-6
tray clg

P

Utility

W
D

Br 3
11-0x11-6

Br 4
11-8x13-4

Porch depth 6-0

First Floor
2,218 sq. ft.

Garage
19-4x21-4

Lower Floor
Optional
1,217 sq. ft.

Up
Atrium

Br 6
14-9x15-2

L

Family Rm
18-7x24-5

Br 5
12-4x15-2

Up

F

Wet Bar

Unfinished Area

Plan 567-0729

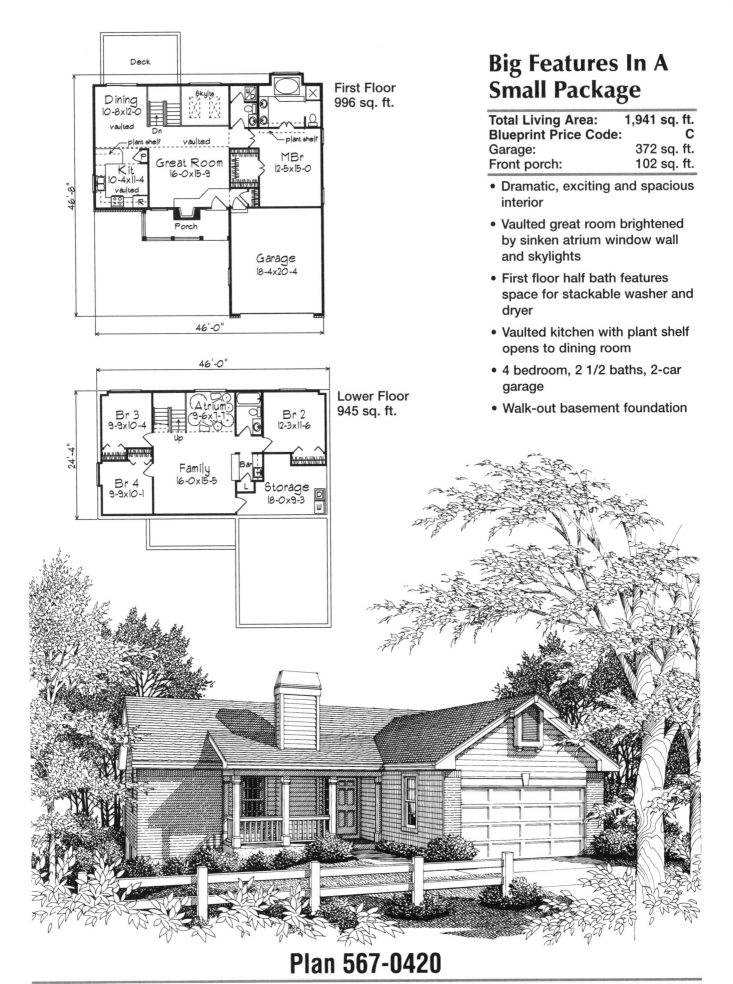

First Floor
996 sq. ft.

Deck

Dining
10-8x12-0
vaulted

Skylts

Dn

plant shelf   vaulted

Kit
10-4x11-4
vaulted

P

R

Great Room
16-0x15-9

plant shelf

MBr
12-5x15-0

Porch

Garage
18-4x20-4

46'-8"

46'-0"

Lower Floor
945 sq. ft.

46'-0"

24'-4"

Br 3
9-9x10-4

Atrium
9-6x7-1

Up

Br 2
12-3x11-6

Br 4
9-9x10-1

Family
16-0x15-5

Bar

L

Storage
18-0x9-3

D

W

Big Features In A Small Package

Total Living Area:	1,941 sq. ft.
Blueprint Price Code:	C
Garage:	372 sq. ft.
Front porch:	102 sq. ft.

- Dramatic, exciting and spacious interior
- Vaulted great room brightened by sinken atrium window wall and skylights
- First floor half bath features space for stackable washer and dryer
- Vaulted kitchen with plant shelf opens to dining room
- 4 bedroom, 2 1/2 baths, 2-car garage
- Walk-out basement foundation

Plan 567-0420

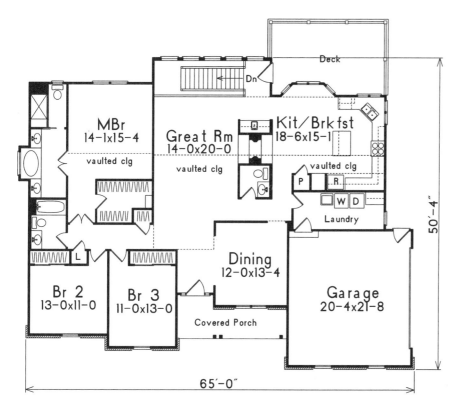

Deck

Dn

MBr
14-1x15-4
vaulted clg

Great Rm
14-0x20-0
vaulted clg

Kit/Brkfst
18-6x15-1
vaulted clg

P

R

W D

Laundry

L

Br 2
13-0x11-0

Br 3
11-0x13-0

Dining
12-0x13-4

Garage
20-4x21-8

Covered Porch

50'-4"

65'-0"

Home Features
Generous
Room Sizes

Total Living Area:	2,164 sq. ft.
Blueprint Price Code:	C
Garage:	440 sq. ft.
Front porch:	90 sq. ft.

- Great design for entertaining with wet bar and see-through fireplace

- Plenty of closet space

- Vaulted ceilings enlarge the master bedroom, great room and kitchen/breakfast area

- Great room features great view to the rear of home

- 3 bedroom, 2 1/2 baths, 2-car side entry garage

- Basement foundation

Plan 567-0744

Bright, Spacious Plan With Many Features

Total Living Area:	2,308 sq. ft.
Blueprint Price Code:	**D**
Garage:	490 sq. ft.
Front porch:	114 sq. ft.

FEATURES

- Efficient kitchen designed with many cabinets and large walk-in pantry adjoins family/breakfast area featuring beautiful fireplace

- Dining area has architectural colonnades that separate it from living area while maintaining spaciousness

- Enter master suite through double-doors and find double walk-in closets and beautiful luxurious bath

- Living room includes vaulted ceiling, fireplace and a sunny atrium window wall creating a dramatic atmosphere

- 3 bedrooms, 2 baths, 2-car side entry garage

- Walk-out basement foundation

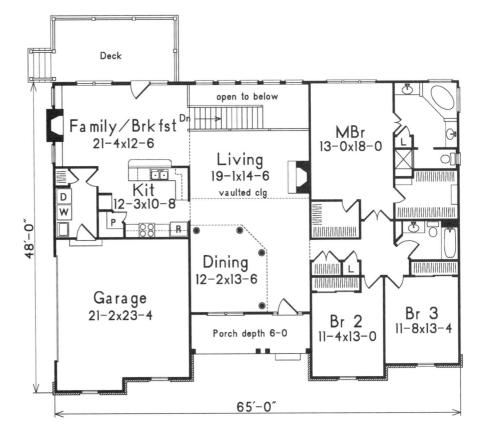

Plan 567-0701

Rear View

Atrium's Dramatic Ambiance, Compliments Of Windows

Total Living Area:	1,721 sq. ft.
Blueprint Price Code:	C
Garage:	625 sq. ft.
Front porch:	138 sq. ft.
Back porch:	150 sq. ft.

FEATURES

- Roof dormers add great curb appeal

- Vaulted great room and dining room immersed in light from atrium window wall

- Breakfast room opens onto covered porch

- Functionally designed kitchen

- 3 bedrooms, 2 baths, 3-car garage

- Walk-out basement foundation, drawings also include crawl space and slab foundations

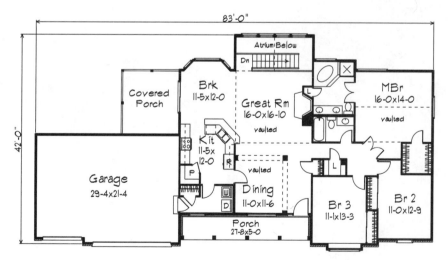

Plan 567-0370

Affordable Atrium Ranch

Total Living Area:	**2,334 sq. ft.**
Blueprint Price Code:	**D**
Garage:	393 sq. ft.
Front porch:	100 sq. ft.

FEATURES

- Roomy front porch gives home a country flavor

- Vaulted great room boasts a fireplace, TV alcove, pass-through bar to kitchen and atrium featuring bayed window wall and stair to family room

- Oversized master bedroom and bath features a vaulted ceiling, double entry doors and large walk-in closet

- 3 bedrooms, 2 baths, 2-car garage

- Walk-out basement foundation

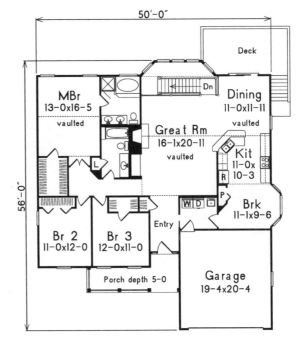

First Floor
1,777 sq. ft.

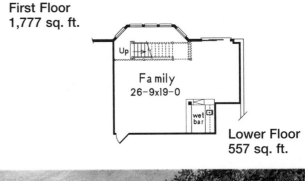

Lower Floor
557 sq. ft.

Rear View

Plan 567-0710

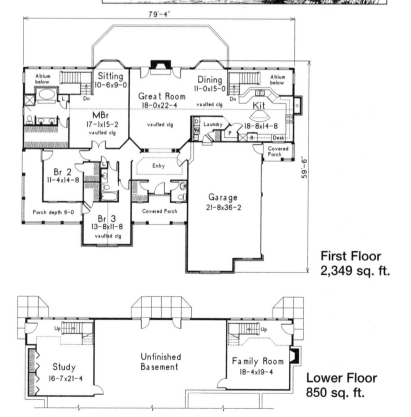

Rear View

Double Atrium Embraces The Sun

Total Living Area:	**3,199 sq. ft.**
Blueprint Price Code:	**E**
Garage:	780 sq. ft.
Front porch:	96 sq. ft.
Left porch:	198 sq. ft.
Right porch:	45 sq. ft.

FEATURES

- Grand scale kitchen features bay-shaped cabinetry built over atrium that overlooks two-story window wall

- A second atrium dominates the master suite which boasts a sitting area with bay window and luxurious bath, which has whirlpool tub open to the garden atrium and lower floor study

- 3 bedrooms, 2 1/2 baths, 3-car side entry garage

- Walk-out basement foundation

First Floor
2,349 sq. ft.

Lower Floor
850 sq. ft.

Plan 567-0713

Rear View

Tranquility Of An Atrium Cottage

Total Living Area:	1,384 sq. ft.
Blueprint Price Code:	A
Garage:	257 sq. ft.
Front porch:	270 sq. ft.

FEATURES

- Wrap-around country porch for peaceful evenings

- Vaulted great room enjoys a large bay window, stone fireplace, pass-through kitchen and awesome rear views through atrium window wall

- Master suite features double entry doors, walk-in closet and a fabulous bath

- 2 bedroom, 2 baths, 1-car side entry garage

- Walk-out basement foundation

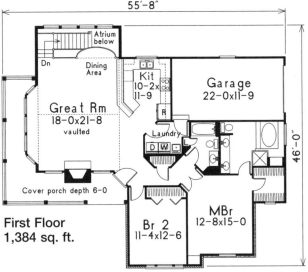

First Floor
1,384 sq. ft.

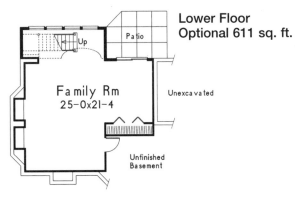

Lower Floor
Optional 611 sq. ft.

Plan 567-0732

Floridian Architecture With In-Law Suite

Total Living Area:	2,408 sq. ft.
Blueprint Price Code:	D
Garage:	637 sq. ft.
Front porch:	96 sq. ft.

FEATURES

- Large vaulted great room overlooks atrium and window wall, adjoins dining, spacious breakfast room with bay and pass-through kitchen

- Private bedroom with bath, separate from other bedrooms is perfect for in-law suite or children home from college

- 4 bedrooms, 2 baths, 2-car side entry garage

- Walk-out basement foundation

First Floor
2,408 sq. ft.

Lower Floor
Optional 1,100 sq. ft.

Plan 567-0730

TO ORDER BLUEPRINTS USE THE FORM ON PAGE 256 OR CALL **TOLL-FREE 1-800-367-7667**

Traditional Exterior Boasts Exciting Interior

Total Living Area:	**2,531 sq. ft.**
Blueprint Price Code:	**D**
Garage:	484 sq. ft.
Front porch:	165 sq. ft.

FEATURES

- Charming porch with dormers leads into vaulted great room with atrium

- Well-designed kitchen and breakfast bar adjoins extra large laundry/mud room

- Double sinks, tub with window above and plant shelf complete vaulted master suite bath

- 4 bedrooms, 2 1/2 baths, 2-car side entry garage

- Walk-out basement foundation

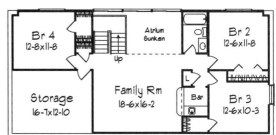

First Floor
1,297 sq. ft.

Lower Floor
1,234 sq. ft.

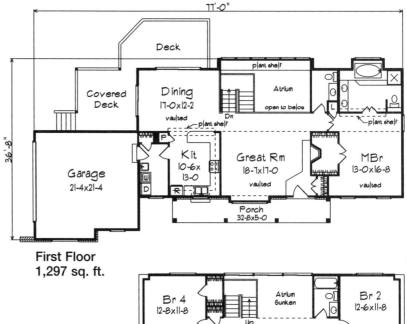

Rear View

Plan 567-0364

TO ORDER BLUEPRINTS USE THE FORM ON PAGE 256 OR CALL **TOLL-FREE 1-800-367-7667**

Country-Style Home With Large Front Porch

Total Living Area:	**1,501 sq. ft.**
Blueprint Price Code:	**B**
Garage:	465 sq. ft.
Front porch:	224 sq. ft.

FEATURES

- Spacious kitchen with dining area open to outdoors

- Convenient utility room adjacent to garage

- Master suite with private bath, dressing area and access to large covered porch

- Large family room creates openness

- 3 bedrooms, 2 baths, 2-car side entry garage

- Basement foundation, drawings also include crawl space and slab foundations

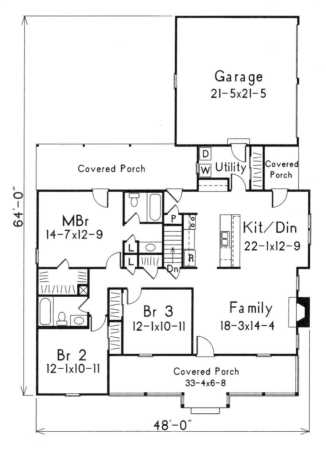

Plan 567-0249

Interesting Plan For Narrow Lot

Total Living Area: 1,516 sq. ft.
Blueprint Price Code: B
Garage: 413 sq. ft.

FEATURES

- Spacious great room is open to dining with a bay and unique stair location

- Attractive and well-planned kitchen offers breakfast bar and built-in pantry

- Smartly designed master suite enjoys patio views

- 3 bedrooms, 2 baths, 2-car garage

- Basement foundation

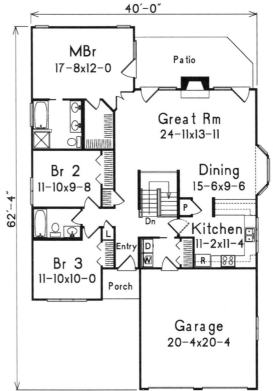

Plan 567-0659

TO ORDER BLUEPRINTS USE THE FORM ON PAGE 256 OR CALL **TOLL-FREE 1-800-367-7667**

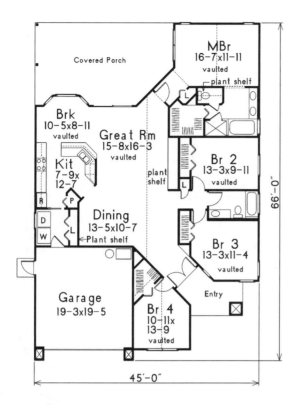

Covered Porch

MBr
16-7x11-11
vaulted

plant shelf

Brk
10-5x8-11
vaulted

Great Rm
15-8x16-3
vaulted

Kit
7-9x
12-7

plant shelf

Br 2
13-3x9-11
vaulted

Dining
13-5x10-7

Plant shelf

Br 3
13-3x11-4
vaulted

Garage
19-3x19-5

Br 4
10-11x
13-9
vaulted

Entry

66'-0"

45'-0"

Wonderful
Great Room

Total Living Area:	**1,865 sq. ft.**
Blueprint Price Code:	**D**
Garage:	372 sq. ft.
Front enty	69 sq. ft.
Back porch:	443 sq. ft.

FEATURES

- Large foyer opens into expansive dining/great room area

- Home features vaulted ceilings throughout

- Master suite features bath with double-bowl vanity, shower, tub and toilet in separate room for privacy

- 4 bedrooms, 2 baths, 2-car garage

- Slab foundation, drawings also include crawl space foundation

Plan 567-0335

Enchanting Country Cottage

Total Living Area:	**1,140 sq. ft.**
Blueprint Price Code:	**AA**
Drive-under garage:	456 sq. ft.
Front porch:	123 sq. ft.

FEATURES

- Open and spacious living and dining area for family gatherings

- Well-organized kitchen with an abundance of cabinetry and built-in pantry

- Roomy master bath features double-bowl vanity

- 3 bedrooms, 2 baths, 2-car drive under garage

- Basement foundation

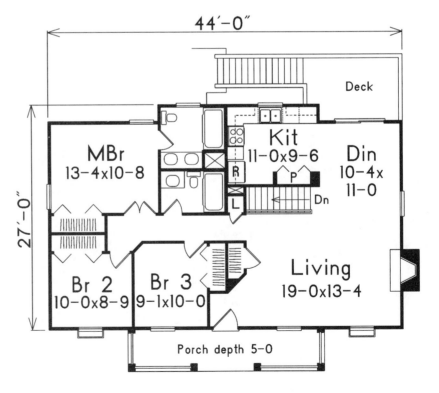

Plan 567-0477

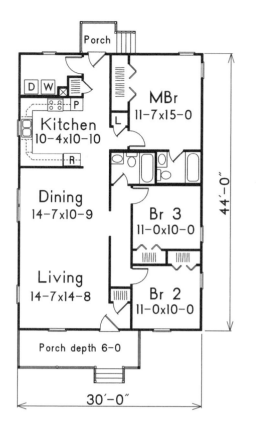

Porch

D W ⊠ P
Kitchen
10-4x10-10
R

MBr
11-7x15-0
L

Dining
14-7x10-9

Br 3
11-0x10-0

Living
14-7x14-8

Br 2
11-0x10-0

Porch depth 6-0

44'-0"

30'-0"

Gabled, Covered Front Porch

Total Living Area: 1,320 sq. ft.
Blueprint Price Code: A
Front porch: 120 sq. ft.

FEATURES

- Functional U-shaped kitchen features pantry

- Large living and dining areas join to create open atmosphere

- Secluded master bedroom includes private full bath

- Covered front porch opens into large living area with convenient coat closet

- Utility/laundry room located near the kitchen

- 3 bedrooms, 2 baths

- Crawl space foundation

Plan 567-0297

Formal Facade

- Formally balanced with twin dormers, gables and bay windows, a charming Southern-style exterior complements this home's informal interior. Its design boasts a compact, efficient plan with highly functional spaces.
- Featuring a fireplace, a built-in media center and a volume ceiling, the pavilion-style Great Room is flooded with light from the home's front and rear porches.
- Sliding glass doors to the back deck and a bay window highlight the dining room, which is easily served by the adjoining U-shaped kitchen.
- With a large walk-in closet, a private bath, a tray ceiling and a bay window, the secluded master bedroom offers wonderful respite from a busy day.
- Across the home, two secondary bedrooms share a full hall bath.
- An unfinished attic provides future expansion space, ideal for an additional bedroom or a home office.

VIEW INTO GREAT ROOM

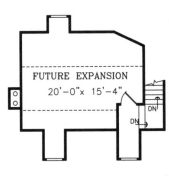

UPPER FLOOR

Plan 567-HAX-97359

Bedrooms: 3+	**Baths:** 2
Living Area:	
Main floor	1,380 sq. ft.
Total Living Area:	**1,380 sq. ft.**
Future upper floor	385 sq. ft.
Standard basement	1,380 sq. ft.
Garage	427 sq. ft.
Exterior Wall Framing:	2x4

Foundation Options:
Standard basement
Crawlspace
Slab
(Please specify foundation type when ordering.)

BLUEPRINT PRICE CODE:	**A**

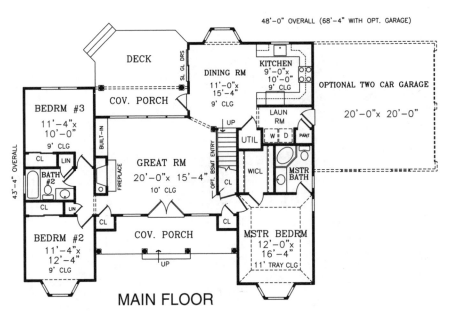

MAIN FLOOR

Plan 567-HAX-97359

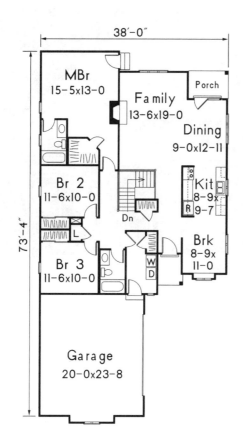

38'-0"

MBr
15-5x13-0

Family
13-6x19-0

Porch

Dining
9-0x12-11

Br 2
11-6x10-0

Dn

Kit
8-9x
9-7

R

73'-4"

L

Br 3
11-6x10-0

W
D

Brk
8-9x
11-0

Garage
20-0x23-8

Ideal Ranch For A Narrow Lot

Total Living Area:	**1,624 sq. ft.**
Blueprint Price Code:	**B**
Garage:	480 sq. ft.
Front entry:	28 sq. ft.
Back porch:	43 sq. ft.

FEATURES

- Complete master bedroom suite with private entry from the outdoors

- Garage adjacent to utility room with convenient storage closet

- Large family/dining area with fireplace and porch access

- Pass-through kitchen opens directly to cozy breakfast area

- 3 bedrooms, 2 baths, 2-car side entry garage

- Basement foundation, drawings also include crawl space and slab foundations

Plan 567-0281

Distinctive Inside and Out

- A decorative columned entry, shuttered windows and a facade of stucco and stone offer a distinctive look to this economical one-story home.
- The focal point of the interior is the huge, central family room. The room is enhanced by a dramatic corner fireplace and a neat serving bar that includes a wet bar.
- A decorative plant shelf adorns the entrance to the adjoining breakfast room, which features a lovely bay window. The kitchen offers a pantry and a pass-through to the family room.
- The formal dining room is easy to reach from both the kitchen and the family room, and is set off with columned arches and a raised ceiling.
- The secluded master suite boasts a vaulted private bath with dual sinks, an oval garden tub, a separate toilet room and a large walk-in closet.
- Two more bedrooms share a second bath at the other end of the home.

Plan 567-HFB-5001-SAVA

Bedrooms: 3	Baths: 2
Living Area:	
Main floor	1,429 sq. ft.
Total Living Area:	**1,429 sq. ft.**
Daylight basement	1,429 sq. ft.
Garage and storage	436 sq. ft.
Exterior Wall Framing:	2x4

Foundation Options:

Daylight basement
Crawlspace
Slab
(Please specify foundation type when ordering.)

BLUEPRINT PRICE CODE:	A

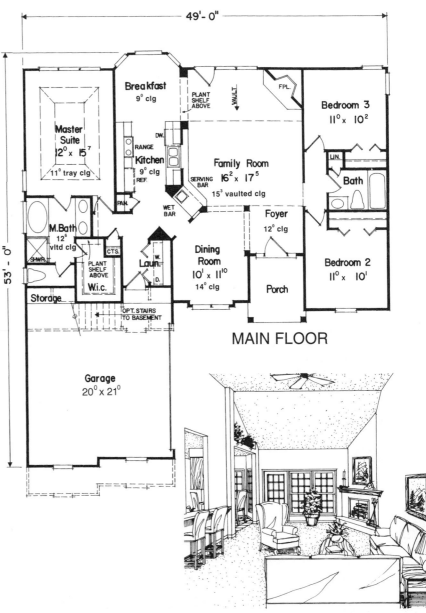

MAIN FLOOR

VIEW INTO FAMILY ROOM

Plan 567-HFB-5001-SAVA

Open Living Area Adds Drama To Home

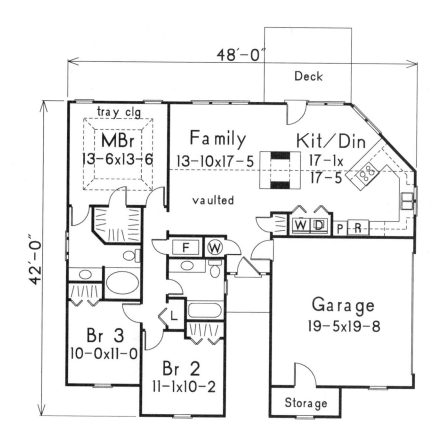

48´-0"

Deck

tray clg

MBr
13-6x13-6

Family
13-10x17-5

vaulted

Kit/Din
17-1x
17-5

42´-0"

W D P R

F W

L

Br 3
10-0x11-0

Br 2
11-1x10-2

Garage
19-5x19-8

Storage

Total Living Area:	1,340 sq. ft.
Blueprint Price Code:	**A**
Garage:	380 sq. ft.
Front entry:	30 sq. ft.

FEATURES

- Master bedroom with private bath and walk-in closet
- Recessed entry leads to vaulted family room with see-through fireplace to dining area
- Garage includes handy storage area
- Convenient laundry closet in the kitchen
- 3 bedrooms, 2 baths, 2-car side entry garage
- Slab foundation, drawings also include crawl space foundation

Plan 567-0255

Unique Step Up
From Entry To
Living Space

Total Living Area: 1,261 sq. ft.
Blueprint Price Code: **A**
Drive-under garage: 506 sq. ft.

FEATURES

• Great room, brightened by windows and doors, features vaulted ceiling, fireplace and access to sun deck

• Vaulted master bedroom with private bath

• Split level foyer leads to living space or basement

• Centrally located laundry area near bedrooms

• 3 bedrooms, 2 baths, 2-car drive under garage

• Basement foundation

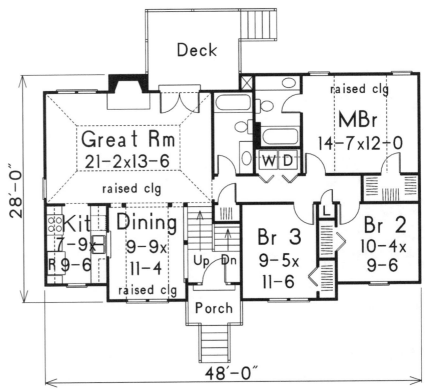

Plan 567-0260

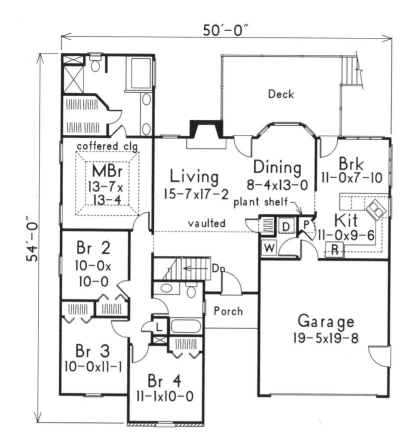

Dormers And Stone Veneer Add Exterior Appeal

Total Living Area:	1,609 sq. ft.
Blueprint Price Code:	B
Garage:	384 sq. ft.
Front porch:	40 sq. ft.

FEATURES

- Efficient kitchen with corner pantry and adjacent laundry room

- Breakfast room boasts plenty of windows and opens onto rear deck

- Master bedroom features tray ceiling and private deluxe bath

- Entry opens into large living area with fireplace

- 4 bedrooms, 2 baths, 2-car garage

- Basement foundation

Plan 567-0295

Family Room With Fireplace Perfect For Central Gathering

Total Living Area:	**1,631 sq. ft.**
Blueprint Price Code:	**B**
Drive-under garage:	620 sq. ft.
Front porch:	115 sq. ft.
Rear deck:	56 sq. ft.

FEATURES

- 9' ceilings throughout this home
- Utility room conveniently located near kitchen
- Roomy kitchen and dining areas boast a breakfast bar and patio access
- Coffered ceiling accents master suite
- 3 bedrooms, 2 baths, 2-car drive under garage
- Basement foundation

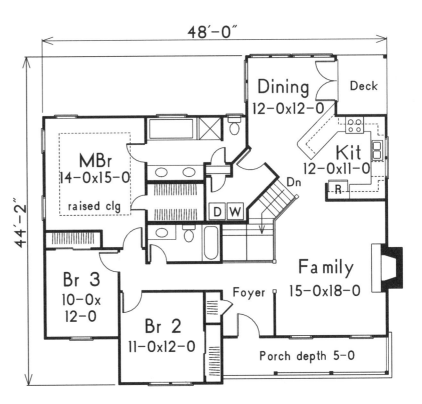

Plan 567-0237

Touches of Luxury

- This European-style home's thoughtful floor plan puts everything within reach, while pretty windows, vaulted ceilings and luxurious amenities lend a touch of opulence.
- A stylish arched entry and a door with an oval window usher you into the foyer. To the right, the formal dining room enjoys a plant shelf and a nearby wet bar.
- In the spacious Great Room, the ceiling soars and bright arched windows flank the fireplace. A long, angled serving bar helps keep company refreshed.
- Another plant shelf graces the angled galley kitchen, and the adjoining vaulted breakfast nook basks in the light of a lovely radius window.
- The luxurious master suite features a tray ceiling and an adjoining sitting room. The private bath boasts a vaulted ceiling, a garden tub, a separate shower, a dual-sink vanity and a generous walk-in closet.

Plan 567-HFB-5276-STAU

Bedrooms: 3	Baths: 2
Living Area:	
Main floor	1,575 sq. ft.
Total Living Area:	**1,575 sq. ft.**
Daylight basement	1,658 sq. ft.
Garage and storage	459 sq. ft.
Exterior Wall Framing:	2x4
Foundation Options:	
Daylight basement	
Crawlspace	
(Please specify foundation type when ordering.)	
BLUEPRINT PRICE CODE:	**B**

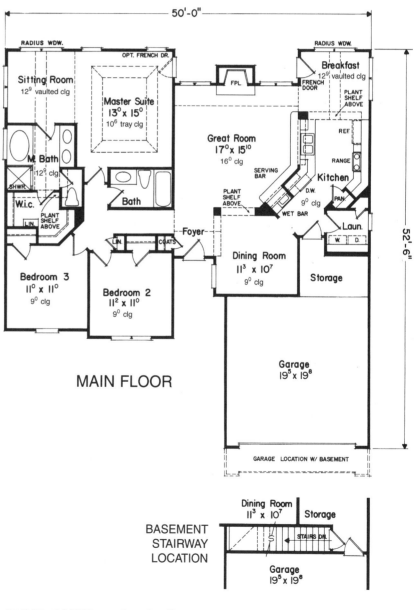

MAIN FLOOR

BASEMENT STAIRWAY LOCATION

Plan 567-HFB-5276-STAU

Large Great Room Perfect For Entertaining

Total Living Area:	**1,862 sq. ft.**
Blueprint Price Code:	**C**
Garage:	**410 sq. ft.**

FEATURES

- Master bedroom includes tray ceiling, bay window, access to patio and a private bath with oversized tub and generous closet space

- Corner sink and breakfast bar faces into breakfast area and great room

- Spacious great room features vaulted ceiling, fireplace and access to rear patio

- 3 bedrooms, 2 baths, 2-car garage

- Slab foundation, drawings also include crawl space foundation

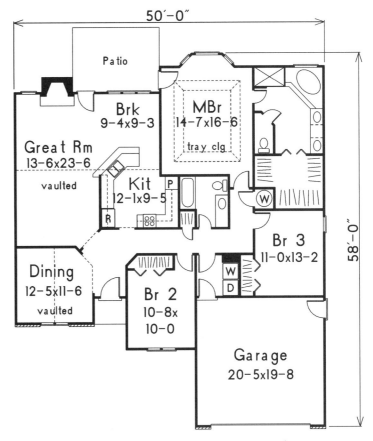

Plan 567-0257

Distinctive Home
For Sloping Terrain

Total Living Area:	**1,340 sq. ft.**
Blueprint Price Code:	**A**
Drive-under garage:	661 sq. ft.
Front porch:	33 sq. ft.

FEATURES

- Grand-sized vaulted living and dining rooms offer fireplace, wet bar and breakfast counter open to spacious kitchen

- Vaulted master suite features double entry doors, walk-in closet and elegant bath

- Basement includes a huge 2-car garage and space for a bedroom/bath expansion

- 3 bedrooms, 2 baths, 2-car drive under garage with storage area

- Basement foundation

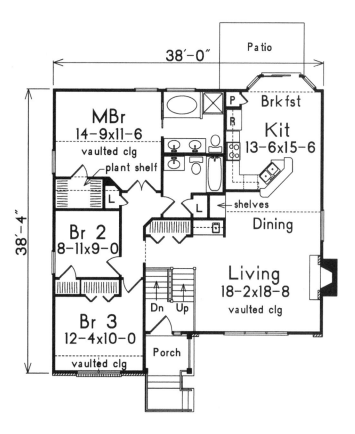

Plan 567-0718

Gable Facade Adds Appeal To This Ranch

Total Living Area:	**1,304 sq. ft.**
Blueprint Price Code:	**A**
Garage:	450 sq. ft.
Front entry:	15 sq. ft.

FEATURES

- Covered entrance leads into family room with 10' ceiling and fireplace

- 10' ceilings in kitchen, dining and family rooms

- Master bedroom features coffered ceiling, walk-in closet and private bath

- Efficient kitchen includes large window over the sink

- 3 bedrooms, 2 baths, 2-car garage

- Slab foundation

Plan 567-0292

All The Essentials For Comfortable Living

Total Living Area:	**1,344 sq. ft.**
Blueprint Price Code:	**A**
Front porch:	50 sq. ft.

FEATURES

- Kitchen has side entry, laundry area, pantry and joins family/dining area

- Master bedroom includes private bath

- Linen and storage closets in hall

- Covered porch opens to spacious living room with handy coat closet

- 3 bedrooms, 2 baths

- Crawl space foundation, drawings also include basement and slab foundations

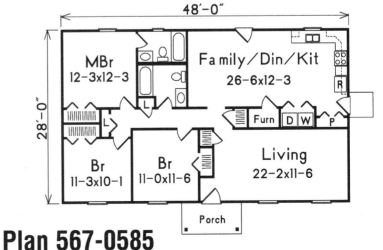

Plan 567-0585

Open Invitation

- The wide front porch of this friendly country-style home extends an open invitation to all who visit.
- Highlighted by a round-topped transom, the home's entrance opens directly into the spacious living room, which shows off a fireplace flanked by windows.
- The large adjoining dining area is enhanced by a lovely bay window and is easily serviced by the updated kitchen's angled snack bar.
- A bright sun room off the kitchen provides a great space for informal meals

or relaxation. Access to a back porch is nearby.
- The good-sized master bedroom is secluded from the other sleeping areas. Its lavish private bath includes a separate shower, a dual-sink vanity, a garden tub and a nice-sized walk-in closet.
- Two more bedrooms share a second full bath. A convenient laundry/utility room is nearby.
- The upper floor offers opportunity for expanding into additional living space.
- The home's high ceilings add spaciousness.

Plan 567-J-91078

Bedrooms: 3+	Baths: 2
Living Area:	
Main floor	1,879 sq. ft.
Total Living Area:	**1,879 sq. ft.**
Future upper floor	1,007 sq. ft.
Standard basement	1,846 sq. ft.
Garage	484 sq. ft.
Storage	132 sq. ft.
Exterior Wall Framing:	2x6

Foundation Options:

Standard basement
Crawlspace
Slab
(Please specify foundation type when ordering.)

BLUEPRINT PRICE CODE:	B

VIEW INTO DINING AND LIVING ROOMS

MAIN FLOOR

45-0

62-0

MASTER BATH
17-9 x 9-0

MASTER BEDROOM
17-9 x 14-0
9-0 ceiling

SUNROOM
12-7 x 9-6
9-0 ceiling

PORCH
10-0 x 10-0

GARAGE
21-2 x 21-5

UTIL.
6-2x9-0

UP

KITCHEN
11-0 x 13-6
9-0 ceiling

DINING
11-0 x 13-6
9-0 ceiling

STORAGE
21-2 x 5-5

BEDROOM
11-2 x 10-6
9-0 ceiling

DN

BATH
11-2 x 5-0

BEDROOM
15-0 x 10-0
9-0 ceiling

LIVING
22-7 x 15-4
9-0 ceiling

PORCH
42-0 x 8-0

UPPER FLOOR

FUTURE
21-0 x 41-0

Plan 567-J-91078

Vaulted Living
Area Adds Appeal

Total Living Area:	**1,689 sq. ft.**
Blueprint Price Code:	**B**
Garage:	550 sq. ft.
Front porch:	70 sq. ft.

FEATURES

- Distinct covered entrance

- Large, open living and dining area including vaulted ceiling, corner fireplace and access to the rear deck

- Stylish angled kitchen offers large counter work space and nook

- Master bedroom boasts spacious bath with step-up tub, separate shower and large walk-in closet

- 3 bedrooms, 2 baths, 2-car garage

- Basement foundation, drawings also include slab and crawl space foundations

50'-0"

68'-0"

Deck

MBr
13-8x14-0

Brk
8-4x
10-0

Kit
8-6x12-0

Br 2
10-0x
10-0

Dining
9-10x
10-10
vaulted

R   P

Dn

D
W

Br 3
10-0x
10-0

Living
18-4x16-6
vaulted

Porch

Garage
23-8x23-8

Plan 567-0264

Vaulted Ceiling Frames Circle-Top Window

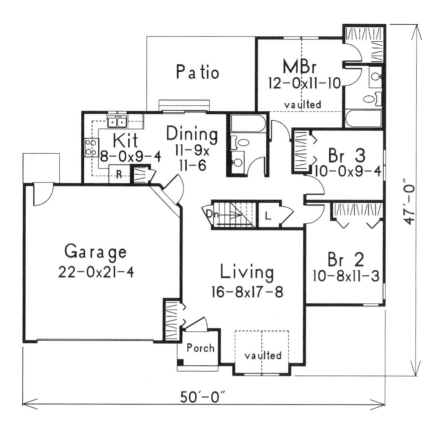

Total Living Area:	**1,195 sq. ft.**
Blueprint Price Code:	**AA**
Garage:	470 sq. ft.
Front porch:	25 sq. ft.

FEATURES

- Kitchen/dining room opens onto the patio

- Master bedroom features vaulted ceiling, private bath and walk-in closet

- Coat closets located by both the entrances

- Convenient secondary entrance at the back of the garage

- 3 bedrooms, 2 baths, 2-car garage

- Basement foundation

Plan 567-0485

Vaulted Ceilings
Show Off
This Ranch

Total Living Area:	**1,135 sq. ft.**
Blueprint Price Code:	**AA**
Garage:	388 sq. ft.
Front porch:	58 sq. ft.

FEATURES

- Living and dining rooms feature vaulted ceilings and a corner fireplace

- Energy efficient home with 2" x 6" exterior walls

- Master bedroom offers vaulted ceilings, private bathroom and generous closet space

- Compact but functional kitchen complete with pantry and adjacent utility room

- 3 bedrooms, 2 baths, 2-car garage

- Basement foundation, drawings also include crawl space foundation

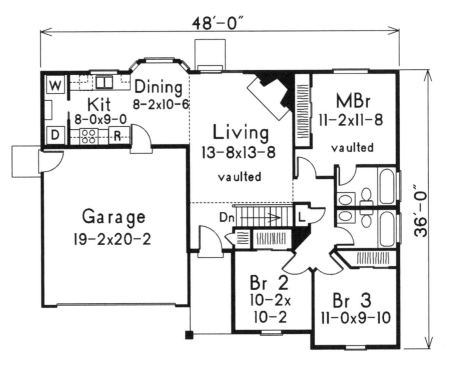

Plan 567-0268

Economical Ranch For Easy Living

Total Living Area:	1,314 sq. ft.
Blueprint Price Code:	**A**
Garage:	450 sq. ft.
Front porch:	93 sq. ft.

FEATURES

- Energy efficient home with 2" x 6" exterior walls
- Covered porch adds immediate appeal and welcoming charm
- Open floor plan combined with vaulted ceiling offers spacious living
- Functional kitchen complete with pantry and eating bar
- Cozy fireplace in the living room
- Private master bedroom features a large walk-in closet and bath
- 3 bedrooms, 2 baths, 2-car garage
- Basement foundation

Plan 567-0265

Convenient Ranch

Total Living Area:	1,120 sq. ft.
Blueprint Price Code:	**AA**
Front porch:	72 sq. ft.

FEATURES

- Master bedroom includes a half bath with laundry area, linen closet and kitchen access
- Kitchen has charming double-door entry, breakfast bar and a convenient walk-in pantry
- Welcoming front porch opens to large living room with coat closet
- 3 bedrooms, 1 1/2 baths
- Crawl space foundation, drawings also include basement and slab foundations

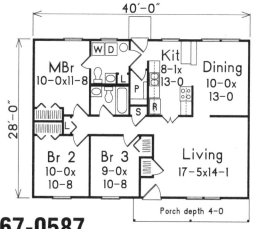

Plan 567-0587

Secluded Master Suite Has Private Patio Area

Total Living Area: 1,438 sq. ft.
Blueprint Price Code: A
Garage: 380 sq. ft.

FEATURES

- Vaulted living and dining rooms unite to provide open space for entertaining

- Secondary bedrooms share full bath

- Compact kitchen

- Vaulted master bedroom includes private bath, large walk-in closet and access to patio

- 3 bedrooms, 2 baths, 2-car side entry garage

- Crawl space foundation, drawings also include slab foundation

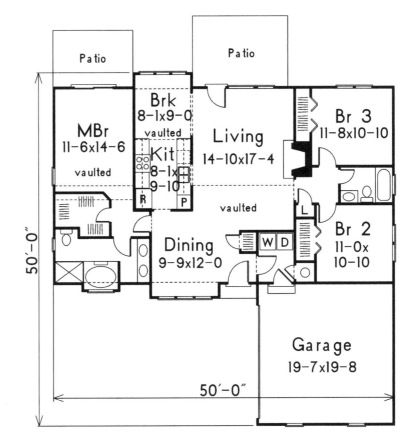

Plan 567-0258

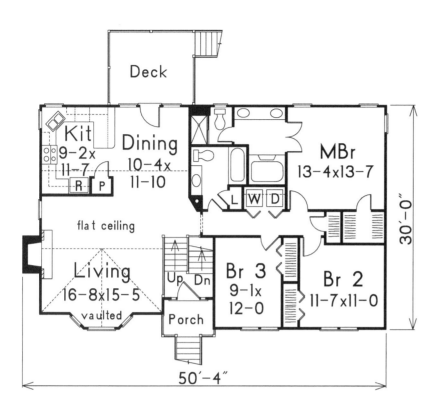

Deck

Kit
9-2x
11-7

R P

Dining
10-4x
11-10

MBr
13-4x13-7

L W D

flat ceiling

Living
16-8x15-5

vaulted

Up Dn

Porch

Br 3
9-1x
12-0

Br 2
11-7x11-0

30'-0"

50'-4"

Compact Home Is Charming And Functional

Total Living Area: 1,404 sq. ft.
Blueprint Price Code: A
Drive-under garage: 667 sq. ft.

FEATURES

- Split foyer entrance

- Bayed living area features unique vaulted ceiling and fireplace

- Wrap-around kitchen has corner windows for added sunlight and a bar that overlooks dining area

- Master suite features a garden tub with separate shower

- Back deck provides handy access to dining room and kitchen

- 3 bedrooms, 2 baths, 2-car drive under garage

- Basement foundation, drawings also include partial crawl space foundation

Plan 567-0176

Bring the Outdoors In!

- This home is filled with features that meld the interior spaces with the outdoors, yet is affordably sized.
- Cathedral ceilings, angled walls, skylights and rear-facing views are key elements that add light, space and intensity to the home.
- The boxed-out kitchen, which overlooks a covered rear deck or patio, is easily reached from the dining room.
- The family room offers a cathedral ceiling, a window wall facing the backyard and access to the deck.
- The living room is highlighted by a beautiful Palladian window. Framed by a cathedral ceiling and a deep ledge, the window floods the living room and the adjoining dining room with light.
- The master suite is enhanced by double doors, angled walls and a large window facing the side yard. A walk-in closet and a private bath are also included.
- Two secondary bedrooms are positioned at the rear of the home for picturesque views as well as for privacy. A full bathroom, a linen closet and a laundry closet are nearby.

Plan 567-NW-864

Bedrooms: 3	Baths: 2
Living Area:	
Main floor	1,449 sq. ft.
Total Living Area:	**1,449 sq. ft.**
Garage	390 sq. ft.
Exterior Wall Framing:	2x6

Foundation Options:
Crawlspace
(Please specify foundation type when ordering.)

BLUEPRINT PRICE CODE: A

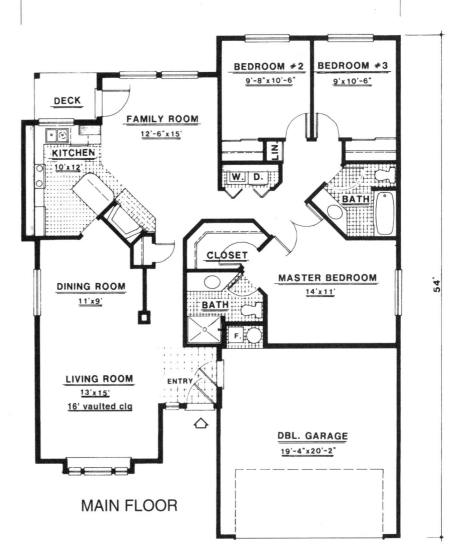

MAIN FLOOR

Plan 567-NW-864

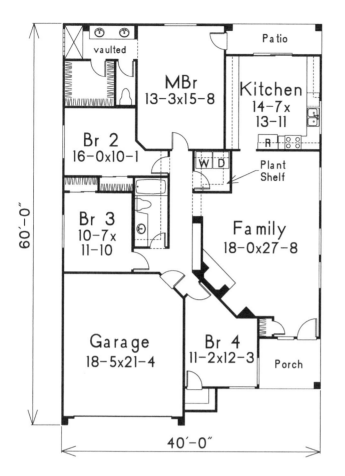

Inviting Covered Corner Entry

Total Living Area:	1,747 sq. ft.
Blueprint Price Code:	B
Garage:	394 sq. ft.
Front porch:	71 sq. ft.
Back patio:	69 sq. ft.

FEATURES

- Entry opens into large family room with coat closet, angled fireplace and attractive plant shelf

- Kitchen and master bedroom access covered patio

- Functional kitchen includes ample workspace

- 4 bedrooms, 2 baths, 2-car garage

- Slab foundation

Plan 567-0441

Perfect Fit For A Narrow Site

Total Living Area:	**1,270 sq. ft.**
Blueprint Price Code:	**A**
Garage:	380 sq. ft.
Front entry:	50 sq. ft.

FEATURES

- Spacious living area features angled stairs, vaulted ceiling, exciting fireplace and deck access

- Master bedroom with walk-in closet and private bath

- Dining and living rooms join to create open atmosphere

- Eat-in kitchen with convenient pass-through to dining room

- 3 bedrooms, 2 baths, 2-car garage

- Basement foundation

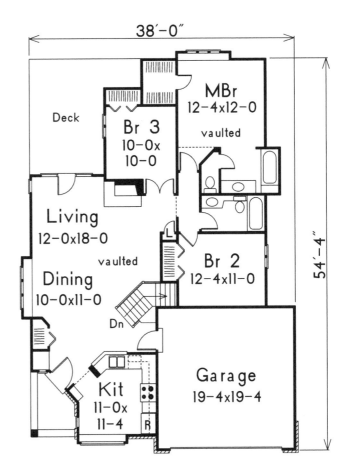

Plan 567-0275

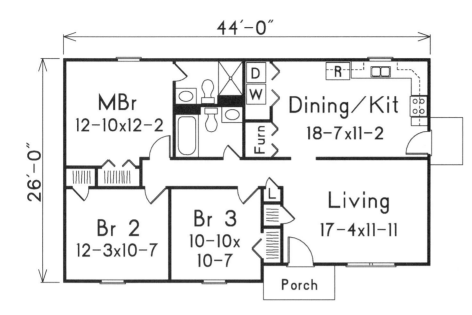

Spacious Dining And Living Areas

Total Living Area: 1,104 sq. ft.
Blueprint Price Code: AA

FEATURES

- Master bedroom includes private bath
- Convenient side entrance to kitchen/dining area
- Laundry area located near kitchen
- Large living area creates comfortable atmosphere
- 3 bedrooms, 2 baths
- Crawl space foundation, drawings also include basement and slab foundations

Plan 567-0505

Exciting Split-Foyer Entrance

Total Living Area: 1,407 sq. ft.
Blueprint Price Code: A
Drive-under garage: 360 sq. ft.

FEATURES

- Large living room with fireplace and access to the rear deck

- Kitchen and dining areas combine to create open gathering area

- Convenient laundry room and broom closet

- Master bedroom includes private bath with large vanity and separate tub and shower

- 3 bedrooms, 2 baths, 2-car drive under garage

- Basement foundation

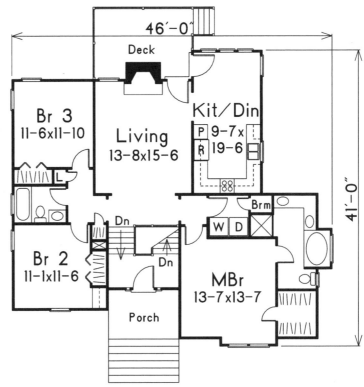

Plan 567-0251

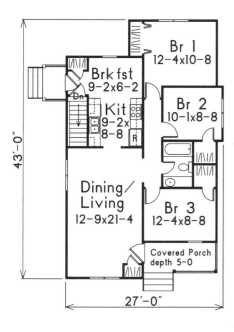

43'-0"

27'-0"

Br 1
12-4x10-8

Brk fst
9-2x6-2

Dn

Kit
9-2x
8-8

R

Br 2
10-1x8-8

Dining/
Living
12-9x21-4

Br 3
12-4x8-8

Covered Porch
depth 5-0

Compact Home Maximizes Space

Total Living Area:	987 sq. ft.
Blueprint Price Code:	AA
Front porch:	62 sq. ft.

FEATURES

- Galley kitchen opens into cozy breakfast room
- Convenient coat closets located by both entrances
- Dining/living room combined for expansive open area
- 3 bedrooms, 1 bath
- Basement foundation

Plan 567-0495

Layout Creates Large Open Living Area

Total Living Area:	1,285 sq. ft.
Blueprint Price Code:	B
Storage:	102 sq. ft.
Front porch:	288 sq. ft.

FEATURES

- Accommodating home with ranch-style porch
- Large storage area on back of home
- Master bedroom includes dressing area, private bath and built-in bookcase
- Kitchen features pantry, break-fast bar and complete view to dining room
- 3 bedrooms, 2 baths
- Crawl space foundation, draw-ings also include basement and slab foundations

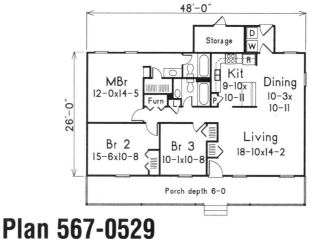

48'-0"

26'-0"

Storage

D
W

MBr
12-0x14-5

Furn

Kit
9-10x
10-11

R

P

Dining
10-3x
10-11

Br 2
15-6x10-8

Br 3
10-1x10-8

Living
18-10x14-2

Porch depth 6-0

Plan 567-0529

Cozy, Rustic Country Home

- This cozy, rustic home offers a modern, open interior that efficiently maximizes the modest square footage.
- A simple front porch offers just enough room to set up a couple of rocking chairs and shoot the breeze.
- The large living room features a sloped ceiling accented by rustic beams. An eye-catching corner fireplace warms this inviting space.
- The living room flows into the adjoining dining room and the efficient U-shaped kitchen for a spacious, open feel.
- The master suite is separated from the two secondary bedrooms by the home's common living areas. The master suite includes a private bath and a separate dressing area with a dual-sink vanity.
- Two good-sized secondary bedrooms share another full bath.

Plan 567-E-1109

Bedrooms: 3	Baths: 2
Living Area:	
Main floor	1,191 sq. ft.
Total Living Area:	**1,191 sq. ft.**
Garage, storage and utility	572 sq. ft.
Exterior Wall Framing:	2x6

Foundation Options:

Crawlspace

Slab

(Please specify foundation type when ordering.)

BLUEPRINT PRICE CODE:	**A**

VIEW INTO LIVING ROOM, DINING ROOM AND KITCHEN

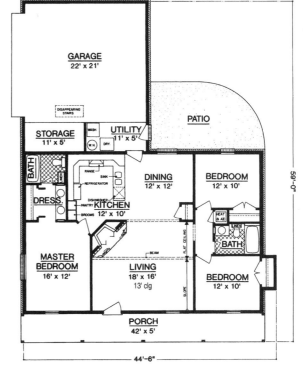

MAIN FLOOR

Plan 567-E-1109

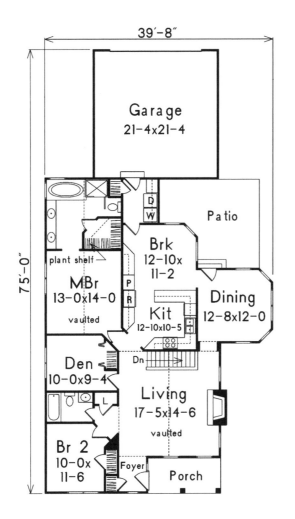

39'-8"

Garage
21-4x21-4

75'-0"

plant shelf

Patio

D
W

Brk
12-10x
11-2

MBr
13-0x14-0
vaulted

P
R

Kit
12-10x10-5

Dining
12-8x12-0

Den
10-0x9-4

Dn

Living
17-5x14-6
vaulted

L

Br 2
10-0x
11-6

Foyer

Porch

Innovative Design For That Narrow Lot

Total Living Area:	**1,558 sq. ft.**
Blueprint Price Code:	**B**
Garage:	455 sq. ft.
Front porch:	78 sq. ft.

FEATURES

- Illuminated spaces created by visual access to outdoor living areas

- Vaulted master bedroom features private bath with whirlpool tub, separate shower and large walk-in closet

- Convenient first floor laundry has garage access

- Practical den or third bedroom

- U-shaped kitchen adjacent to sunny breakfast area

- 2 bedrooms, 2 baths, 2-car rear entry garage

- Basement foundation

Plan 567-0394

Efficient Kitchen Layout

Total Living Area:	**1,598 sq. ft.**
Blueprint Price Code:	**B**
Garage:	456 sq. ft.
Front porch:	53 sq. ft.
Rear porch:	53 sq. ft.

FEATURES

- Additional storage area in garage

- Double-door entry into master bedroom with luxurious master bath

- Entry opens into large family room with vaulted ceiling and open stairway to basement

- 3 bedroom, 2 baths, 2-car garage

- Basement foundation

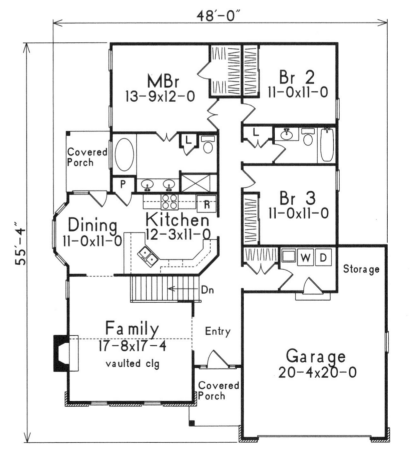

Plan 567-0743

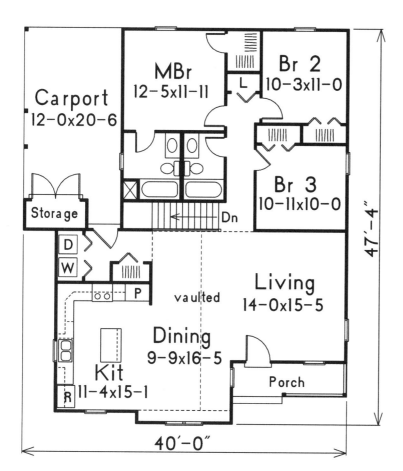

Carport
12-0x20-6

MBr
12-5x11-11

Br 2
10-3x11-0

L

Storage

D
W

P

Kit
11-4x15-1

R

vaulted

Dining
9-9x16-5

Living
14-0x15-5

Br 3
10-11x10-0

Dn

Porch

47'-4"

40'-0"

Compact Home With Functional Design

Total Living Area:	**1,396 sq. ft.**
Blueprint Price Code:	**A**
Carport:	246 sq. ft.
Storage:	28 sq. ft.
Front porch:	56 sq. ft.

FEATURES

- Gabled front adds interest to facade
- Living and dining rooms share a vaulted ceiling
- Master bedroom features a walk-in closet and private bath
- Functional kitchen with a center work island and convenient pantry
- 3 bedrooms, 2 baths, 1-car carport
- Basement foundation, drawings also include crawl space foundation

Plan 567-0296

Soaring Spaces

- This charming home is filled with large spaces and soaring ceilings.
- The exterior offers a covered front porch and lap siding with brick accents.
- Inside, the huge family room features a 15½-ft. vaulted ceiling.
- The family room flows into the spacious breakfast room and kitchen, which are brightened by plenty of windows.
- The master bedroom boasts an 11-ft. tray ceiling and a vaulted private bath.

Plan 567-HFB-1070

Bedrooms: 3	Baths: 2
Living Area:	
Main floor	1,070 sq. ft.
Total Living Area:	**1,070 sq. ft.**
Daylight basement	1,070 sq. ft.
Garage	484 sq. ft.
Exterior Wall Framing:	2x4
Foundation Options:	
Daylight basement	
Crawlspace	
Slab	
(Please specify foundation type when ordering.)	
BLUEPRINT PRICE CODE:	**A**

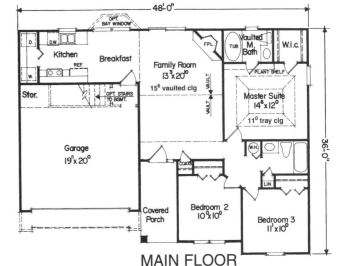

MAIN FLOOR

Plan 567-HFB-1070

Simple Yet Stylish

- With its simple yet stylish exterior, this modest-sized design is suitable for country or urban settings.
- A covered front porch and a gabled roof extension accent the facade, allowing plenty of space for outdoor relaxation.
- The living room, which boasts a warm fireplace, is expanded by a 10½-ft. cathedral ceiling. The addition of the kitchen and the bayed dining room creates an expansive gathering space.

Plan 567-J-86155

Bedrooms: 3	Baths: 2
Living Area:	
Main floor	1,385 sq. ft.
Total Living Area:	**1,385 sq. ft.**
Standard basement	1,385 sq. ft.
Carport	380 sq. ft.
Storage	40 sq. ft.
Exterior Wall Framing:	2x4
Foundation Options:	
Standard basement	
Crawlspace	
Slab	
(Please specify foundation type when ordering.)	
BLUEPRINT PRICE CODE:	**A**

VIEW INTO LIVING ROOM AND DINING ROOM

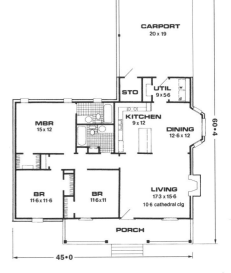

MAIN FLOOR

Plan 567-J-86155

The Essence of Elegance

- This home's stunning facade and masterful interior details reflect your love for all that is elegant in life.
- The soaring foyer basks in natural light. Arched doorways flanked by decorative columns and topped by plant shelves lead you to the heart of the design.
- Generous in proportion, the Great Room is warmed by a no-fuss gas fireplace. A French door leads to the backyard, and an archway introduces the adjoining formal dining room.
- The kitchen boasts a center island, a cozy breakfast nook and a serving bar that accommodates the Great Room.
- A haven from the stresses of daily life, the master suite includes a private bath with a garden tub, a separate shower, a dual-sink vanity and a walk-in closet. A plant shelf hugs one corner of the bath.
- A striking arched window brightens the foremost secondary bedroom.

Plan 567-HFB-5493-SCOT

Bedrooms: 3	Baths: 2½
Living Area:	
Main floor	1,884 sq. ft.
Total Living Area:	**1,884 sq. ft.**
Daylight basement	1,884 sq. ft.
Garage and storage	463 sq. ft.
Exterior Wall Framing:	2x4

Foundation Options:
Daylight basement
Crawlspace
Slab
(Please specify foundation type when ordering.)

BLUEPRINT PRICE CODE:	B

MAIN FLOOR

Plan 567-HFB-5493-SCOT

...ntral Fireplace ...cuses ...amily Living

Total Living Area:	**1,408 sq. ft.**
Blueprint Price Code:	**A**
Garage:	**440 sq. ft.**

FEATURES

- Handsome see-through fireplace offers a gathering point for the family room and breakfast/kitchen area

- Vaulted ceiling and large bay window in the master bedroom add charm to this room

- A dramatic angular wall and large windows add brightness to the kitchen/breakfast area

- Family room and breakfast/kitchen area have vaulted ceilings, adding to this central living area

- 3 bedrooms, 2 baths, 2-car garage

- Crawl space foundation, drawings also include slab foundation

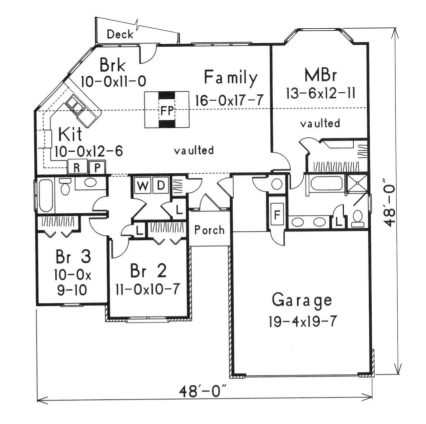

Plan 567-0181

Covered Porch Invites Visitors

- This nice home welcomes visitors with its covered front porch and its wide-open living areas.
- Detailed columns, railings and shutters decorate the front porch that guides guests to the central entry.
- Just off the entry, the bright living room merges with the dining room. The side wall is lined with glass, including a glass door that opens to the yard.
- The angled kitchen features a serving counter facing the dining room. A handy laundry closet and access to a storage area and the garage are nearby.
- An angled hall leads to the bedroom wing. The master suite offers a private bath, a walk-in closet and a dressing area with a vanity. Two additional bedrooms and another full bath are located down the hall.

Plan 567-E-1217

Bedrooms: 3	Baths: 2
Living Area:	
Main floor	1,266 sq. ft.
Total Living Area:	**1,266 sq. ft.**
Garage and storage	550 sq. ft.
Exterior Wall Framing:	2x6

Foundation Options:

Crawlspace

Slab
(Please specify foundation type when ordering.)

BLUEPRINT PRICE CODE:	**A**

VIEW INTO KITCHEN AND LIVING ROOM FROM DINING ROOM

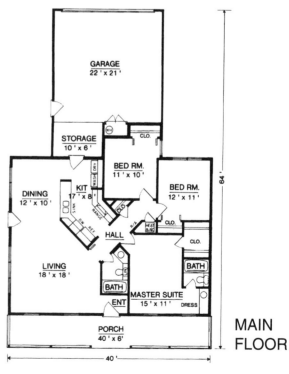

MAIN FLOOR

Plan 567-E-1217

Good Things, Small Package

- This compact design offers plenty of fine amenities, proving that good things do, indeed, come in small packages.
- With soaring vaulted ceilings, the family and dining rooms flaunt the look and feel of elegance.
- Imagine get-togethers with close friends in the spacious family room.
- Double doors introduce the master suite, which is topped by a lovely tray ceiling.

Plan 567-HFB-5036-MABR

Bedrooms: 3	Baths: 2
Living Area:	
Main floor	1,277 sq. ft.
Total Living Area:	**1,277 sq. ft.**
Daylight basement	528 sq. ft.
Tuck-under garage	473 sq. ft.
Storage	276 sq. ft.
Exterior Wall Framing:	2x4
Foundation Options:	
Daylight basement	
Crawlspace	
Slab	
(Please specify foundation type when ordering.)	
BLUEPRINT PRICE CODE:	**A**

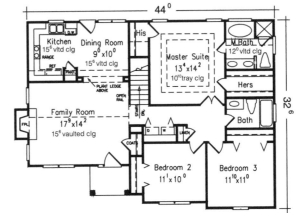

MAIN FLOOR

Plan 567-HFB-5036-MABR

Quaint Details

- This quaint home features a handsome exterior and an exciting floor plan that maximizes square footage.
- The foyer flows to the Great Room, which features a fireplace, backyard access and a 16½-ft. vaulted ceiling.
- Sharing the vaulted ceiling, the galley-style kitchen leads to a breakfast area with a convenient laundry closet.
- The master suite boasts a 15-ft., 8-in. tray ceiling and a garden bath with a 13-ft.-high vaulted ceiling.

Plan 567-HFB-1289

Bedrooms: 3	Baths: 2
Living Area:	
Main floor	1,289 sq. ft.
Total Living Area:	**1,289 sq. ft.**
Daylight basement	1,289 sq. ft.
Garage	430 sq. ft.
Exterior Wall Framing:	2x4
Foundation Options:	
Daylight basement	
Crawlspace	
Slab	
(Please specify foundation type when ordering.)	
BLUEPRINT PRICE CODE:	**A**

MAIN FLOOR

Plan 567-HFB-1289

Family Tradition

- This quaint home basks in tradition, with beautiful gables facing the street and vaulted family spaces inside.
- The columned front porch opens to a spacious family room, where a vaulted ceiling soars above a striking fireplace flanked by arched windows. The high ceiling continues into the dining room and the kitchen.
- The sunny dining room opens to the backyard through a French door. The walk-through kitchen offers a bright, angled sink, a snack bar and a large pantry closet topped by a plant shelf.
- The master bedroom boasts a tray ceiling, while the garden bath flaunts a high vaulted ceiling.
- Two secondary bedrooms share another full bath. A handy laundry closet is close to the bedrooms and the garage.
- For added spaciousness, all ceilings are raised unless otherwise specified.

Plan 567-HFB-5115-CLAI

Bedrooms: 3	Baths: 2
Living Area:	
Main floor	1,198 sq. ft.
Total Living Area:	**1,198 sq. ft.**
Daylight basement	1,198 sq. ft.
Garage	484 sq. ft.
Exterior Wall Framing:	2x4
Foundation Options:	

Daylight basement
Crawlspace
(Please specify foundation type when ordering.)

BLUEPRINT PRICE CODE:	A

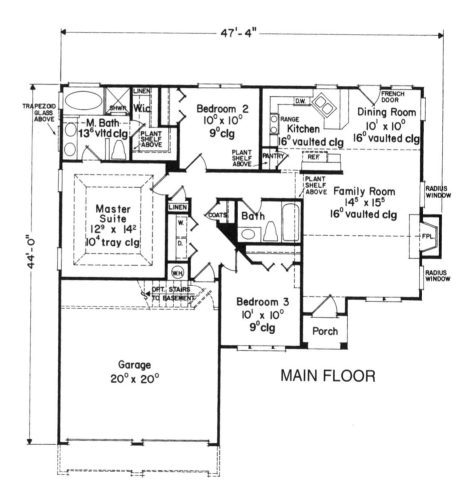

MAIN FLOOR

Plan 567-HFB-5115-CLAI

Captivating Country

- A modest front porch and dormer windows lend this single-story home a distinctly country look that neatly matches its hospitable interior.
- Inside, the main living area is formed by the open family and dining rooms. Both rooms are crowned by a vaulted ceiling; the family room boasts a cozy fireplace and an arched transom window overlooking the front yard.
- The gourmet kitchen features a pass-through to the family room. Nearby, a wonderful windowed breakfast room provides access to a secluded porch.
- A tray ceiling tops the master bedroom, which is brightened by a wall of windows and includes a walk-in closet. The master bath is luxurious, with a garden tub and a separate shower.
- Two additional bedrooms share another full bath.

Plan 567-HFB-5373-BARN

Bedrooms: 3	Baths: 2
Living Area:	
Main floor	1,373 sq. ft.
Total Living Area:	**1,373 sq. ft.**
Daylight basement	1,386 sq. ft.
Garage	400 sq. ft.
Exterior Wall Framing:	2x4

Foundation Options:

Daylight basement
Crawlspace
(Please specify foundation type when ordering.)

BLUEPRINT PRICE CODE:	**A**

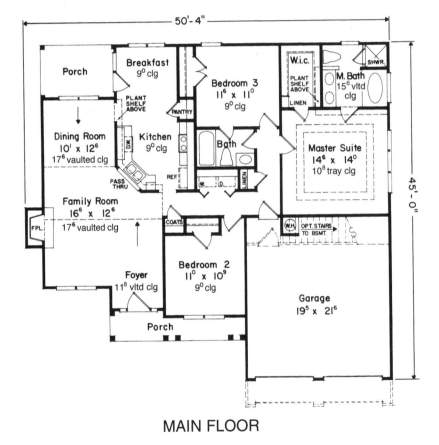

MAIN FLOOR

Plan 567-HFB-5373-BARN

Rustic Ranch

- A rustic exterior and a relaxed interior define this warm ranch-style home.
- The living room flows into the bayed dining room, which opens to a patio. Both rooms are enhanced by 14-ft. vaulted ceilings and a central fireplace.
- The functional kitchen includes a snack bar to the dining room, a pantry and plenty of cabinet space.
- The master bedroom boasts a mirrored dressing area, a private bath and abundant closet space.
- The third bedroom includes a cozy window seat.

Plan 567-NW-521

Bedrooms: 3	Baths: 2
Living Area:	
Main floor	1,187 sq. ft.
Total Living Area:	**1,187 sq. ft.**
Garage	448 sq. ft.
Exterior Wall Framing:	2x6
Foundation Options:	
Crawlspace (Please specify foundation type when ordering.)	
BLUEPRINT PRICE CODE:	A

MAIN FLOOR

Plan 567-NW-521

Ritzy Rambler

- This inviting one-story home is full of fancy touches not usually associated with such an economical floor plan!
- A quaint, covered porch adorns the entry, which leads first to two secondary bedrooms and the well-placed laundry facilities between them.
- At the back of the home, the family room faces a warm fireplace.
- With a versatile center island, the adjoining kitchen and breakfast nook promise easy food preparation. Sliding glass doors lead to a backyard patio.
- The master bedroom boasts a roomy walk-in closet and a private bath.

Plan 567-NW-531

Bedrooms: 3	Baths: 2
Living Area:	
Main floor	1,214 sq. ft.
Total Living Area:	**1,214 sq. ft.**
Garage	380 sq. ft.
Exterior Wall Framing:	2x6
Foundation Options:	
Crawlspace (Please specify foundation type when ordering.)	
BLUEPRINT PRICE CODE:	A

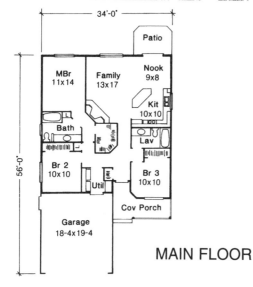

MAIN FLOOR

Plan 567-NW-531

Distinguished Styling For A Small Lot

Total Living Area:	**1,268 sq. ft.**
Blueprint Price Code:	**A**
Garage:	373 sq. ft.
Front porch:	63 sq. ft.

FEATURES

- Multiple gables, large porch and arched windows create classy exterior

- Innovative design provides openness in great room, kitchen and breakfast room

- Secondary bedrooms have private hall with bath

- 3 bedrooms, 2 baths, 2-car garage

- Basement foundation

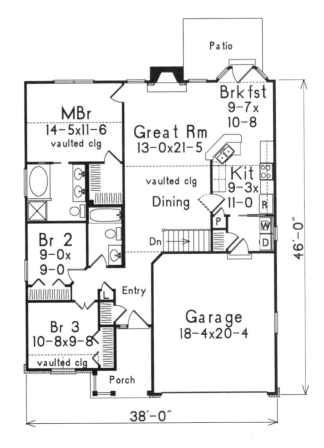

Plan 567-0717

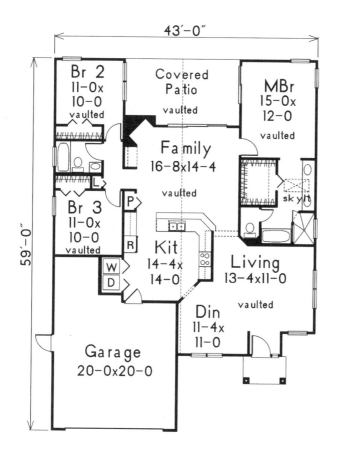

43'-0"

Br 2
11-0x
10-0
vaulted

Covered Patio
vaulted

MBr
15-0x
12-0
vaulted

Family
16-8x14-4
vaulted

sk lt

Br 3
11-0x
10-0
vaulted

P

R

Kit
14-4x
14-0

W
D

Living
13-4x11-0
vaulted

Din
11-4x
11-0

59'-0"

Garage
20-0x20-0

Vaulted Ceilings
Add Dimension

Total Living Area:	1,550 sq. ft.
Blueprint Price Code:	B
Garage:	400 sq. ft.
Front entry:	28 sq. ft.
Back patio:	202 sq. ft.

FEATURES

- Cozy corner fireplace provides focal point in family room

- Master bedroom features large walk-in closet, skylight and separate tub and shower

- Convenient laundry closet

- Kitchen with pantry and breakfast bar connects to family room

- Family room and master bedroom access covered patio

- 3 bedrooms, 2 baths, 2-car garage

- Slab foundation

Plan 567-0357

Front Porch Adds Style To This Ranch

Total Living Area:	**1,496 sq. ft.**
Blueprint Price Code:	**A**
Drive-under garage:	238 sq. ft.
Front porch:	162 sq. ft.
Rear porch:	77 sq. ft.

FEATURES

- Master bedroom features coffered ceiling, walk-in-closet and spacious bath

- Vaulted ceiling and fireplace grace family room

- Dining room adjacent to kitchen and features access to rear porch

- Convenient access to utility room from kitchen

- 3 bedrooms, 2 baths, 2-car drive under garage

- Basement foundation

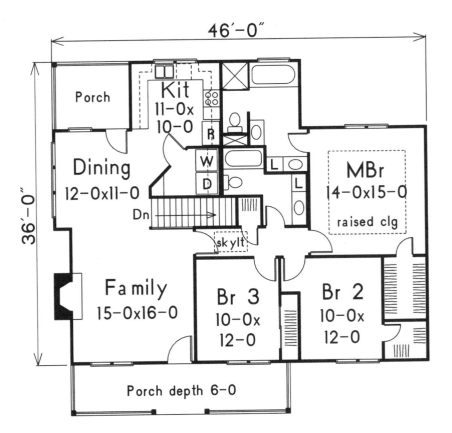

Plan 567-0239

Compact Ranch

- Repeating gables, wood siding and brick accents adorn this compact ranch-style home.
- The entry opens into the family room, which is enhanced by a 21-ft. vaulted ceiling and a striking corner fireplace.
- A serving bar is open to the efficient kitchen, which has a handy pantry and a sunny breakfast room.
- The luxurious master suite boasts a 10½-ft. tray ceiling, a walk-in closet and a luxurious garden bath.
- Two more bedrooms, one with a 14½-ft. vaulted ceiling, share another full bath.

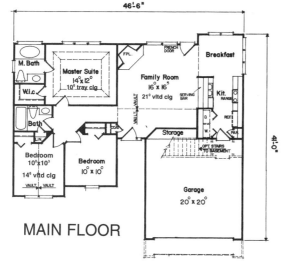

MAIN FLOOR

Plan 567-HFB-1104

Bedrooms: 3	Baths: 2
Living Area:	
Main floor	1,104 sq. ft.
Total Living Area:	**1,104 sq. ft.**
Daylight basement	1,104 sq. ft.
Garage	400 sq. ft.
Exterior Wall Framing:	2x4
Foundation Options:	
Daylight basement	
Crawlspace	
(Please specify foundation type when ordering.)	
BLUEPRINT PRICE CODE:	A

Plan 567-HFB-1104

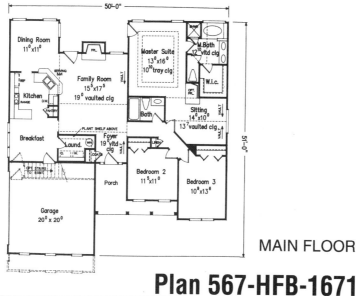

Smashing Master Suite!

- Corniced gables accented with arched louvers and striking columns take this one-story design beyond the ordinary.
- The vaulted ceiling in the foyer rises to join the family room's 19-ft. vaulted ceiling. A central fireplace is framed by a window and a French door.
- The master suite is smashing, with a 10-ft. ceiling and private access to the backyard. The 13-ft.-high vaulted sitting area offers an optional fireplace.

Plan 567-HFB-1671

Bedrooms: 3	Baths: 2
Living Area:	
Main floor	1,671 sq. ft.
Total Living Area:	**1,671 sq. ft.**
Daylight basement	1,671 sq. ft.
Garage	240 sq. ft.
Exterior Wall Framing:	2x4
Foundation Options:	
Daylight basement	
Crawlspace	
(Please specify foundation type when ordering.)	
BLUEPRINT PRICE CODE:	B

MAIN FLOOR

Plan 567-HFB-1671

An Enhancement To Any Neighborhood

Total Living Area:	**1,440 sq. ft.**
Blueprint Price Code:	**A**
Garage:	504 sq. ft.
Front porch:	84 sq. ft.

FEATURES

- Foyer adjoins massive-sized great room with sloping ceilings and tall masonry fireplace

- Kitchen adjoins spacious dining room and features pass-through breakfast bar

- Master suite enjoys private bath and two closets

- An oversized two-car side entry garage offers plenty of storage for bicycles, lawn equipment, etc.

- 3 bedrooms, 2 baths, 2-car side entry garage

- Basement, crawl space or slab foundation available, please specify when ordering

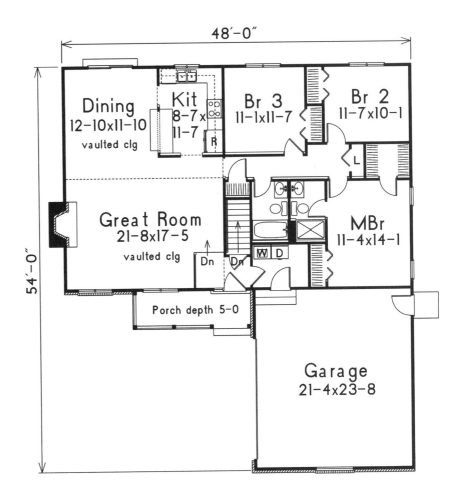

Plan 567-1117

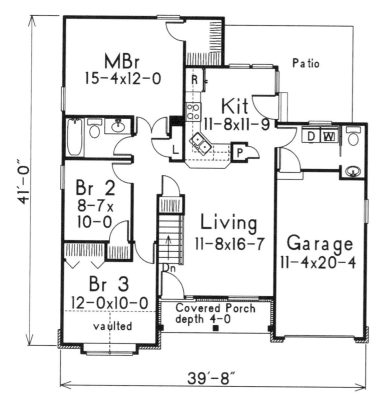

MBr
15-4x12-0

Patio

Kit
11-8x11-9

R

D W

L P

Br 2
8-7x
10-0

Living
11-8x16-7

Garage
11-4x20-4

Dn

Br 3
12-0x10-0

Covered Porch
depth 4-0

vaulted

41'-0"

39'-8"

Innovative Ranch Has Cozy Corner Patio

Total Living Area:	1,092 sq. ft.
Blueprint Price Code:	**AA**
Garage:	230 sq. ft.
Front porch:	56 sq. ft.

FEATURES

- Box window and inviting porch with dormers create a charming facade

- Eat-in kitchen offers a pass-through breakfast bar, corner window wall to patio, pantry and convenient laundry with half bath

- Master bedroom features double entry doors and walk-in closet

- 3 bedrooms, 1 1/2 baths, 1-car garage

- Basement foundation

Plan 567-0478

Bold Stucco and Stone

- Stone and stucco join forces to create this dapper home's bold facade.
- Windows and high ceilings command attention inside and add a vertical dimension to the sprawling layout.
- The foyer's 20½-ft.-high vaulted ceiling is echoed by the family room ahead. Nestled between two windows, the family room's handsome fireplace further attracts your eye.
- At the center of the living spaces, the kitchen offers its users a stylish wrap-around serving bar and a neat five-shelf pantry.
- Four bedrooms make up the sleeping wing. The foremost bedroom boasts a 15-ft. vaulted ceiling, while the master bedroom offers a 10-ft. tray ceiling.
- The master bath's 13-ft. vaulted ceiling hovers above a garden tub, a dual-sink vanity and a dramatic arched window.
- Unless otherwise mentioned, each room has a 9-ft. ceiling.

Plan 567-HFB-1688

Bedrooms: 4	Baths: 2
Living Area:	
Main floor	1,702 sq. ft.
Total Living Area:	**1,702 sq. ft.**
Daylight basement	1,702 sq. ft.
Garage	400 sq. ft.
Exterior Wall Framing:	2x4
Foundation Options:	

Daylight basement
Crawlspace
(Please specify foundation type when ordering.)

BLUEPRINT PRICE CODE:	**B**

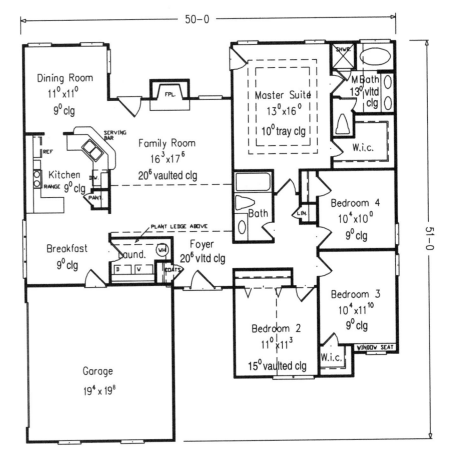

MAIN FLOOR

Plan 567-HFB-1688

Planned to Perfection

- This attractive and stylish home offers an interior design that is planned to perfection.
- The vaulted Great Room features a corner fireplace and lots of windows. The adjoining dining room offers a bay window and access to a covered patio.
- The gourmet kitchen includes an island cooktop, a garden window above the sink and a built-in desk.
- The master suite boasts a tray ceiling and a peaceful reading area.

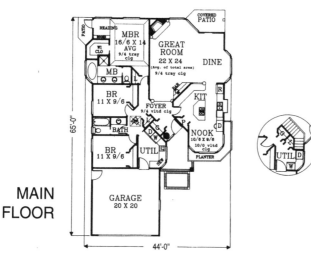

MAIN FLOOR

Plan 567-S-4789

Plan 567-S-4789

Bedrooms: 3	Baths: 2
Living Area:	
Main floor	1,665 sq. ft.
Total Living Area:	**1,665 sq. ft.**
Standard basement	1,665 sq. ft.
Garage	400 sq. ft.
Exterior Wall Framing:	2x6
Foundation Options:	

Standard basement, crawlspace or slab
(Please specify foundation type when ordering.)

BLUEPRINT PRICE CODE:	B

Elegant Facade

- A stucco facade with corner quoins and keystone accents adds a refined look to this elegant one-story home.
- The foyer leads to the family room, where an 11-ft., 8-in. ceiling and a window-flanked fireplace are featured.
- The kitchen showcases an angled serving bar that faces the sunny breakfast room.
- The fantastic master suite features an elegant 10-ft. tray ceiling and a superb bath with 13-ft. vaulted ceiling, a garden tub and an overhead plant shelf.

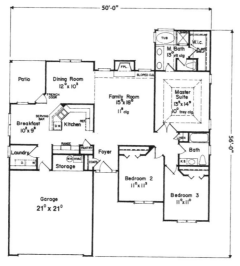

MAIN FLOOR

Plan 567-HFB-1531

Bedrooms: 3	Baths: 2
Living Area:	
Main floor	1,531 sq. ft.
Total Living Area:	**1,531 sq. ft.**
Garage and storage	471 sq. ft.
Exterior Wall Framing:	2x4
Foundation Options:	

Crawlspace
Slab
(Please specify foundation type when ordering.)

BLUEPRINT PRICE CODE:	B

Plan 567-HFB-1531

A Trim Arrangement Of Living Areas

Total Living Area: 1,770 sq. ft.
Blueprint Price Code: B
Garage: 400 sq. ft.
Front porch: 64 sq. ft.

FEATURES

- Distinctive covered entrance leads into spacious foyer

- Master bedroom, living and dining rooms all feature large windows for plenty of light

- Oversized living room has a high ceiling and large windows that flank the fireplace

- Kitchen includes pantry and large planning center

- 3 bedrooms, 2 baths, 2-car garage

- Slab foundation

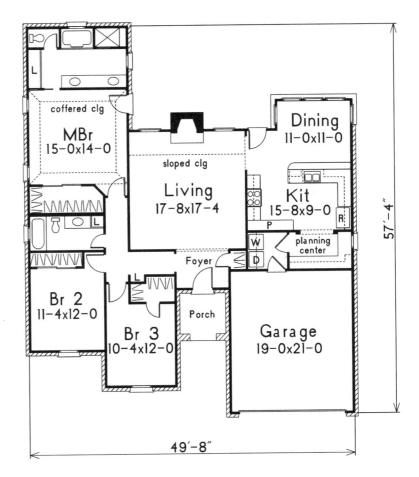

Plan 567-0214

Built-In Media Center Focal Point In Living Room

Total Living Area: 1,539 sq. ft.
Blueprint Price Code: B
Garage: 503 sq. ft.
Front entry: 14 sq. ft.
Back porch: 102 sq. ft.

FEATURE

- Standard 9' ceilings

- Master bedroom features 10' tray ceiling, access to porch, ample closet space and full bath

- Serving counter separates kitchen and dining room

- Foyer with handy coat closet opens to living area with fireplace

- Handy utility room near kitchen

- 3 bedrooms, 2 baths, 2-car garage

- Slab foundation

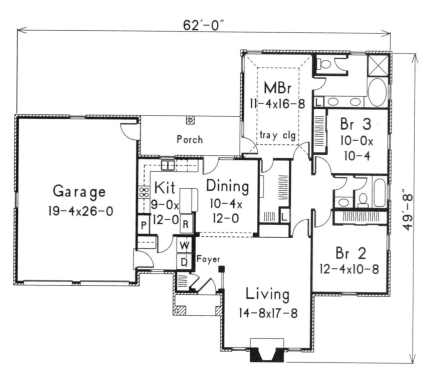

62'-0"

49'-8"

Garage 19-4x26-0

Porch

Kit 9-0x 12-0

Dining 10-4x 12-0

MBr 11-4x16-8
tray clg

Br 3 10-0x 10-4

P

R

W

D

Foyer

Living 14-8x17-8

Br 2 12-4x10-8

Plan 567-0246

UP TO 1,799 SQ. FT.

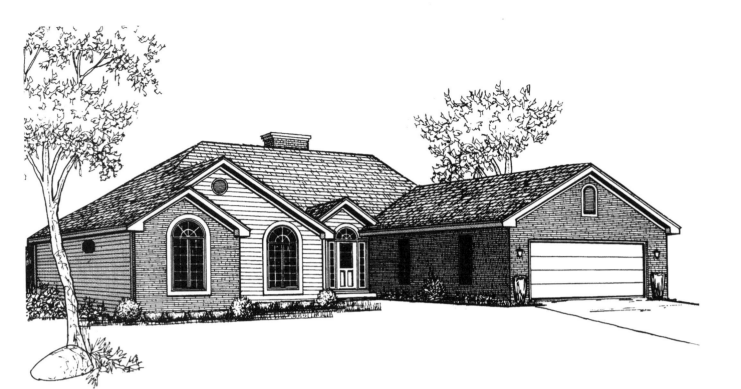

Palladian Windows Dominate Facade

Total Living Area:	1,500 sq. ft.
Blueprint Price Code:	B
Garage:	462 sq. ft.

FEATURES

- Living room features a cathedral ceiling and opens to breakfast room

- Breakfast room has a spectacular bay window and adjoins a well-appointed kitchen with generous storage

- Laundry is convenient to kitchen and includes a large closet

- Large walk-in closet gives the master bedroom abundant storage

- 3 bedrooms, 2 baths, 2-car garage

- Basement foundation

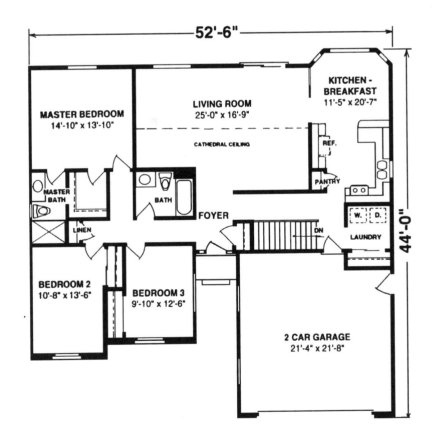

Plan 567-1429

Terrific Design For Family Living

Total Living Area:	1,345 sq. ft.
Blueprint Price Code:	A
Garage:	531 sq. ft.
Storage:	100 sq. ft.
Front porch:	92 sq. ft.

FEATURES

- Brick front details add a touch of elegance

- Master suite has private full bath

- Great room combined wih dining area adds spaciousness

- Functional kitchen complete with pantry and eating bar

- Storage area in garage

- 3 bedrooms, 2 baths, 2-car side entry garage

- Basement foundation, crawl space or slab foundation available, please specify when ordering

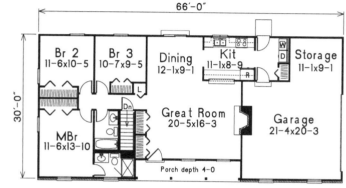

Plan 567-1124

Multi-Roof Levels Create Attractive Colonial Home

Total Living Area:	1,364 sq. ft.
Blueprint Price Code:	A
Garage	459 sq. ft.
Front porch:	140 sq. ft.

FEATURES

- A large porch and entry door with sidelights lead into a generous living room

- Well-planned kitchen features a laundry closet, built-in pantry and open peninsula

- Master bedroom has its own bath with 4' shower

- 3 bedrooms, 2 baths, 2-car garage

- Basement, crawl space and slab foundation, please specify when ordering

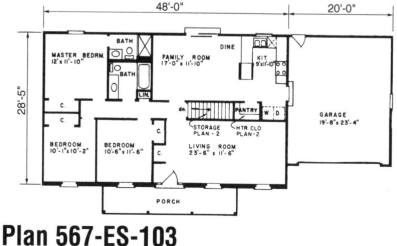

Plan 567-ES-103

Central Fireplace Dominates Living Area

Total Living Area: 1,444 sq. ft.
Blueprint Price Code: A
Garage: 515 sq. ft.
Front porch: 80 sq. ft.
Back porch: 71 sq. ft.

FEATURES

- 11' ceilings in living and dining rooms combine with a central fireplace to create large open living area

- Both secondary bedrooms have large walk-in closets

- Large storage area in garage suitable for a work shop or play area

- Front and rear covered porches add cozy touch

- U-shaped kitchen includes a laundry closet and serving bar

- 3 bedrooms, 2 baths, 2-car side entry garage

- Slab foundation, drawings also include crawl space foundation

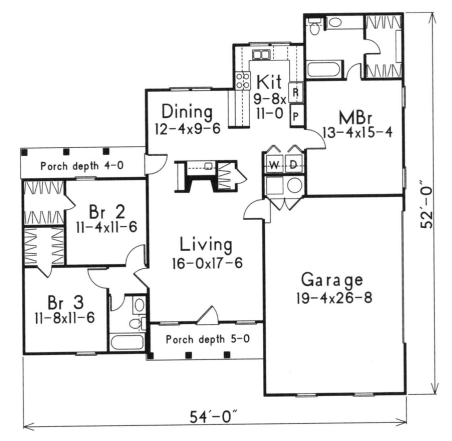

Plan 567-0194

Classic Styling
With Framed Entry

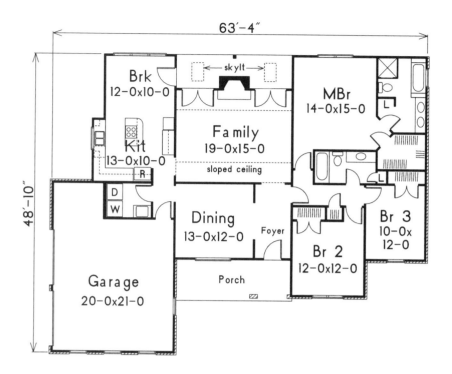

Total Living Area:	1,739 sq. ft.
Blueprint Price Code:	B
Garage:	420 sq. ft.
Storage:	51 sq. ft.
Front porch:	133 sq. ft.
Back porch:	91 sq. ft.

FEATURES

- Utility room has convenient work area, laundry sink and storage space

- Vaulted ceiling lends drama to the family room with fireplace and double French doors

- Island kitchen is enhanced by adjoining breakfast area with access to the patio

- Formal dining room features a 10' ceiling

- Private hallway separates bedrooms from living area

- 3 bedrooms, 2 baths, 2-car side entry garage

- Slab foundation

Plan 567-0240

Lighted Charm

Total Living Area:	1,540 sq. ft.
Blueprint Price Code:	B
Garage:	462 sq. ft.
Front porch:	34 sq. ft.

FEATURES

- Porch entrance into foyer leads to an impressive dining area with full window and a half-circle window above

- Kitchen/breakfast room features a center island and cathedral ceiling

- Great room with cathedral ceiling and exposed beams accessible from foyer

- Master bedroom includes full bath and walk-in closet

- Two additional bedrooms share a full bath

- 3 bedrooms, 2 baths, 2-car garage

- Basement, crawl space or slab foundation available, please specify when ordering

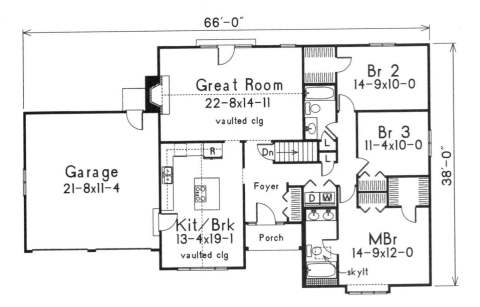

Plan 567-1220

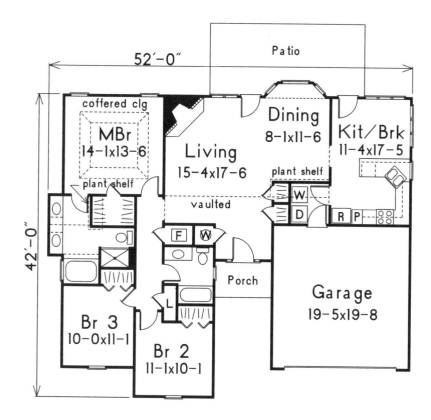

Impressive Corner Fireplace Highlights The Living Area

Total Living Area:	1,458 sq. ft.
Blueprint Price Code:	**A**
Garage:	382 sq. ft.
Front porch:	35 sq. ft.

FEATURES

- Convenient snack bar joins kitchen with breakfast room

- Large living/dining room with fireplace, plenty of windows, vaulted ceiling and plant shelves

- Master bedroom offers a private bath with vaulted ceiling, walk-in closet, plant shelf and coffered ceiling

- Corner windows provide abundant light in breakfast room

- 3 bedrooms, 2 baths, 2-car garage

- Crawl space foundation, drawings also include slab foundation

Plan 567-0253

High-Style Vaulted Ranch

Total Living Area:	**1,453 sq. ft.**
Blueprint Price Code:	**A**
Garage:	**504 sq. ft.**

FEATURES

- Decorative vents, window trim, shutters and brick blend to create dramatic curb appeal

- Energy efficient home with 2" x 6" exterior walls

- Kitchen opens to living area and includes salad sink in the island, pantry and handy laundry room

- Exquisite master bedroom highlighted by vaulted ceiling

- 3 bedrooms, 2 baths, 2-car garage

- Basement foundation, drawings also include crawl space foundation

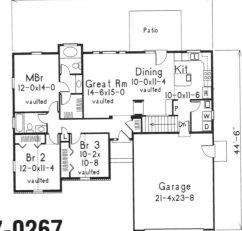

Plan 567-0267

Vaulted Ceilings Throughout

Total Living Area:	**1,428 sq. ft.**
Blueprint Price Code:	**A**
Garage:	**505 sq. ft.**
Front entry:	**78 sq. ft.**

FEATURES

- 10' ceiling in entry and hallway

- Vaulted dining room combines a desk area near the see-through fireplace

- Energy efficient home with 2" x 6" exterior walls

- Kitchen boasts an island with salad sink and pantry

- Master bedroom with vaulted ceilings includes large walk-in closet and private master bath

- 3 bedrooms, 2 baths, 2-car garage

- Basement foundation, drawings also include crawl space foundation

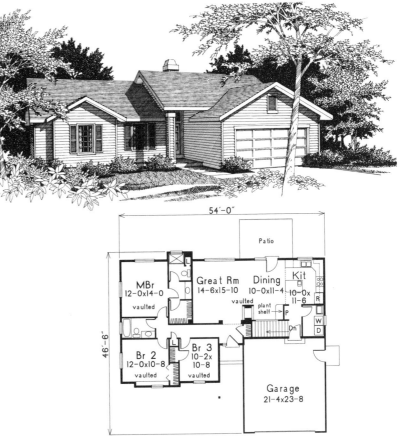

Plan 567-0269

Large Corner Deck Lends Way To Outside Living Area

Total Living Area:	**1,283 sq. ft.**
Blueprint Price Code:	**A**
Garage:	374 sq. ft.
Front porch:	25 sq. ft.

FEATURES

- Vaulted breakfast room with sliding doors that open onto deck

- Kitchen features convenient corner sink and pass-through to dining room

- Open living atmosphere in dining area and great room

- Vaulted great room features a fireplace

- 3 bedrooms, 2 baths, 2-car garage

- Basement foundation

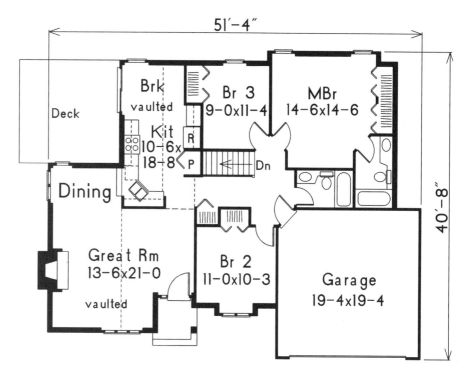

Plan 567-0272

A Home for All Seasons

- As a starter home, a vacation retreat or a quiet place to spend your retirement years, this versatile design stands ready to accommodate your needs in all seasons of life.
- Past the covered entry, a tiled foyer introduces the expansive Great Room. With a vaulted ceiling lending an added feeling of spaciousness, the Great Room unfolds to the backyard. A

door at the rear opens to the patio or garden that you'll be eager to add for outdoor enjoyment.
- Off the convenient U-shaped kitchen, an eating bar serves casual meals with comfortable ease.
- A main-floor laundry room just off the kitchen means no more trips to the basement with baskets of washing.
- At the rear of the home, the master bedroom offers a vaulted ceiling, a large walk-in closet and a private bath.
- Two secondary bedrooms, one with a lovely arched window, share an additional full bath.

Plan 567-HUD-102-B	
Bedrooms: 3	**Baths:** 2
Living Area:	
Main floor	1,200 sq. ft.
Total Living Area:	**1,200 sq. ft.**
Standard basement	1,257 sq. ft.
Garage	440 sq. ft.
Exterior Wall Framing:	2x4
Foundation Options:	
Standard basement	
Crawlspace	
Slab	
(Please specify foundation type when ordering.)	
BLUEPRINT PRICE CODE:	**A**

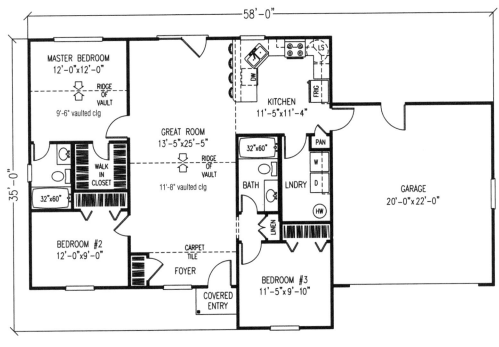

MAIN FLOOR

Plan 567-HUD-102-B

Pillared Front Porch Generates Charm And Warmth

Total Living Area:	**1,567 sq. ft.**
Blueprint Price Code:	**B**
Garage:	420 sq. ft.
Sorage:	72 sq. ft.
Front porch:	138 sq. ft.

FEATURES

- Living room flows into dining room shaped by an angled pass-through into the kitchen

- Cheerful, windowed dining area

- Second floor has 338 square feet for future space and is well-lit from four dormers

- Master suite separated from other bedrooms for privacy

- 3 bedrooms, 2 baths, 2-car side entry garage

- Basement foundation, drawings also include slab foundation

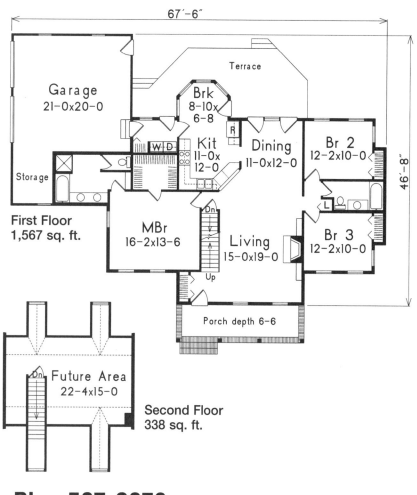

Garage
21-0x20-0

Storage

First Floor
1,567 sq. ft.

Terrace

Brk
8-10x
6-8

W D

Kit
11-0x
12-0

R

Dining
11-0x12-0

Br 2
12-2x10-0

MBr
16-2x13-6

Dn

Up

Living
15-0x19-0

Br 3
12-2x10-0

L

67'-6"

46'-8"

Porch depth 6-6

Dn Future Area
22-4x15-0

Second Floor
338 sq. ft.

Plan 567-0678

Rustic
Stone Exterior

Total Living Area:	**1,466 sq. ft.**
Blueprint Price Code:	**A**
Garage:	390 sq. ft.
Storage:	65 sq. ft.
Front porch:	137 sq. ft.

FEATURES

- Energy efficient home with 2" x 6" exterior walls

- Foyer separates the living room from the dining room and contains a generous coat closet

- Large living room with corner fireplace, bay window and pass-through to the kitchen

- Informal breakfast area opens out to large terrace through sliding glass doors which lets light into area

- Master bedroom has a large walk-in closet and private bath

- 3 bedrooms, 2 baths, 2-car garage

- Basement foundation, drawings also include slab foundation

56'-4"

49'-8"

Br 3
10-4x
10-0

Br 2
13-4x10-0

MBr
14-10x14-4

L

R

Brk
8-8x
9-0

Porch

Kit
11-0x9-0

Dn

D
W

Living
14-10x14-4

Dining
10-0x11-0

shelf

Porch depth 6-0

Garage
20-0x19-6

Plan 567-0679

Fine Details

- The attractive facade of this home is marked by delicate detailing and eye-catching window and door treatments.
- French doors in the living room provide a stunning view of the rear porch and patio. The living room also boasts a 12½-ft. ceiling and a corner fireplace.
- A bayed dining area and a U-shaped kitchen adjoin the living room. Patio views and an eating bar are nice extras.
- The master suite includes a big walk-in closet and a private bath with a dual-sink vanity.

MAIN FLOOR

Plan 567-E-1428

Bedrooms: 3	Baths: 2
Living Area:	
Main floor	1,415 sq. ft.
Total Living Area:	**1,415 sq. ft.**
Garage	484 sq. ft.
Storage	60 sq. ft.
Exterior Wall Framing:	2x6
Foundation Options:	
Crawlspace, slab (Please specify foundation type when ordering.)	
BLUEPRINT PRICE CODE:	**A**

Plan 567-E-1428

Comfortable L-Shaped Ranch

- The covered entry of this beautiful and spacious ranch-style home leads to many extras lying within.
- A fireplace and a bright bay window highlight the living and dining area.
- The combination kitchen/family room features a large eating bar.
- In the sleeping wing, the master bedroom boasts a private bath, while two additional bedrooms share another full bath.

VIEW INTO LIVING ROOM

MAIN FLOOR

Plan 567-K-276-R

Bedrooms: 3	Baths: 2–2½
Living Area:	
Main floor	1,245 sq. ft.
Total Living Area:	**1,245 sq. ft.**
Standard basement	1,245 sq. ft.
Garage	499 sq. ft.
Exterior Wall Framing:	2x4 or 2x6
Foundation Options:	
Standard basement, crawlspace or slab (Please specify foundation type when ordering.)	
BLUEPRINT PRICE CODE:	**A**

Plan 567-K-276-R

Openness In A Split-Bedroom Ranch

Total Living Area:	**1,574 sq. ft.**
Blueprint Price Code:	**B**
Garage:	420 sq. ft.
Front porch:	28 sq. ft.

FEATURES

- Foyer enters into open great room with corner fireplace and rear dining room with adjoining kitchen

- Two secondary bedrooms share a full bath

- Master bedroom has a spacious private bath with tub and shower and double bowl vanity

- Garage accesses home through mud room/laundry

- 3 bedrooms, 2 baths, 2-car garage

- Basement or crawl space foundation available, please specify when ordering

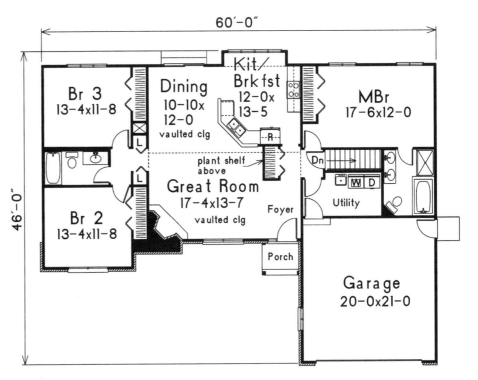

Plan 567-1248

Central Living Area Keeps Bedrooms Private

Total Living Area: 1,546 sq. ft.
Blueprint Price Code: B
Garage: 440 sq. ft.
Front porch: 60 sq. ft.

FEATURES

- Spacious, open rooms create casual atmosphere

- Master suite secluded for privacy

- Dining room features large bay window

- Kitchen/dinette combination offers access to the outdoors

- Large laundry room includes convenient sink

- 3 bedrooms, 2 baths, 2-car garage

- Basement foundation

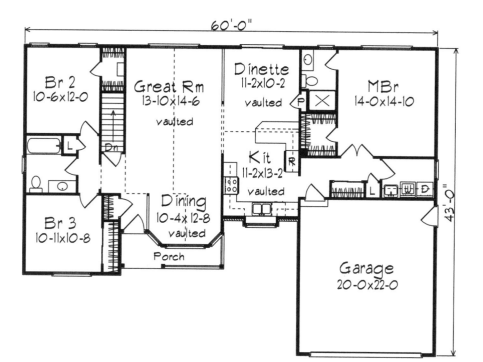

60'-0"

43'-0"

Br 2
10-6x12-0

Great Rm
13-10x14-6
vaulted

Dinette
11-2x10-2
vaulted

MBr
14-0x14-10

Kit
11-2x13-2
vaulted

Dining
10-4x12-8
vaulted

Br 3
10-11x10-8

Porch

Garage
20-0x22-0

Plan 567-0382

Stylish Ranch With Rustic Charm

Total Living Area:	**1,344 sq. ft.**
Blueprint Price Code:	**A**
Garage:	506 sq. ft.
Front porch:	140 sq. ft.

FEATURES

- Family/dining room with sliding door
- Master bedroom and private bath with shower
- Hall bath includes double vanity for added convenience
- Kitchen features U-shaped design, large pantry and laundry area
- 3 bedrooms, 2 baths, 2-car garage
- Crawl space foundation, drawings also include basement and slab foundations

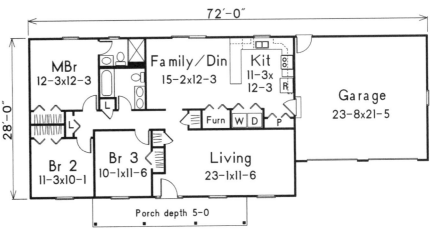

Plan 567-0515

Old Santa Fe Adobe Look

Total Living Area:	**1,689 sq. ft.**
Blueprint Price Code:	**B**
Garage:	506 sq. ft.
Front porch:	100 sq. ft.
Back Patio:	256 sq. ft.

FEATURES

- Traditional beamed ceilings with rough sawn planking at living, dining, front and rear portals
- Unique angled floor plan
- "Kiva" or beehive style fireplace
- Secluded master suite with bath
- Herringbone latilla ceiling at entry
- Large covered patio for outside entertaining
- Energy efficient home with 2" x 6" exterior walls
- 3 bedrooms, 2 baths, 2-car side entry garage
- Slab foundation

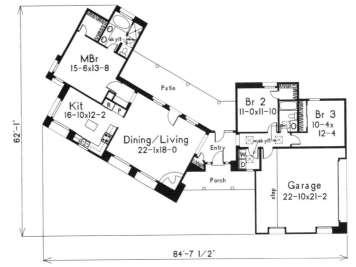

Plan 567-0424

TO ORDER BLUEPRINTS USE THE FORM ON PAGE 256 OR CALL **TOLL-FREE 1-800-367-7667**

See-Through Fireplace Joins Gathering Rooms

Total Living Area:	**1,684 sq. ft.**
Blueprint Price Code:	**B**
Garage:	485 sq. ft.
Front porch:	84 sq. ft.

FEATURES

- Convenient double-doors in dining area provide access to large deck

- Family room features several large windows for brightness

- Bedrooms separate from living areas for privacy

- Master bedroom suite offers bath with walk-in closet, double-bowl vanity and both shower and whirlpool tub

- 3 bedrooms, 2 1/2 baths, 2-car garage

- Basement foundation

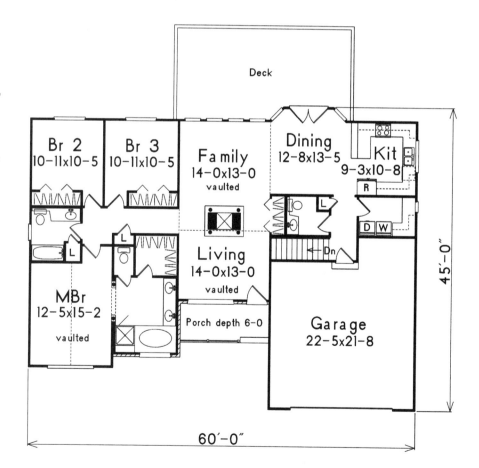

Plan 567-0393

Single-Story with Sparkle

- A lovely facade with a cameo front door, bay windows and dormers give this country-style home extra sparkle.
- The Great Room is at the center of the floor plan, where it merges with the dining room and a screened porch. The Great Room features a tray ceiling, a fireplace and a built-in wet bar.
- The eat-in kitchen has a half-wall that keeps it open to the Great Room and hallway. The dining room offers a half-wall facing the foyer and a bay window overlooking the front porch.
- The delectable master suite is isolated from the other bedrooms and includes a charming bay window, a tray ceiling and a luxurious private bath.
- The two smaller bedrooms are off the main foyer and separated by a full bath.
- A mudroom with a washer and dryer is accessible from the two-car garage.

Plan 567-HAX-91312

Bedrooms: 3	Baths: 2
Living Area:	
Main floor	1,595 sq. ft.
Total Living Area:	**1,595 sq. ft.**
Screened porch	178 sq. ft.
Basement	1,595 sq. ft.
Garage	469 sq. ft.
Storage	21 sq. ft.
Utility room	18 sq. ft.
Exterior Wall Framing:	2x4

Foundation Options:

Daylight basement
Standard basement
Crawlspace
Slab
(Please specify foundation type when ordering.)

BLUEPRINT PRICE CODE:	B

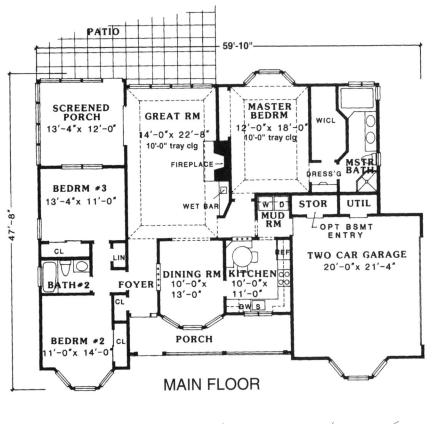

MAIN FLOOR

VIEW INTO GREAT ROOM

Plan 567-HAX-91312

Contemporary Elegance With Efficiency

Total Living Area:	1,321 sq. ft.
Blueprint Price Code:	A
Garage:	265 sq. ft.
Front porch:	30 sq. ft.

FEATURES

- Rear garage and elongated brick wall adds to appealing facade

- Dramatic vaulted living room includes corner fireplace and towering feature windows

- Kitchen/breakfast room is immersed in light from two large windows and glass sliding doors

- 3 bedrooms, 2 baths, 1-car rear entry garage

- Basement foundation

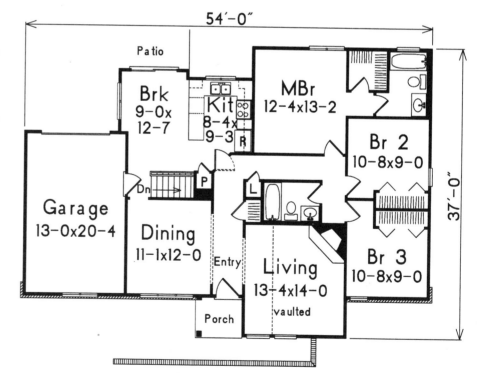

Plan 567-0660

Rustic Ranch

- This ranch-style home offers a warm facade featuring a railed front porch and stone accents.
- Inside, the inviting living room includes an eye-catching fireplace, patio access and a sloped, beamed ceiling.
- The dining room adjoins the efficient U-shaped kitchen, which includes a pantry and a broom closet.
- The master suite offers a large walk-in closet and a roomy master bath.
- At the other end of the home, two secondary bedrooms with abundant closet space share another full bath.

Plan 567-E-1410

Bedrooms: 3	Baths: 2
Living Area:	
Main floor	1,418 sq. ft.
Total Living Area:	**1,418 sq. ft.**
Garage	484 sq. ft.
Storage	38 sq. ft.
Exterior Wall Framing:	2x4
Foundation Options:	
Crawlspace	
Slab	

(Please specify foundation type when ordering.)

BLUEPRINT PRICE CODE: A

MAIN FLOOR

Plan 567-E-1410

Rustic Welcome

- This appealing home boasts a rustic exterior offering guests a friendly welcome. Inside, the Great Room boasts a massive fireplace and an 11-ft., 8-in. cathedral ceiling.
- Off the dining room, the galley-style kitchen flows into the breakfast room.
- The master suite features a walk-in closet and a compartmentalized bath.
- On the opposite side of the home, two additional bedrooms share a second full bath.

Plan 567-C-8460

Bedrooms: 3	Baths: 2
Living Area:	
Main floor	1,670 sq. ft.
Total Living Area:	**1,670 sq. ft.**
Daylight basement	1,600 sq. ft.
Garage	427 sq. ft.
Storage	63 sq. ft.
Exterior Wall Framing:	2x4
Foundation Options:	
Daylight basement	
Crawlspace	
Slab	

(Please specify foundation type when ordering.)

BLUEPRINT PRICE CODE: B

MAIN FLOOR

Plan 567-C-8460

Perfect Repose

- This perfectly planned home is well suited to serve as the haven your family retreats to for repose and relaxation.
- Out front, a covered porch includes just the right amount of space for your favorite two rockers and a side table.
- Inside, the foyer flows right into the Great Room, which will serve as home base for family gatherings. A fireplace flanked by a media center turns this room into a home theater.
- Nearby, sunlight pours into the versatile dining room. Along one wall, a beautiful built-in cabinet holds linens, china and other fine collectibles.
- Afternoon treats take on a fun twist at the kitchen's snack bar. For easy serving, the snack bar extends to a peninsula counter.
- A tray ceiling and a cheery bay window in the master suite turn this space into a stylish oasis. A dressing area with a vanity table for morning preening leads to the master bath, where a skylight and a vaulted ceiling brighten the room.

Plan 567-HAX-95347

Bedrooms: 3	Baths: 2½
Living Area:	
Main floor	1,709 sq. ft.
Total Living Area:	**1,709 sq. ft.**
Standard basement	1,709 sq. ft.
Garage and storage	448 sq. ft.
Enclosed storage	12 sq. ft.
Utility room	13 sq. ft.
Exterior Wall Framing:	2x4

Foundation Options:
Standard basement
Crawlspace
Slab
(Please specify foundation type when ordering.)

BLUEPRINT PRICE CODE:	B

REAR VIEW

MAIN FLOOR

Plan 567-HAX-95347

Graciously Designed Traditional Ranch

Total Living Area:	**1,477 sq. ft.**
Blueprint Price Code:	**A**
Garage:	424 sq. ft.
Storage:	94 sq. ft.
Front porch:	161 sq. ft.

FEATURES

- Oversized porch provides protection from the elements

- Innovative kitchen employs step-saving design

- Breakfast room offers bay window and snack bar open to kitchen with convenient laundry nearby

- 3 bedroom, 2 baths, 2-car side entry garage with storage area

- Basement foundation

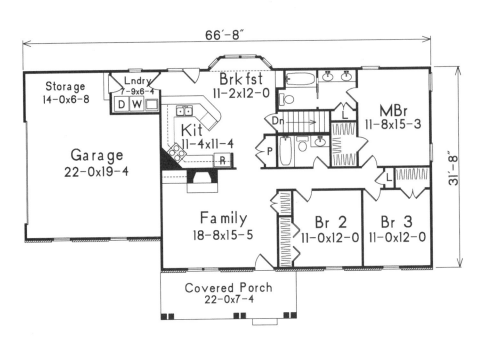

Plan 567-0727

Spacious Interior For Open Living

Total Living Area: 1,400 sq. ft.
Blueprint Price Code: A
Garage: 554 sq. ft.
Front porch: 140 sq. ft.

FEATURES

- Front porch offers warmth and welcome

- Large great room opens into dining room creating open living atmosphere

- Kitchen features convenient laundry area, pantry and breakfast bar

- 3 bedrooms, 2 baths, 2-car garage

- Crawl space foundation, drawings also include basement and slab foundations

74'-0"

28'-0"

MBr 12-3x13-6

Kit 8-1x 13-6

Dining 18-1x13-6

Garage 23-8x23-5

Br 2 12-3x10-3

Br 3 12-1x10-3

Great Rm 22-1x13-7

Porch 28-0x5-0

Plan 567-0510

Breathtaking Open Space

- Soaring ceilings and an open floor plan add breathtaking volume to this charming country-style home.
- The inviting covered-porch entrance opens into the spacious living room, which boasts a spectacular 17-ft.-high cathedral ceiling. Two overhead dormers fill the area with natural light, while a fireplace adds warmth.
- Also under the cathedral ceiling, the kitchen and bayed breakfast room share an eating bar. Skylights brighten the convenient laundry room and the computer room, which provides access to a covered rear porch.
- The secluded master bedroom offers private access to another covered porch. The skylighted master bath has a walk-in closet and a 10-ft. sloped ceiling above a whirlpool tub.
- Optional upper-floor areas provide future expansion space for the needs of a growing family.

Plan 567-J-9302

Bedrooms: 3+	Baths: 2
Living Area:	
Main floor	1,745 sq. ft.
Total Living Area:	**1,745 sq. ft.**
Upper floor (future area)	500 sq. ft.
Future area above garage	241 sq. ft.
Standard basement	1,745 sq. ft.
Garage and storage	559 sq. ft.
Exterior Wall Framing:	2x4

Foundation Options:

Standard basement
Crawlspace
Slab
(Please specify foundation type when ordering.)

BLUEPRINT PRICE CODE: B

VIEW INTO LIVING ROOM

UPPER FLOOR

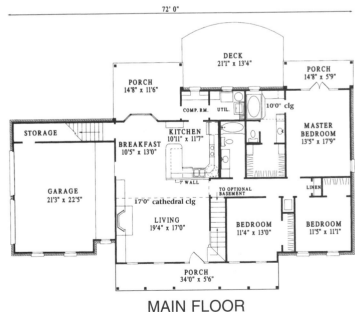

MAIN FLOOR

Plan 567-J-9302

Simply Beautiful

- This four-bedroom design offers simplistic beauty, economical construction and ample space for both family life and formal entertaining—all on one floor.
- The charming cottage-style exterior gives way to a spacious interior. A vaulted, beamed ceiling soars above the huge living room, which features a massive fireplace, built-in bookshelves and access to a backyard patio.
- The deluxe master suite includes a dressing room, a large walk-in closet and a private bath.
- The three remaining bedrooms are larger than average and offer ample closet space.
- The efficient galley-style kitchen flows between a sunny bayed eating area and the formal dining room.
- A nice-sized storage area and a deluxe utility room are accessible from the two-car garage.

VIEW
INTO
LIVING
ROOM

Plan 567-E-1702

Bedrooms: 4	Baths: 2
Living Area:	
Main floor	1,751 sq. ft.
Total Living Area:	**1,751 sq. ft.**
Garage	484 sq. ft.
Storage	105 sq. ft.
Exterior Wall Framing:	2x4

Foundation Options:
Crawlspace
Slab
(Please specify foundation type when ordering.)

BLUEPRINT PRICE CODE:	B

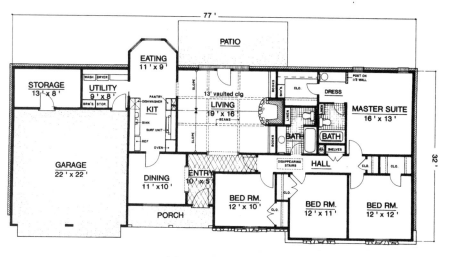

MAIN FLOOR

Plan 567-E-1702

Vaulted Ceilings Create Spacious Feeling

Total Living Area:	**1,605 sq. ft.**
Blueprint Price Code:	**B**
Garage:	405 sq. ft.
Front porch:	36 sq. ft.

FEATURES

- Vaulted ceilings in great room and kitchen/breakfast area

- Spacious great room features large bay window, fireplace, built-in bookshelves and a convenient wet bar

- Dine in formal dining room or breakfast room overlooking rear yard, perfect for entertaining or everyday living

- Master bedroom has a spacious master bath with oval tub and separate shower

- 3 bedrooms, 2 baths, 2-car garage

- Basement foundation, drawings also include slab and crawl space foundations

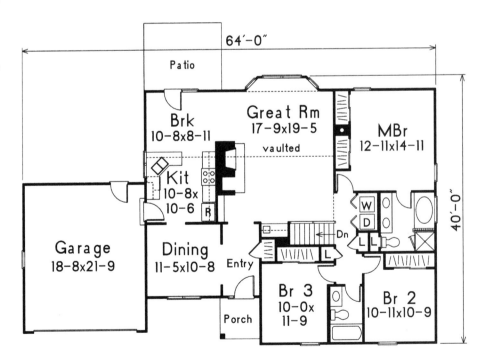

Plan 567-0110

Circletop Transom Window Graces This Exterior

Total Living Area:	1,588 sq. ft.
Blueprint Price Code:	B
Garage:	548 sq. ft.

FEATURES

- Family and dining rooms access rear patio

- Angled walkway leads guests by an attractive landscape area

- Master bedroom with separate dressing area and private bath

- Sunken living room features an attractive railing on two sides

- Kitchen complete with large pantry and eating bar

- 3 bedrooms, 2 baths, 2-car garage

- Basement foundation, drawings also include crawl space and slab foundations

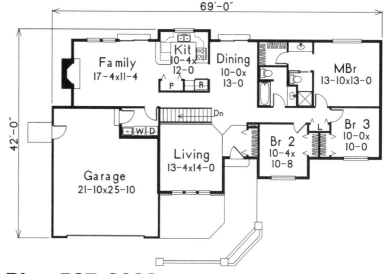

Plan 567-0266

Balance Of Style And Functional Design

Total Living Area:	1,698 sq. ft.
Blueprint Price Code:	B
Drive-under garage:	405 sq. ft.

FEATURES

- Kitchen includes walk-in pantry and corner sink that faces living area

- Breakfast room highlighted by expanse of windows and access to sun deck

- Recessed foyer opens into vaulted living room with fireplace

- Master suite features private bath with large walk-in closet

- 3 bedrooms, 2 baths, 2-car drive under garage

- Basement foundation

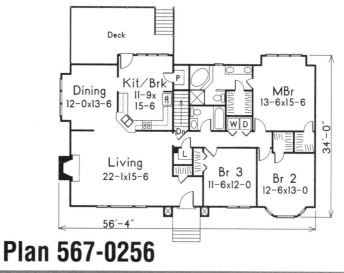

Plan 567-0256

Central Fireplace Brightens Family Living

Total Living Area:	1,260 sq. ft.
Blueprint Price Code:	A
Garage:	460 sq. ft.
Front porch:	162 sq. ft.

FEATURES

- Spacious kitchen and dining area features large pantry, storage area, easy access to garage and laundry room

- Pleasant covered front porch adds a practical touch

- Master bedroom with a private bath adjoins two other bedrooms, all with plenty of closet space

- 3 bedrooms, 2 baths, 2-car garage

- Basement foundaiton, drawings also include crawl space and slab foundations

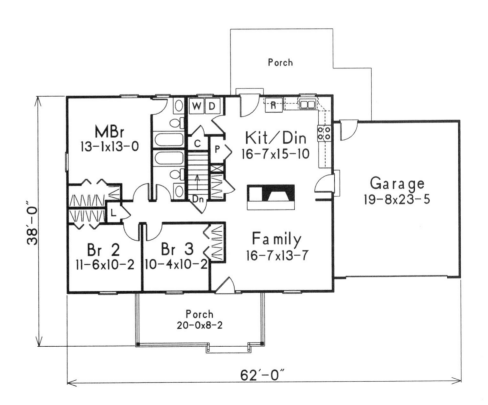

Plan 567-0225

Sculptured Roof Line And Facade Add Charm

Total Living Area:	**1,674 sq. ft.**
Blueprint Price Code:	**B**
Garage:	487 sq. ft.
Front porch:	192 sq. ft.
Screened porch:	140 sq. ft.

FEATURES

- Great room, dining area and kitchen, surrounded with vaulted ceiling, central fireplace and log bin

- Convenient laundry/mud room located between garage and family area with handy stairs to basement

- Easily expandable screened porch and adjacent patio with access from dining area

- Master bedroom features full bath with tub, separate shower and walk-in closet

- 3 bedrooms, 2 baths, 2-car garage

- Basement foundation, drawings also include crawl space and slab foundations

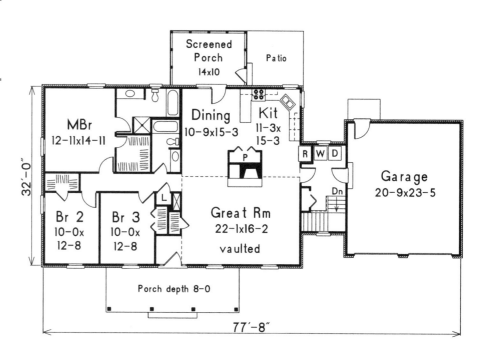

Plan 567-0227

Well Arranged For Cozy Open Living

Total Living Area: 1,527 sq. ft.
Blueprint Price Code: B
Garage: 384 sq. ft.

FEATURES

- Convenient laundry room located off the garage

- Vaulted ceiling in living room slopes to dining and foyer areas creating a spacious entrance

- Galley kitchen provides easy passage to both breakfast and dining areas

- Master suite complete with a large master bath, platform tub and shower, plus roomy walk-in closets

- 3 bedrooms, 2 baths, 2-car side entry garage

- Basement foundation, drawings also include slab and crawl space foundations

50'-0"

50'-0"

Deck

MBr
11-6x16-6

Kit/Brk
8-2x19-0

Living
14-8x22-0

vaulted

Dn

Br 3
10-6x10-6

L

Dining
10-0x12-0

Br 2
11-8x10-10

W
D

Garage
19-5x19-8

Plan 567-0179

Efficient Ranch With Country Charm

Total Living Area: 1,364 sq. ft.
Blueprint Price Code: A
Optional Garage: 505 sq. ft.
Front porch: 120 sq. ft.

FEATURES

- Master suite features spacious walk-in closet and private bath

- Great room highlighted with several windows

- Kitchen with snack bar adjacent to dining area

- Plenty of storage space throughout

- 3 bedrooms, 2 baths, optional 2-car garage

- Basement or crawl space foundation available, please specify when ordering

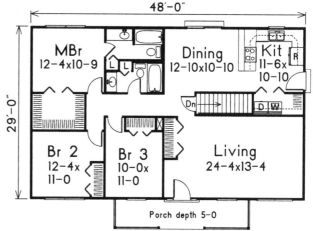

Plan 567-1336

Charming Country Facade

Total Living Area: 1,643 sq. ft.
Blueprint Price Code: B
Garage: 462 sq. ft.
Front porch: 168 sq. ft.

FEATURES

- Attractive front entry porch gives this ranch a country accent

- Spacious family room is the focal point of this design

- Kitchen and utility rooms are conveniently located near gathering areas

- Formal living room in the front of the home provides area for quiet and privacy

- Master suite has view to the rear of the home and a generous walk-in closet

- 3 bedrooms, 2 baths, 2-car garage

- Basement, crawl space or slab foundation available, please specify when ordering

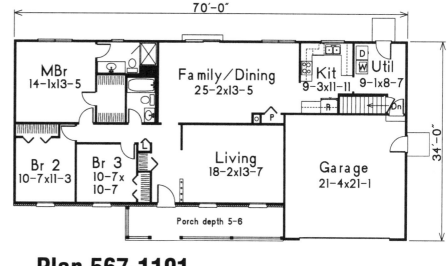

Plan 567-1101

Welcome Home

- An inviting covered porch welcomes you home to this country-kissed ranch.
- Inside, a cathedral ceiling soars over the expansive living room, which boasts a fireplace flanked by windows.
- Bathed in sunlight from more windows, the dining room flaunts an elegant French door that opens to a delightful backyard porch.
- The gourmet kitchen features a planning desk, a pantry and a unique, angled bar—a great place to settle for an afternoon snack. Garage access is conveniently nearby.

- Smartly secluded in one corner of the home is the lovely and spacious master bedroom, crowned by a tray ceiling. Other amenities include huge his-and-hers walk-in closets and a private bath with a garden tub and a dual-sink vanity.
- Just outside the door to the master bedroom, a neat laundry closet is handy for last-minute loads.
- Two secondary bedrooms round out this wonderful design. The front-facing bedroom is complemented by a vaulted ceiling, while the rear bedroom offers a sunny window seat. A full bath accented by a stylish round window is shared by both rooms.

Plan 567-J-91085

Bedrooms: 3	Baths: 2
Living Area:	
Main floor	1,643 sq. ft.
Total Living Area:	**1,643 sq. ft.**
Standard basement	1,643 sq. ft.
Garage and storage	480 sq. ft.
Exterior Wall Framing:	2x4

Foundation Options:
Standard basement
Crawlspace
Slab
(Please specify foundation type when ordering.)

BLUEPRINT PRICE CODE: B

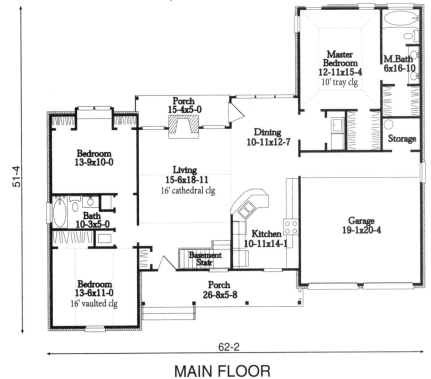

MAIN FLOOR

Plan 567-J-91085

Center of Activity

- At the center of this well-designed home is the generous Great Room, which is sure to be the hub of all family activity. This room's high, sloped ceiling and large corner fireplace make it a place where family and guests will naturally want to gather.
- The Great Room flows right into the adjoining dining room, a spot that is just right for formal entertaining.

- The eat-in kitchen boasts a window above the sink to brighten daily chores, plus a closed-off utility area and sliding glass doors that lead to the backyard.
- The master bedroom features a large walk-in closet and a deluxe master bath that includes a dual-sink vanity and a soaking tub tucked under a window.
- The larger of two secondary bedrooms has a vaulted ceiling and a stunning front window. Both bedrooms share easy access to a hall bath.
- The position of the home's garage doors may be altered to fit the requirements of your lot.

Plan 567-HHFL-3050-FO	
Bedrooms: 3	**Baths:** 2
Living Area:	
Main floor	1,366 sq. ft.
Total Living Area:	**1,366 sq. ft.**
Standard basement	1,366 sq. ft.
Garage	430 sq. ft.
Exterior Wall Framing:	2x6
Foundation Options:	
Standard basement	
Crawlspace	
Slab	
(Please specify foundation type when ordering.)	
BLUEPRINT PRICE CODE:	A

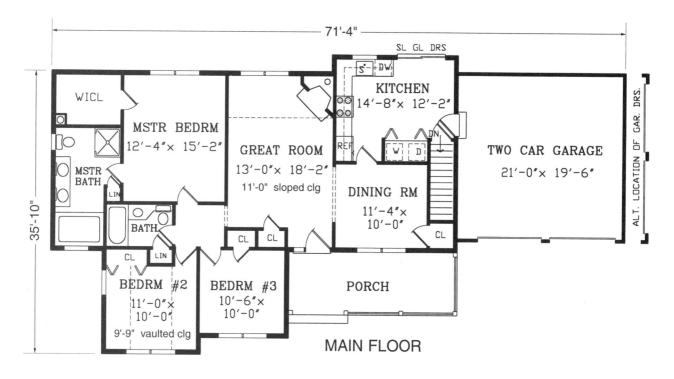

MAIN FLOOR

Plan 567-HHFL-3050-FO

Front Features Corner Accents and Striking Window Treatment

Total Living Area:	1,740 sq. ft.
Blueprint Price Code:	B
Drive-under garage:	780 sq. ft.

FEATURES

- Coffered ceilings in dining room, specially treated ceilings in living room and master bedroom

- Master bedroom features large master bath with walk-in closet, double-vanity, separate shower and tub

- Both secondary bedrooms have ample closet space

- Large breakfast area convenient to the laundry, pantry and rear deck

- 3 bedrooms, 2 baths, 2-car drive under garage

- Basement foundation

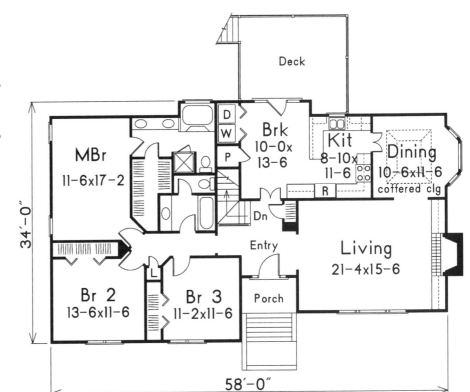

Plan 567-0117

Spacious And Open Family Living Area

Total Living Area:	1,416 sq. ft.
Blueprint Price Code:	**A**
Garage:	433 sq. ft.

FEATURES

- Family room includes fireplace, elevated plant shelf and vaulted ceiling

- Patio is accessible from dining area and garage

- Centrally located laundry area

- Oversized walk-in pantry

- 3 bedrooms, 2 baths, 2-car garage

- Basement foundation, drawings also include crawl space and slab foundations

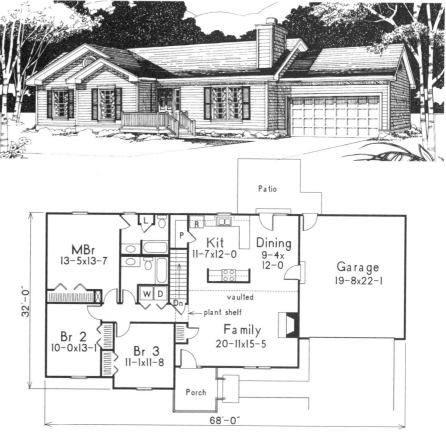

Plan 567-0226

Classic Ranch, Pleasant Covered Front Porch

Total Living Area:	1,416 sq. ft.
Blueprint Price Code:	**A**
Garage:	507 sq. ft.
Front porch:	162 sq. ft.

FEATURES

- Excellent floor plan eases traffic

- Master bedroom features private bath

- Foyer opens to both formal living room and informal family room

- Great room has access to the outdoors through sliding doors

- 3 bedrooms, 2 baths, 2-car garage

- Basement foundation, drawings also include crawl space foundation

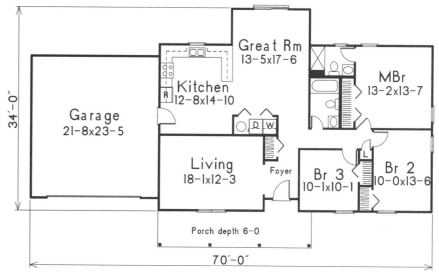

Plan 567-0198

Distinctive Turret Surrounds The Dining Bay

Total Living Area: 1,742 sq. ft.
Blueprint Price Code: B
Garage: 440 sq. ft.

FEATURES

- Efficient kitchen combines with breakfast and great room creating spacious living area

- Master bedroom includes private bath with huge walk-in closet, shower and corner tub

- Great room boasts a fireplace and outdoor access

- Laundry room conveniently located near kitchen and garage

- 3 bedrooms, 2 baths, 2-car garage

- Slab foundation, drawings also include crawl space foundation

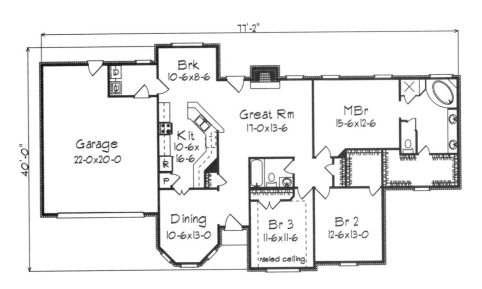

Plan 567-0410

Great Room Forms Core Of This Home

Total Living Area:	**2,076 sq. ft.**
Blueprint Price Code:	**C**
Garage:	374 sq. ft.
Front porch:	96 sq. ft.

FEATURES

- Vaulted great room fireplace flanked by windows and sky-lights that welcome the sun

- Kitchen leads to vaulted break-fast room and rear deck

- Study located off foyer provides great location for home office

- Large bay windows grace mas-ter bedroom and bath

- 3 bedrooms, 2 baths, 2-car garage

- Basement foundation

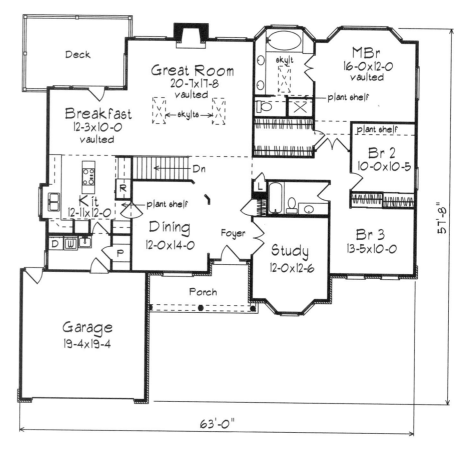

Plan 567-0425

Sweet Sanctuary

- A clean-cut brick-and-siding facade accented by gables, shutters, a single dormer and a sidelighted entry beckons you into this efficient traditional home. Make it your sanctuary from the chaos of modern life!
- A vaulted ceiling tops the expansive family room, anchored by a cozy corner fireplace. Display plants or treasured collectibles on the plant shelf

above the entrance to the dining room, which also boasts a vaulted ceiling. Enjoy a view of the backyard landscaping through sliding glass doors.
- Adjacent to the space-saving kitchen, the utility room makes laundry duty seem like less of a chore.
- After a long day, retreat to the comforts of the master suite, which is crowned by an elegant tray ceiling. A walk-in closet and a private bath are added luxuries.
- Two secondary bedrooms share a full hall bath.

Plan 567-HFB-5035-SOUT	
Bedrooms: 3	**Baths:** 2
Living Area:	
Main floor	1,042 sq. ft.
Total Living Area:	**1,042 sq. ft.**
Daylight basement	998 sq. ft.
Garage	400 sq. ft.
Exterior Wall Framing:	2x4
Foundation Options:	
Daylight basement	
Crawlspace	
(Please specify foundation type when ordering.)	
BLUEPRINT PRICE CODE:	**A**

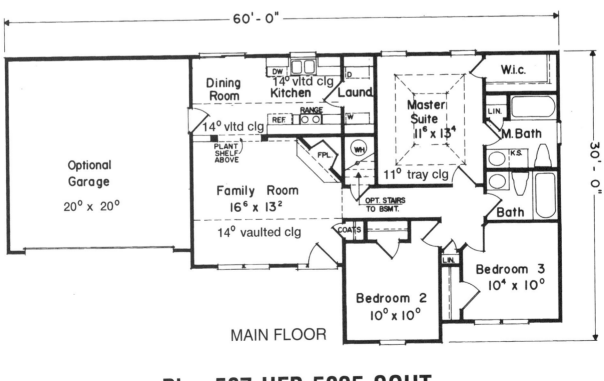

Plan 567-HFB-5035-SOUT

Quality Details

- Quality details are the hallmarks of this inviting home, from the covered front porch to the 16-ft. cathedral ceilings that grace the entire living area.
- Just inside the stone-tiled foyer, a three-sided fireplace is the center of attention. Skylights brighten both the family room and the island kitchen.
- The master suite boasts a walk-in closet and a skylighted bath with a soaking tub and a separate shower. Two additional bedrooms share another centrally located full bath.

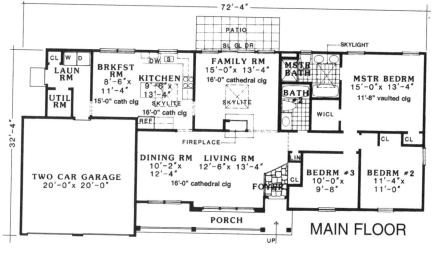

MAIN FLOOR

Plan 567-HAX-90303-A

Bedrooms: 3	Baths: 2
Living Area:	
Main floor	1,615 sq. ft.
Total Living Area:	**1,615 sq. ft.**
Basement	1,615 sq. ft.
Garage	412 sq. ft.
Exterior Wall Framing:	2x4

Foundation Options:
Daylight basement, standard basement, crawlspace, slab
(Please specify foundation type when ordering.)

BLUEPRINT PRICE CODE:	B

Plan 567-HAX-90303-A

Fall in Love

- A classic facade makes it easy to fall in love with this adorable home.
- The family room has a decorative plant shelf and a cozy fireplace. The dining room is great for casual or formal occasions. The sliding glass doors that access the backyard may be built into a sunny window bay.
- The efficient kitchen offers a handy pantry and an attached laundry room.
- The master bedroom includes a roomy walk-in closet. The master bath features a garden tub and a dual-sink vanity.

Plan 567-APS-1103

Bedrooms: 3	Baths: 2
Living Area:	
Main floor	1,197 sq. ft.
Total Living Area:	**1,197 sq. ft.**
Garage	380 sq. ft.
Exterior Wall Framing:	2x4

Foundation Options:
Crawlspace
Slab
(Please specify foundation type when ordering.)

BLUEPRINT PRICE CODE:	A

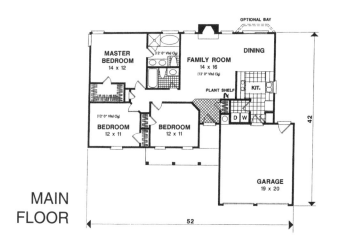

MAIN FLOOR

Plan 567-APS-1103

Affordable Upscale, Amenity Full

Total Living Area:	1,643 sq. ft.
Blueprint Price Code:	B
Garage:	510 sq. ft.
Front porch:	117 sq. ft.

FEATURES

- Family room has vaulted ceiling, open staircase and arched windows allowing for plenty of light

- Kitchen captures full use of space, with pantry, storage, ample counter space and work island

- Large closets and storage areas throughout

- Roomy master bath has a skylight for natural lighting plus separate tub and shower

- Rear of house provides ideal location for future screened-in porch

- 3 bedrooms, 2 baths, 2-car side entry garage

- Basement foundation, drawings also include slab and crawl space foundations

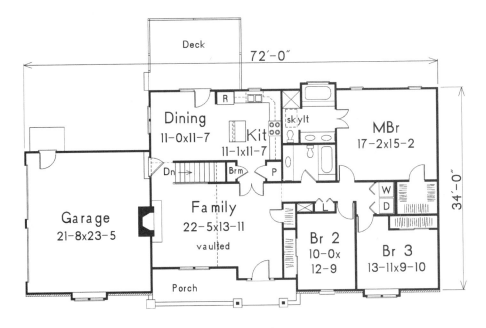

Plan 567-0172

Bay Window Graces Luxury Master Bedroom

Total Living Area: 1,668 sq. ft.
Blueprint Price Code: C
Drive-under garage: 756 sq. ft.
Front porch: 224 sq. ft.

FEATURES

- Large bay windows in breakfast area, master bedroom and dining room
- Extensive walk-in closets and storage spaces throughout the home
- Handy entry covered porch
- Large living room has fireplace, built-in bookshelves and sloped ceiling
- 3 bedrooms, 2 baths, 2-car drive under garage
- Basement foundation

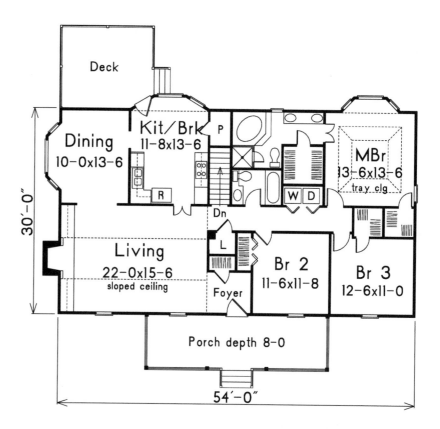

Plan 567-0112

Classic Ranch Has Grand Appeal With Expansive Porch

Total Living Area:	**1,400 sq. ft.**
Blueprint Price Code:	**A**
Garage:	592 sq. ft.
Front porch:	216 sq. ft.

FEATURES

- Master bedroom is secluded for privacy
- Large utility room with additional cabinet space
- Covered porch provides an outdoor seating area
- Roof dormers add great curb appeal
- Vaulted ceilings in living room and master bedroom
- Oversized garage with storage
- 3 bedrooms, 2 baths, 2-car garage
- Basement foundation, drawings also include crawl space foundation

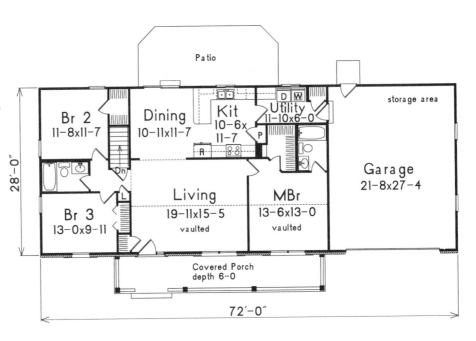

Plan 567-0690

Private Breakfast Room Provides Casual Dining

Total Living Area:	**1,708 sq. ft.**
Blueprint Price Code:	**B**
Garage:	555 sq. ft.
Front porch:	72 sq. ft.

FEATURES

- Massive family room enhanced with several windows, fireplace and access to porch

- Deluxe master bath accented by step-up corner tub flanked by double vanities

- Closets throughout maintain organized living

- Bedrooms isolated from living areas

- 3 bedrooms, 2 baths, 2-car garage

- Basement foundation, drawings also include crawl space foundation

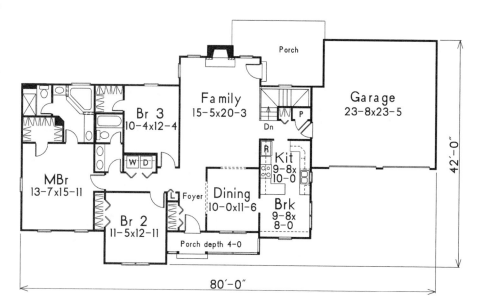

Plan 567-0450

It's All in the Details

- It's the mouthwatering details that give this home its distinctively country character. Its facade is a marvel; the graceful columns, railings, dormer windows and high transoms accentuate the inviting porch.
- Brightened by radiant windows, the large living room hosts a warming fireplace. Two high dormers admit additional natural light.

- Straight back, a bay window punctuated by French doors livens the dining area. A snack bar links it to the kitchen, which you'll find adaptable to both casual and formal meals.
- A sizable terrace overlooking the backyard is the perfect arena for lazy summer picnics and frolicsome Sunday afternoons.
- The sprawling master bedroom is blessed with a pair of windows in the sleeping chamber that wake you with morning light. A private bath offers a zesty whirlpool tub and a separate shower for busy weekday mornings.

Plan 567-AHP-9615

Bedrooms: 3	Baths: 2
Living Area:	
Main floor	1,331 sq. ft.
Total Living Area:	**1,331 sq. ft.**
Standard basement	1,377 sq. ft.
Garage	459 sq. ft.
Exterior Wall Framing:	2x4 or 2x6

Foundation Options:

Standard basement
Crawlspace
Slab
(Please specify foundation type when ordering.)

BLUEPRINT PRICE CODE:	A

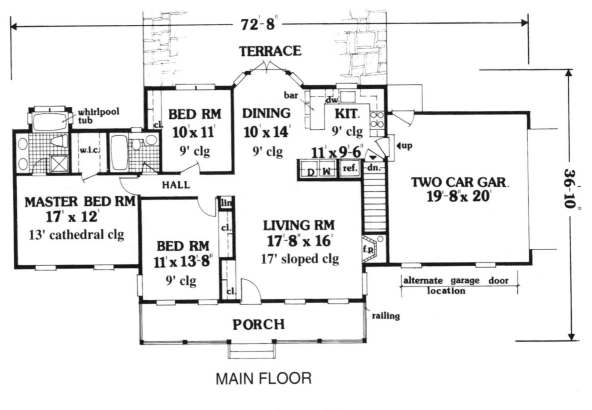

MAIN FLOOR

Plan 567-AHP-9615

Fresh Air

- With its nostalgic look and country style, this lovely home brings a breath of fresh air into any neighborhood.
- Past the inviting wraparound porch, the foyer is brightened by an elliptical transom window above the front door.
- The adjoining formal dining room is defined by decorative columns and a stylish stepped ceiling.
- The bright and airy kitchen includes a pantry, a windowed sink and a sunny breakfast area with porch access.
- A stepped ceiling enhances the spacious Great Room, where a fireplace warms the area. Two sets of sliding glass doors open to a back porch.
- The lush master bedroom and a bayed sitting area boast high ceilings. The master bath showcases a circular spa tub embraced by a glass-block wall.
- Two more bedrooms share a second bath. The protruding bedroom includes a dramatic vaulted ceiling.
- Additional living space can be made available by finishing the upper floor.

Plan 567-HAX-93308

Bedrooms: 3+	Baths: 2
Living Area:	
Main floor	1,793 sq. ft.
Total Living Area:	**1,793 sq. ft.**
Future upper floor	779 sq. ft.
Standard basement	1,793 sq. ft.
Garage	451 sq. ft.
Utility	20 sq. ft.
Exterior Wall Framing:	2x4

Foundation Options:

Standard basement
Crawlspace
Slab
(Please specify foundation type when ordering.)

BLUEPRINT PRICE CODE: B

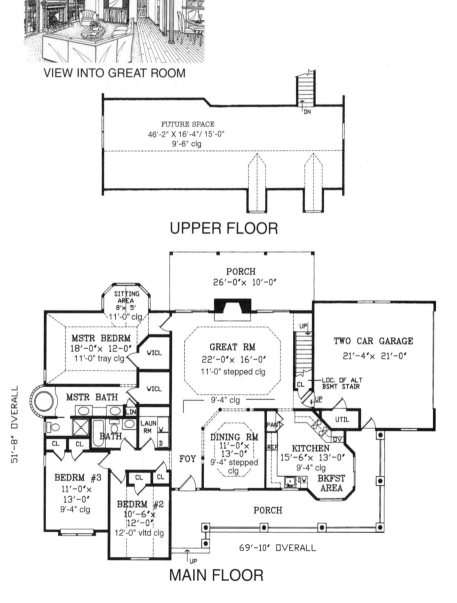

VIEW INTO GREAT ROOM

UPPER FLOOR

MAIN FLOOR

Plan 567-HAX-93308

Small Ranch For A Perfect Country Haven

Total Living Area:	1,761 sq. ft.
Blueprint Price Code:	B
Garage:	423 sq. ft.
Front porch:	66 sq. ft.

FEATURES

- Exterior window dressing, roof dormers and planter boxes provide visual warmth and charm

- Great room boasts a vaulted ceiling, fireplace and opens to pass-through kitchen

- Master bedroom is vaulted with luxury bath and walk-in closet

- Home features eight separate closets with an abundance of storage

- 4 bedrooms, 2 baths, 2-car side entry garage

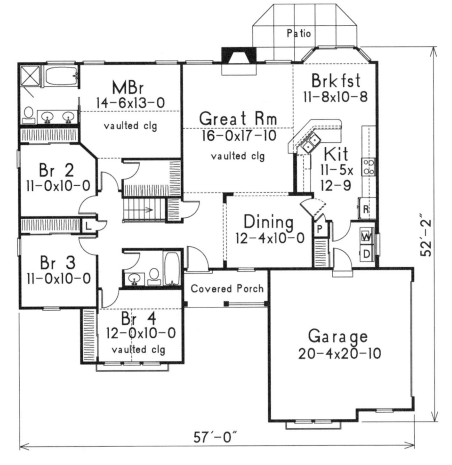

Plan 567-0731

Classic Exterior Employs Innovative Planning

Total Living Area:	1,791 sq. ft.
Blueprint Price Code:	**B**
Garage:	405 sq. ft.
Front porch:	125 sq. ft.
Back patio:	130 sq. ft.

FEATURES

- Vaulted great room and octa-gon-shaped dining area enjoy views of covered patio

- Kitchen features a pass-through to dining, center island, large walk-in pantry and breakfast room with large bay window

- Master bedroom is vaulted with sitting area

- 4 bedrooms, 2 baths, 2-car garage with storage

- Basement foundation

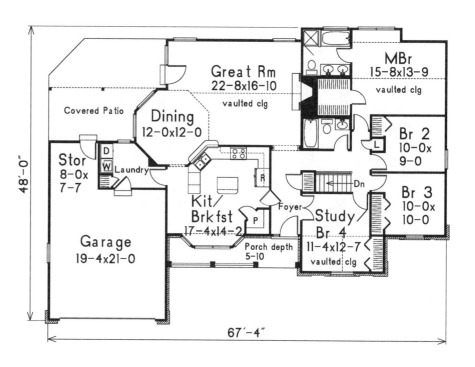

Plan 567-0706

Mark Englund/HomeStyles

Porch Offers Three Entries

- Showy window treatments, stately columns and three sets of French doors give this Plantation-style home an inviting exterior.
- High ceilings in the living room, dining room and kitchen add volume to the economically-sized home.
- A corner fireplace and a view to the back porch are found in the living room. The porch is accessed from a door in the dining room.
- The adjoining kitchen features an angled snack bar that easily serves the dining room and the casual eating area.
- The secluded master suite offers a cathedral ceiling, a walk-in closet and a luxurious private bath with a spa tub and a separate shower.
- Across the home, two additional bedrooms share a second full bath.

Plan 567-E-1602

Bedrooms: 3	Baths: 2
Living Area:	
Main floor	1,672 sq. ft.
Total Living Area:	**1,672 sq. ft.**
Standard basement	1,672 sq. ft.
Garage	484 sq. ft.
Storage	96 sq. ft.
Exterior Wall Framing:	2x6

Foundation Options:

Standard basement

Crawlspace

Slab

(Please specify foundation type when ordering.)

BLUEPRINT PRICE CODE: **B**

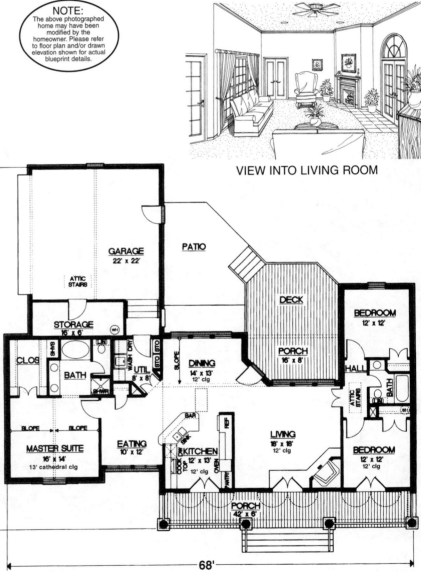

VIEW INTO LIVING ROOM

MAIN FLOOR

Plan 567-E-1602

Rustic Comfort

- Rustic charm highlights the exterior of this design, while the interior is filled with all the latest comforts.
- The wide, covered porch opens to a roomy entry, where two 7-ft.-high openings with decorative railings view into the dining room.
- Straight ahead lies the sunken living room, which features a 16-ft.-high vaulted ceiling with exposed beams. The fireplace is faced with floor-to-ceiling fieldstone, adding to the rustic look. A rear door opens to a large patio with twin plant areas.

- The large U-shaped kitchen has such nice extras as a china niche with glass shelves. Other bonuses include the adjacent sewing/hobby room, the over-sized utility room and the storage area and built-in workbench in the side-entry garage.
- The secluded master suite hosts a sunken sleeping area with built-in bookshelves. One step up is a cozy sitting area that is outlined by brick columns and a railed room divider. Double doors open to the deluxe bath, which offers a niche with glass shelves.
- Double doors conceal two more bedrooms and a full bath.

Plan 567-E-1607

Bedrooms: 3	Baths: 2
Living Area:	
Main floor	1,600 sq. ft.
Total Living Area:	**1,600 sq. ft.**
Standard basement	1,600 sq. ft.
Garage	484 sq. ft.
Storage	132 sq. ft.
Exterior Wall Framing:	2x6

Foundation Options:
Standard basement
Crawlspace
Slab
(Please specify foundation type when ordering.)

BLUEPRINT PRICE CODE:	B

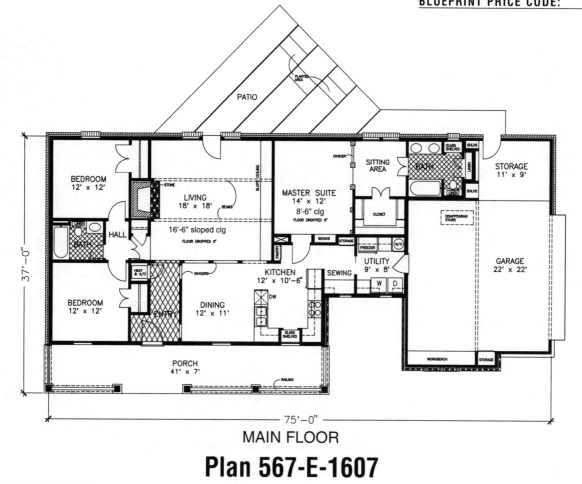

MAIN FLOOR

Plan 567-E-1607

Functional Layout For Comfortable Living

Total Living Area:	**1,360 sq. ft.**
Blueprint Price Code:	**A**
Garage:	523 sq. ft.
Workshop:	64 sq. ft.
Front porch:	184 sq. ft.

FEATURES

- Kitchen/dining room features island work space and plenty of dining area

- Master bedroom with large walk-in closet and private bath

- Laundry room adjacent to the kitchen for easy access

- Convenient workshop in garage

- Large closets in secondary bedrooms

- 3 bedrooms, 2 baths, 2-car side entry garage

- Basement foundation, drawings also include crawl space and slab foundations

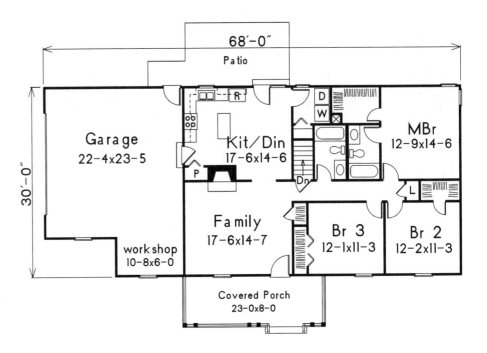

Plan 567-0217

TO ORDER BLUEPRINTS USE THE FORM ON PAGE 256 OR CALL **TOLL-FREE 1-800-367-7667**

Vaulted Ceilings
And Light Add
Dimension

Total Living Area:	1,676 sq. ft.
Blueprint Price Code:	**B**
Garage:	514 sq. ft.
Front porch:	48 sq. ft.

FEATURES

- The living area skylights and large breakfast room with bay window provide plenty of sunlight

- The master bedroom has a walk-in closet and the secondary bedrooms have large closets in both

- Vaulted ceilings, plant shelving and a fireplace provide a quality living area

- 3 bedrooms, 2 baths, 2-car garage

- Basement foundation, drawings also include crawl space and slab foundations

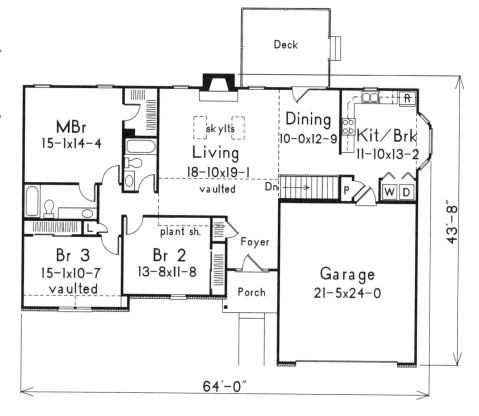

Plan 567-0229

Mark Englund/HomeStyles

Free-Flowing Floor Plan

- A fluid floor plan with open indoor/ outdoor living spaces characterizes this exciting luxury home.
- The stylish columned porch opens to a spacious living room and dining room expanse that overlooks the outdoor spaces. The breathtaking view also includes a dramatic corner fireplace.
- The dining area opens to a bright kitchen with an angled eating bar. The overall spaciousness of the living areas is increased with high ceilings.
- A sunny, informal eating area adjoins the kitchen, and an angled set of doors opens to a convenient main-floor laundry room near the garage entrance.
- The vaulted master bedroom has a walk-in closet and a sumptuous bath with an oval tub.
- A separate wing houses two additional bedrooms and another full bath.
- Attic space is accessible from stairs in the garage and in the bedroom wing.

Plan 567-E-1710

Bedrooms: 3	Baths: 2
Living Area:	
Main floor	1,792 sq. ft.
Total Living Area:	**1,792 sq. ft.**
Standard basement	1,792 sq. ft.
Garage	484 sq. ft.
Storage	96 sq. ft.
Exterior Wall Framing:	2x6

Foundation Options:

Standard basement

Crawlspace

Slab

(Please specify foundation type when ordering.)

BLUEPRINT PRICE CODE: B

REAR VIEW

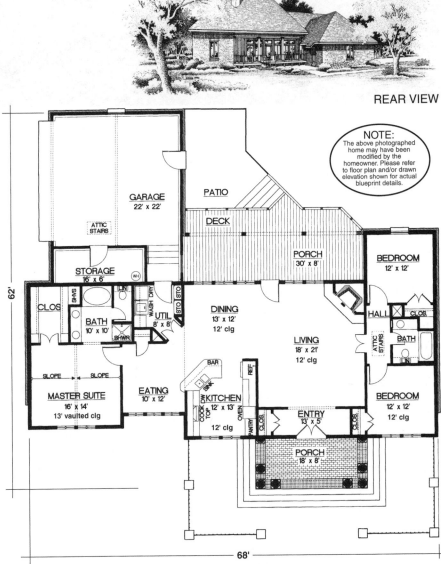

NOTE:
The above photographed home may have been modified by the homeowner. Please refer to floor plan and/or drawn elevation shown for actual blueprint details.

MAIN FLOOR

Plan 567-E-1710

Dramatic Dining Room

- The highlight of this lovely one-story design is its dramatic dining room, which boasts a high ceiling and a soaring window wall.
- The airy foyer ushers guests through an arched opening and into the vaulted Great Room, which is warmed by an inviting fireplace. This room will easily host both formal receptions and casual evenings of conversation.
- The gourmet kitchen features a handy pantry, a versatile serving bar and a pass-through to the Great Room.
- The bright breakfast area offers a laundry closet and outdoor access.
- Two secondary bedrooms share a compartmentalized bath.
- Across the home, the removed master suite boasts a tray ceiling, overhead plant shelves and an adjoining vaulted sitting room. An exciting garden tub is found in the luxurious master bath.

Plan 567-HFB-5008-ALLE

Bedrooms: 3	Baths: 2
Living Area:	
Main floor	1,715 sq. ft.
Total Living Area:	**1,715 sq. ft.**
Daylight basement	1,715 sq. ft.
Garage	400 sq. ft.
Exterior Wall Framing:	2x4
Foundation Options:	
Daylight basement	
Crawlspace	
Slab	
(Please specify foundation type when ordering.)	
BLUEPRINT PRICE CODE:	B

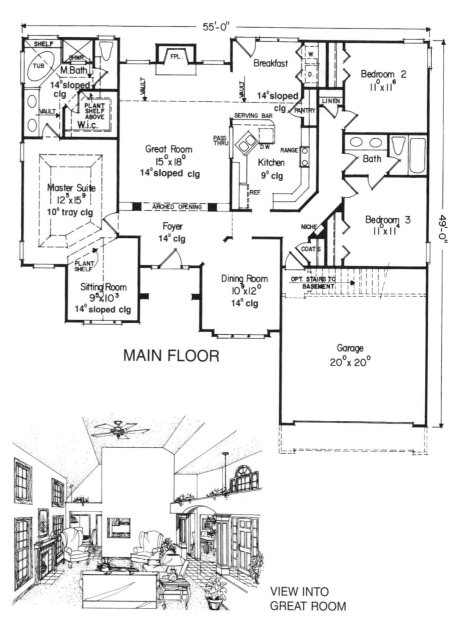

MAIN FLOOR

VIEW INTO GREAT ROOM

Plan 567-HFB-5008-ALLE

Luxury in a Small Package

- The elegant exterior of this design sets the tone for the luxurious spaces within.
- The foyer opens to the centrally located living room, which features a cathedral ceiling, a handsome fireplace and access to a lovely rear terrace.
- The unusual kitchen design includes an angled snack bar that lies between the bayed breakfast den and the formal dining room. Sliding glass doors open to another terrace.
- The master suite is a dream come true, with its romantic fireplace, built-in desk and tray ceiling. The private bath includes a whirlpool tub and a dual-sink vanity.
- Another full bath serves the remaining two bedrooms, one of which boasts a cathedral ceiling and a tall arched window.

Plan 567-AHP-9300

Bedrooms: 3	Baths: 2
Living Area:	
Main floor	1,513 sq. ft.
Total Living Area:	**1,513 sq. ft.**
Standard basement	1,360 sq. ft.
Garage	400 sq. ft.
Exterior Wall Framing:	2x4 or 2x6
Foundation Options:	
Standard basement	
Crawlspace	
Slab	
(Please specify foundation type when ordering.)	
BLUEPRINT PRICE CODE:	**B**

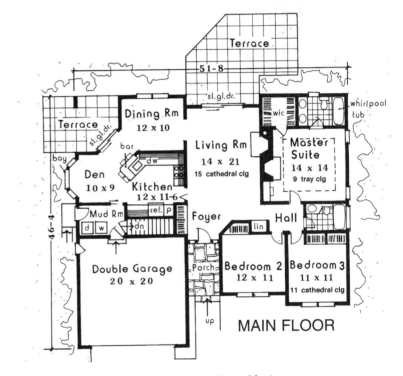

MAIN FLOOR

VIEW INTO MASTER SUITE

Plan 567-AHP-9300

Enchanting!

- This gracious French-style home is the picture of enchantment, with its striking Palladian window and its beautiful brick facade with lovely corner quoins.
- Beyond the leaded-glass front door, the open entry introduces the versatile living room. Guests will enjoy visiting for hours in front of the crackling fire!
- Visible over a half-wall, the formal dining room is worthy of any festive occasion. A wall of windows offers delightful views to a porch and your backyard's award-winning landscaping.
- The bayed morning room is the perfect spot for orange juice and waffles. If the weather permits, open the French door and dine alfresco on the porch.
- A snack bar frames the kitchen. The sink is positioned for backyard views, to brighten those daily chores.
- The two-car garage is ideally located for easy unloading of groceries.
- Across the home, the master suite is a restful haven. Soak away your cares in the fabulous garden tub!
- Two secondary bedrooms, a nice hall bath and a central laundry room round out this enchanting plan.

Plan 567-L-709-FA

Bedrooms: 3	Baths: 2
Living Area:	
Main floor	1,707 sq. ft.
Total Living Area:	**1,707 sq. ft.**
Garage	572 sq. ft.
Exterior Wall Framing:	2x4

Foundation Options:

Slab
(Please specify foundation type when ordering.)

BLUEPRINT PRICE CODE:	B

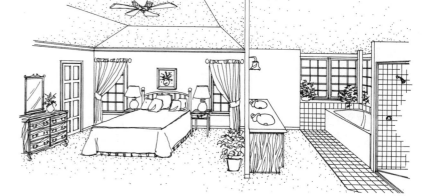

VIEW INTO MASTER SUITE

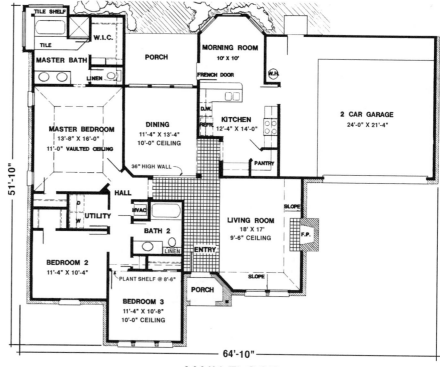

MAIN FLOOR

Plan 567-L-709-FA

Great Room And Kitchen Symmetry Dominates Design

Total Living Area: 1,712 sq. ft.
Blueprint Price Code: B
Garage: 420 sq. ft.
Front porch: 100 sq. ft.

FEATURES

- Stylish stucco exterior enhances curb appeal

- Sunken great room offers corner fireplace flanked by 9' wide patio doors

- Well-designed kitchen features ideal view of great room and fireplace through breakfast bar opening

- 3 bedrooms, 2 1/2 baths, 2-car garage

- Crawl space foundation

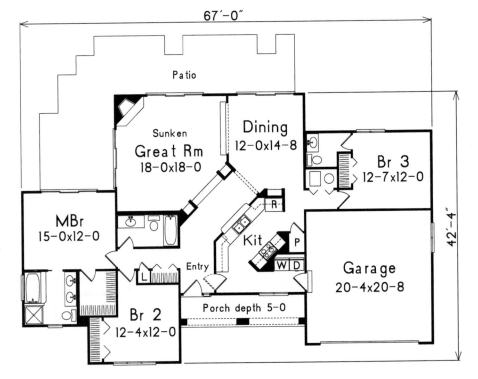

Plan 567-0661

Vaulted Living Area Centers Family Gathering

Total Living Area: 1,697 sq. ft.
Blueprint Price Code: B
Drive-under garage: 336 sq. ft.

FEATURES

- Secondary bedrooms share bath with private dressing area
- Large living room with fireplace and vaulted ceiling
- Secluded master suite boasts a private deluxe bath
- Open kitchen and breakfast area includes a pantry and rear access to sun deck
- 3 bedrooms, 2 baths, 2-car drive under garage
- Basement foundation

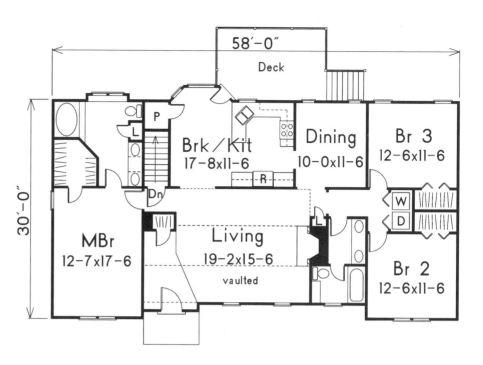

Plan 567-0259

Fine Dining

- This fine stucco home showcases a huge round-top window arrangement that brightens the central dining room.
- A cute covered porch opens to the side-lighted foyer, where a high ceiling extends past a decorative column to the airy Great Room.
- The Great Room, which is the focal point of the home, features a warm fire-place, a pass-through to the kitchen and a French door to the backyard.
- The kitchen hosts a pantry closet, a nice serving bar and an angled sink. The vaulted breakfast nook may be expanded with an optional bay.
- The master suite boasts a tray ceiling and a private bath with a garden tub, a dual-sink vanity and a vaulted ceiling.
- Across the home, two secondary bedrooms share a full bath.

Plan 567-HFB-5351-GENE

Bedrooms: 3	Baths: 2
Living Area:	
Main floor	1,670 sq. ft.
Total Living Area:	**1,670 sq. ft.**
Daylight basement	1,670 sq. ft.
Garage	462 sq. ft.
Exterior Wall Framing:	2x4

Foundation Options:

Daylight basement
Crawlspace
Slab
(Please specify foundation type when ordering.)

BLUEPRINT PRICE CODE:	B

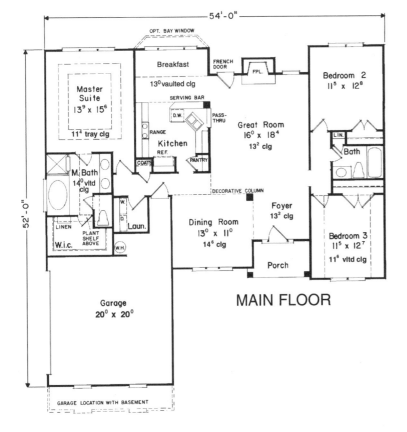

MAIN FLOOR

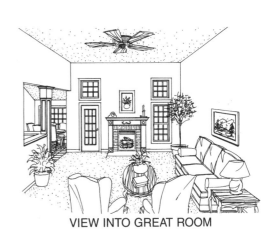

VIEW INTO GREAT ROOM

BASEMENT STAIRWAY LOCATION

Plan 567-HFB-5351-GENE

Mature Design

- With the separation of the master suite, this four-bedroom home is ideal for the maturing family.
- The formal dining room expands to the living room, set off by a column and plant shelves.
- The kitchen offers a morning room and a pantry closet. A bay is created by the morning room and the sitting area of the master suite.
- The master bath boasts an exciting oval garden tub and a separate shower.

Plan 567-DD-1696

Bedrooms: 4	Baths: 2
Living Area:	
Main floor	1,748 sq. ft.
Total Living Area:	**1,748 sq. ft.**
Standard basement	1,748 sq. ft.
Garage	393 sq. ft.
Exterior Wall Framing:	2x4
Foundation Options:	
Standard basement	
Crawlspace	
Slab	
(Please specify foundation type when ordering.)	
BLUEPRINT PRICE CODE:	**B**

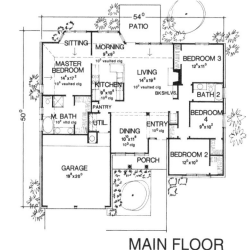

MAIN FLOOR

Plan 567-DD-1696

Rustic, Relaxed Living

- With its warm fireplace and surrounding windows, this home's spacious living room is ideal for unwinding indoors.
- The centrally located, U-shaped kitchen features a nice windowed sink.
- The master bedroom boasts a private bath with a step-up spa tub, a separate shower and two walk-in closets.

Plan 567-C-8650

Bedrooms: 3	Baths: 2
Living Area:	
Main floor	1,773 sq. ft.
Total Living Area:	**1,773 sq. ft.**
Screened porch	246 sq. ft.
Daylight basement	1,773 sq. ft.
Garage	441 sq. ft.
Exterior Wall Framing:	2x4
Foundation Options:	
Daylight basement, crawlspace or slab	
(Please specify foundation type when ordering.)	
BLUEPRINT PRICE CODE:	**B**

MAIN FLOOR

Plan 567-C-8650

Inviting Country Porch

- A columned porch with double doors invites you into the rustic living areas of this ranch-style home.
- Inside, the entry allows views back to the expansive, central living room and the backyard beyond.
- The living room boasts an exposed-beam ceiling and a massive fireplace with a wide stone hearth, a wood box and built-in bookshelves. A sunny patio offers additional entertaining space.
- The dining room and the efficient kitchen combine for easy meal service, with a serving bar separating the two.
- The main hallway leads to the sleeping wing, which offers a large master bedroom with a walk-in closet and a private bath.
- Two additional bedrooms share another full bath, and a laundry closet is easily accessible to the entire bedroom wing.

Plan 567-E-1304

Bedrooms: 3	Baths: 2
Living Area:	
Main floor	1,395 sq. ft.
Total Living Area:	**1,395 sq. ft.**
Garage and storage	481 sq. ft.
Exterior Wall Framing:	2x4

Foundation Options:

Crawlspace
Slab
(Please specify foundation type when ordering.)

BLUEPRINT PRICE CODE:	A

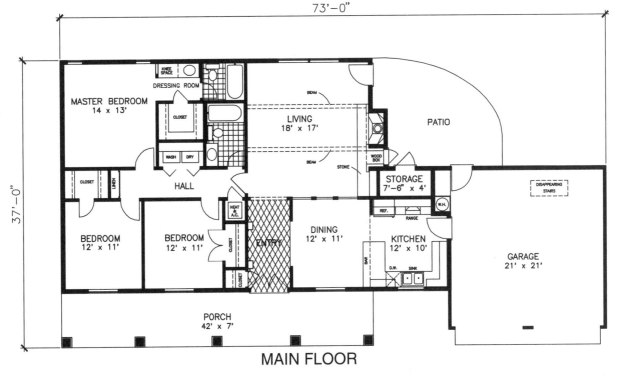

MAIN FLOOR

Plan 567-E-1304

Pastoral Perfection

- An expansive front porch, quaint shutters and warm wood siding lend this home its look of pastoral perfection.
- With a striking stepped ceiling, a cozy fireplace and a built-in entertainment area, the Great Room is a natural gathering spot. Three sets of sliding French doors offer a view to the gentle beauty of the outdoors.
- The nearby dining room shares a snack counter with the kitchen. Here, a windowed sink brightens daily chores.
- Cleverly separated from the other bedrooms for privacy, the master suite is topped by a dramatic stepped ceiling. The bath offers a large walk-in closet and ample preparation space.
- Across the home, two secondary bedrooms look out to the backyard and share another full bath.
- The laundry room is quietly and conveniently tucked between these bedrooms and the foyer.

Plan 567-HAX-5380

Bedrooms: 3	Baths: 2
Living Area:	
Main floor	1,480 sq. ft.
Total Living Area:	**1,480 sq. ft.**
Standard basement	1,493 sq. ft.
Garage and storage	610 sq. ft.
Exterior Wall Framing:	2x4

Foundation Options:
Standard basement
Crawlspace
Slab
(Please specify foundation type when ordering.)

BLUEPRINT PRICE CODE: A

VIEW INTO GREAT ROOM

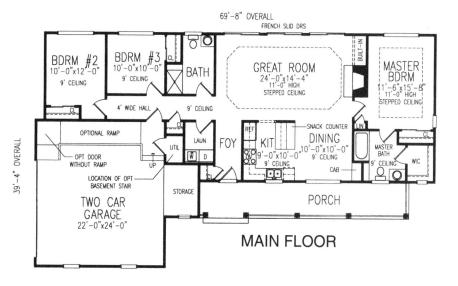

MAIN FLOOR

Plan 567-HAX-5380

Compact Home For Functional Living

Total Living Area:	**1,220 sq. ft.**
Blueprint Price Code:	**A**
Drive-under garage:	439 sq. ft.
Front porch:	45 sq. ft.

FEATURES

- Vaulted ceilings add luxury to living room and master suite

- Spacious living room accented with a large fireplace and hearth

- Dining area adjacent to convenient wrap-around kitchen

- Washer and dryer handy to the bedrooms

- Covered porch entry adds appeal

- 3 bedrooms, 2 baths, 2-car drive under garage

- Basement foundation

Plan 567-0173

Compact Layout, Amenity Full

Total Living Area:	**1,567 sq. ft.**
Blueprint Price Code:	**B**
Drive-under garage:	700 sq. ft.

FEATURES

- Front gables and extended porch add charm to facade

- Large bay windows add brightness to breakfast and dining rooms

- The master bath boasts an oversized tub, separate shower, double sinks and large walk-in closet

- Living room features a vaulted ceiling and a prominent fireplace

- 3 bedrooms, 2 baths, 2-car drive under garage

- Basement foundation

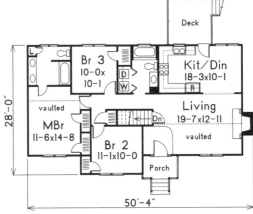

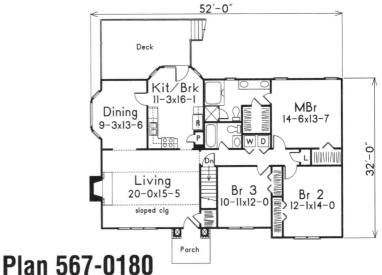

Plan 567-0180

Well-Designed Floor Plan Has Many Extras

Total Living Area:	2,437 sq. ft.
Blueprint Price Code:	**D**
Garage:	584 sq. ft.
Front porch:	45 sq. ft.
Back porch:	213 sq. ft.

FEATURES

- Spacious breakfast area with access to the covered porch is adjacent to kitchen and great room

- Elegant dining area has columned entrance and built-in corner cabinets

- Cozy study has handsome double-door entrance off a large foyer

- Raised ceiling and lots of windows in master suite create a spacious, open feel

- 3 bedrooms, 2 baths, 2-car side entry garage

- Slab foundation, drawings also include crawl space foundation

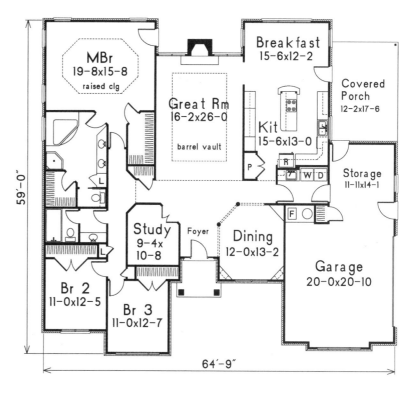

Plan 567-0721

1,800 SQ. FT. & UP

Country Charm, Cottage Look

- An interesting combination of stone and stucco gives a charming cottage look to this attractive country home.
- Off the inviting sidelighted entry, the formal dining room is defined by striking columns.
- The dining room expands into the living room, which boasts a fireplace and built-in shelves. A French door provides access to a cute backyard patio.
- The galley-style kitchen unfolds to a sunny morning room.
- All of the living areas are expanded by 10-ft. ceilings.
- The master bedroom features a 10-ft. ceiling and a nice bayed sitting area. The luxurious master bath boasts an exciting garden tub and a glass-block shower, as well as a big walk-in closet and a dressing area with two sinks.
- Across the home, two additional bedrooms with walk-in closets and private dressing areas share a tidy compartmentalized bath.

Plan 567-DD-1790

Bedrooms: 3	Baths: 2½
Living Area:	
Main floor	1,812 sq. ft.
Total Living Area:	**1,812 sq. ft.**
Standard basement	1,812 sq. ft.
Garage	438 sq. ft.
Exterior Wall Framing:	2x4

Foundation Options:
Standard basement
Crawlspace
Slab
(Please specify foundation type when ordering.)

BLUEPRINT PRICE CODE:	B

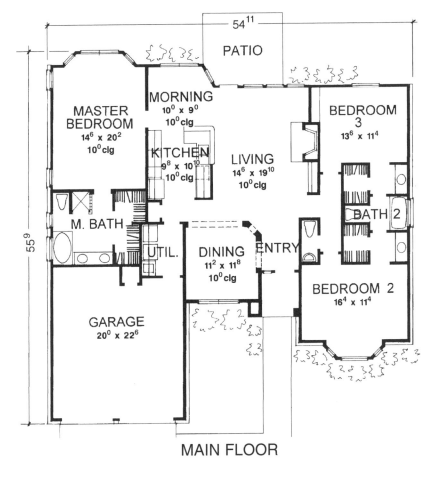

REAR VIEW

MAIN FLOOR

Plan 567-DD-1790

Secluded
Master Suite

Total Living Area:	**1,819 sq. ft.**
Blueprint Price Code:	**C**
Garage:	477 sq. ft.
Front porch:	80 sq. ft.

FEATURES

- Master suite features access to the outdoors, large walk-in closet and private bath

- 9' ceilings throughout

- Formal foyer with coat closet opens into vaulted great room with fireplace and formal dining room

- Kitchen and breakfast room create cozy casual area

- 3 bedroom, 2 baths, 2-car side entry garage

- Basement foundation

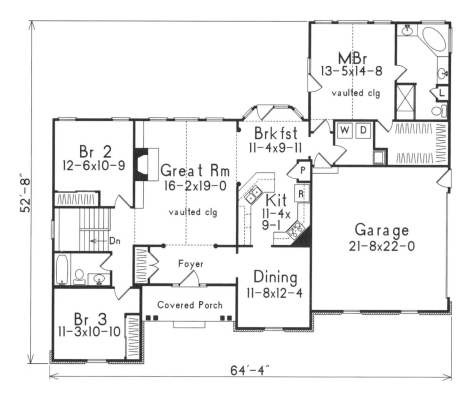

Plan 567-0745

Front Entrance Framed By Triple Gables

Total Living Area:	1,976 sq. ft.
Blueprint Price Code:	C
Garage:	462 sq. ft.
Front porch:	69 sq. ft.

FEATURES

- Compact ranch features garage entry near front door

- Vaulted living area has large balcony above

- Isolated master bedroom with coffered ceiling and luxurious bath

- Loft area has access to plenty of attic storage and future play room

- 3 bedrooms, 2 baths, 2-car side entry garage

- Basement foundation

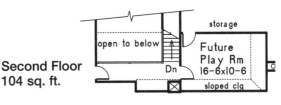

Second Floor
104 sq. ft.

storage

open to below

Future Play Rm
16-6x10-6

Dn

sloped clg

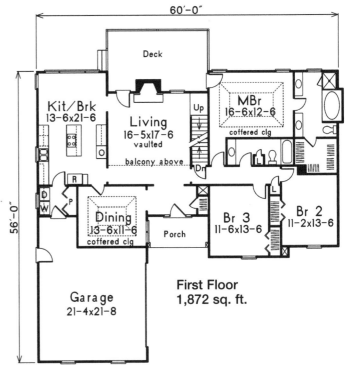

60'-0"

56'-0"

Deck

Kit/Brk
13-6x21-6

Living
16-5x17-6
vaulted

balcony above

Up

Dn

MBr
16-6x12-6

coffered clg

Dining
13-6x11-6
coffered clg

Porch

Br 3
11-6x13-6

Br 2
11-2x13-6

Garage
21-4x21-8

First Floor
1,872 sq. ft.

Plan 567-0121

Practical Layout With Inviting Front Porch

Total Living Area: 1,883 sq. ft.
Blueprint Price Code: C
Garage: 505 sq. ft.
Front porch: 200 sq. ft.
Back porch: 95 sq. ft.

FEATURES

- Large laundry room located off the garage has coat closet and half bath

- Large family room with fireplace and access to covered porch is great central gathering room

- U-shaped kitchen has breakfast bar, large pantry and swing door to dining room for convenient serving

- 3 bedroom, 2 1/2 baths, 2-car side entry garage

- Basement foundation

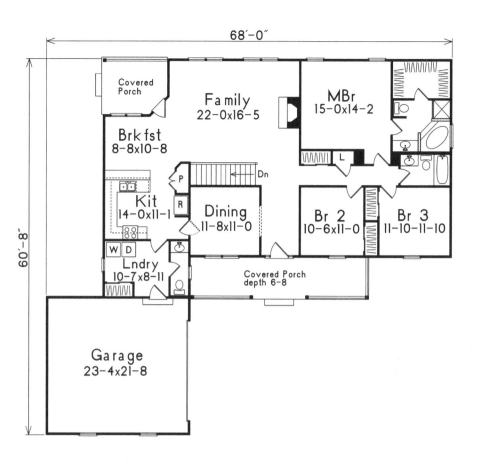

Plan 567-0742

Protected Entry Landscapes Well

Total Living Area: 2,468 sq. ft.
Blueprint Price Code: D
Garage: 462 sq. ft.
Storage: 54 sq. ft.

FEATURES

- Entry, flanked by gables, creates an interesting walkway
- Open entry foyer with access to the upstairs future guest suite, work or play area
- Sunny breakfast room with full windows
- Bay window and garden tub add elegance to master bedroom suite
- Private loft area with bath and generous storage space
- 3 bedrooms, 3 baths, 2-car garage
- Partial basement/crawl space foundation

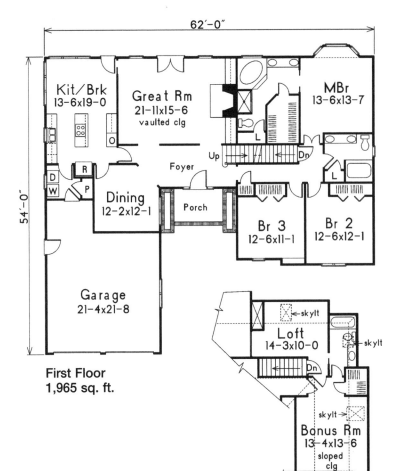

First Floor
1,965 sq. ft.

Second Floor
503 sq. ft.

Plan 567-0125

TO ORDER BLUEPRINTS USE THE FORM ON PAGE 256 OR CALL **TOLL-FREE 1-800-367-7667**

Angled Walls Create Dramatic Layout

Total Living Area:	**2,080 sq. ft.**
Blueprint Price Code:	**C**
Garage:	554 sq. ft.
Storage:	32 sq. ft.
Front porch:	48 sq. ft.
Back patio:	143 sq. ft.

FEATURES

- Combined design elements create unique facade

- Foyer leads into large living room and direct view to patio

- Master bedroom includes spacious bath with garden tub, separate shower, walk-in closet and dressing area

- 4 bedrooms, 2 baths, 2-car side-entry garage

- Crawl space foundation, drawings also include basement and slab foundations

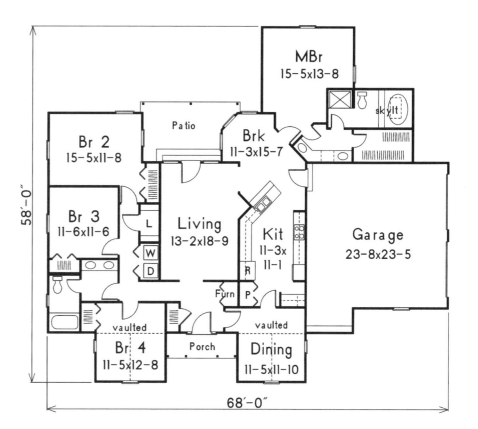

Plan 567-0541

High Ceilings
Create Openness

Total Living Area:	**2,516 sq. ft.**
Blueprint Price Code:	**D**
Garage:	825 sq. ft.
Storage:	218 sq. ft.
Front porch:	80 sq. ft.

FEATURES

- 12' ceiling in living areas

- Plenty of closet space in this open ranch plan

- Large kitchen/breakfast area joins great room via see-through fireplace creating large entering space

- Large garage has extra storage area

- Master bedroom has eye-catching bay window

- 3 bedroom, 2 1/2 baths, 3-car garage

- Basement foundation

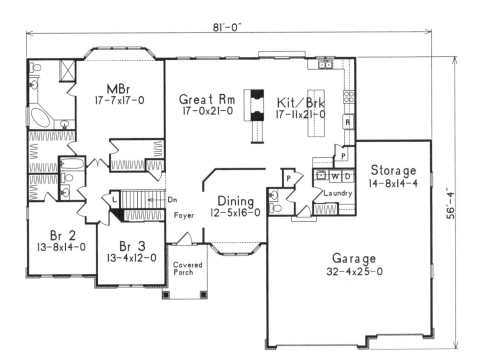

Plan 567-0746

Porch Paradise

- You'll be tempted to spend all your time on the huge front porch of this perfect one-story home!
- The sizable Great Room features a tray ceiling and access to a back patio.
- Centrally located, the island kitchen serves both the casual breakfast nook and the formal dining room.
- With a bubbly whirlpool bath and a sizable walk-in closet, the master suite adds a pleasant dose of luxury.

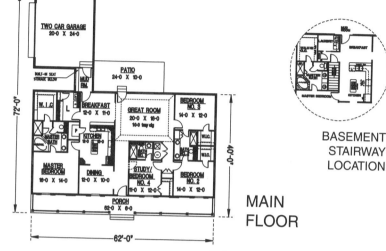

BASEMENT STAIRWAY LOCATION

MAIN FLOOR

Plan 567-DP-2108

Bedrooms: 3+	Baths: 3
Living Area:	
Main floor	2,156 sq. ft.
Total Living Area:	**2,156 sq. ft.**
Standard basement	2,156 sq. ft.
Garage	480 sq. ft.
Exterior Wall Framing:	2x4
Foundation Options:	
Standard basement	
Crawlspace	
Slab	
(Please specify foundation type when ordering.)	
BLUEPRINT PRICE CODE:	C

Plan 567-DP-2108

Breezy Beauty

- Three pleasant outdoor spaces combine to make this beautiful one-story home a breezy delight.
- The front entry opens into the Great Room, which is crowned by a soaring cathedral ceiling.
- The nearby kitchen boasts plenty of counter space and a handy built-in recipe desk.
- The secluded master bedroom is enhanced by a private master bath, which includes a lovely garden tub, a separate shower and dual vanities.

MAIN FLOOR

Plan 567-C-8905

Bedrooms: 3	Baths: 2
Living Area:	
Main floor	1,811 sq. ft.
Total Living Area:	**1,811 sq. ft.**
Screened porch	240 sq. ft.
Daylight basement	1,811 sq. ft.
Garage	484 sq. ft.
Exterior Wall Framing:	2x4
Foundation Options:	
Daylight basement	
Crawlspace	
Slab	
(Please specify foundation type when ordering.)	
BLUEPRINT PRICE CODE:	B

Plan 567-C-8905

Innovative Use of Space

- Strategic angles, built-in shelving and multi-access rooms exemplify the innovative use of space in this exciting stucco and stone home.
- Elaborate ceilings and windows further enhance the volume of the living areas.
- Adjacent to the airy foyer, the living room's built-in cabinets, shelves and plant niches add function to its beautiful fireplace wall.

- More shelves display your personal library in the double-doored study.
- Wraparound counter space frames the octagonal kitchen, which can be accessed from the foyer and formal dining room, as well as from the casual spaces on the other side.
- A luxurious garden bath and a winding walk-in closet adjoin the spacious master bedroom; a compartmentalized bath serves the secondary bedrooms.
- The unfinished bonus room upstairs is available for future use as an extra bedroom, game room or hobby area.

Plan 567-KLF-9710

Bedrooms: 3+	Baths: 2½
Living Area:	
Main floor	2,747 sq. ft.
Total Living Area:	**2,747 sq. ft.**
Future area	391 sq. ft.
Garage and storage	504 sq. ft.
Exterior Wall Framing:	2x4
Foundation Options:	

Slab
(Please specify foundation type when ordering.)

BLUEPRINT PRICE CODE:	**D**

MAIN FLOOR

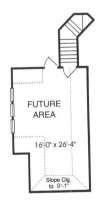

FUTURE AREA

Plan 567-KLF-9710

Handsome Facade Welcomes Guests

Total Living Area: 1,908 sq. ft.
Blueprint Price Code: C
Garage: 470 sq. ft.
Storage: 72 sq. ft.

FEATURES

- Distinguished front entry features circle-top window and prominent center gable

- Sundeck/patio is nestled between living space for easy access from adjacent room

- Oversized garage has large work/storage area and convenient laundry room

- Vaulted ceiling and floor-to-ceiling windows in family and breakfast rooms create an open, unrestricted space

- Master suite with deluxe bath, large walk-in closet and recessed ceiling

- 3 bedrooms, 2 baths, 2-car garage

- Crawl space foundation, drawings also include slab foundation

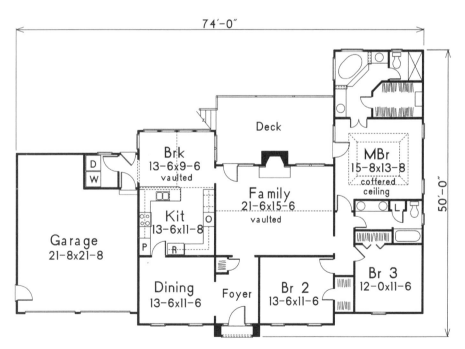

Plan 567-0175

From the Past to Your Future

- With a trio of dormers up top and a classic porch out front, this stately traditional-style home steps straight from the past and into your future.
- Pass through the foyer into the living room, which features a tray ceiling and a window-flanked fireplace that warms not just that space, but the adjoining breakfast room, too.
- Mealtime is easy with a roomy kitchen offering lots of counter space, and with an angled counter serving both the living and breakfast rooms, you'll still be close by when guests come over.
- The owner's bedroom includes backyard views, two walk-in closets and a private bath with a dual-sink vanity, while two secondary bedrooms share a full hall bath.
- Upstairs, future space abounds, with enough room for a wacky game room and even a home office.

Plan 567-J-9513

Bedrooms: 3+	Baths: 2½
Living Area:	
Main floor	1,969 sq. ft.
Bonus room	158 sq. ft.
Total Living Area:	**2,127 sq. ft.**
Future upper floor	1,095 sq. ft.
Standard basement	2,127 sq. ft.
Garage and storage	546 sq. ft.
Exterior Wall Framing:	2x4
Foundation Options:	
Standard basement	
Crawlspace	
Slab	
(Please specify foundation type when ordering.)	
BLUEPRINT PRICE CODE:	C

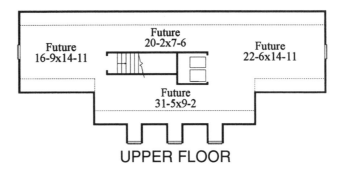

UPPER FLOOR

MAIN FLOOR

Plan 567-J-9513

Cozy Covered Porches

- Twin dormers give this raised one-story design the appearance of a two-story. Two covered porches and a deck supplement the main living areas with plenty of outdoor entertaining space.
- The large central living room features a dramatic fireplace, a high ceiling with a skylight and access to both porch areas.
- Double doors open to a bayed eating area, which overlooks the adjoining deck and includes a sloped ceiling in the kitchen. An angled snack bar and a pantry are also featured.
- The elegant master suite is tucked to one side of the home and also overlooks the backyard and deck. Laundry facilities and garage access are nearby.
- Across the home, two additional bedrooms share another full bath.

Plan 567-E-1826

Bedrooms: 3	Baths: 2
Living Area:	
Main floor	1,800 sq. ft.
Total Living Area:	**1,800 sq. ft.**
Garage and storage	574 sq. ft.
Enclosed storage	60 sq. ft.
Exterior Wall Framing:	2x6

Foundation Options:
Crawlspace
Slab
(Please specify foundation type when ordering.)

BLUEPRINT PRICE CODE:	B

VIEW INTO LIVING ROOM

MAIN FLOOR

Plan 567-E-1826

Sophisticated One-Story

- Beautiful windows accentuated by elegant keystones highlight the exterior of this sophisticated one-story design.
- An open floor plan is the hallmark of the interior. The foyer gives views of the study and the dining and living rooms.
- The spacious living room boasts a fireplace with built-in bookshelves and a rear window wall that stretches into the morning room.
- The sunny morning room has a snack bar to the kitchen. The island kitchen includes a walk-in pantry, a built-in desk and easy access to the utility room and the convenient half-bath.
- The master suite features private access to a nice covered patio, plus an enormous walk-in closet and a posh bath with a spa tub and glass-block shower.
- A hall bath serves the two secondary bedrooms. These three rooms, plus the utility area, have standard 8-ft. ceilings. Other ceilings are 10 ft. high.

Plan 567-DD-2455

Bedrooms: 3+	Baths: 2½
Living Area:	
Main floor	2,387 sq. ft.
Total Living Area:	**2,387 sq. ft.**
Standard basement	2,387 sq. ft.
Garage	585 sq. ft.
Exterior Wall Framing:	2x4
Foundation Options:	
Standard basement	
Crawlspace	
Slab	
(Please specify foundation type when ordering.)	
BLUEPRINT PRICE CODE:	C

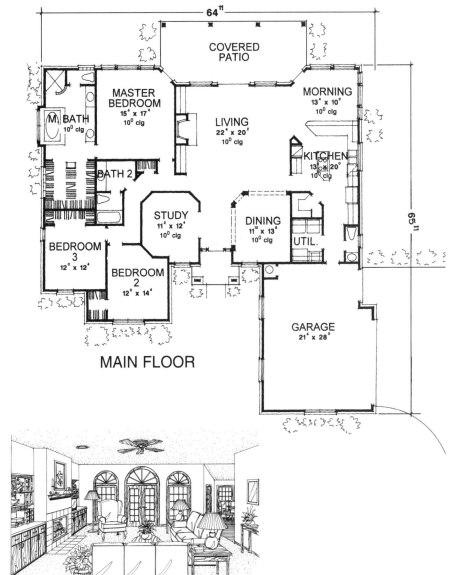

MAIN FLOOR

VIEW INTO LIVING ROOM

Plan 567-DD-2455

Divided Bedroom Areas Lend Privacy

Total Living Area:	**1,833 sq. ft.**
Blueprint Price Code:	**C**
Drive-under garage:	650 sq. ft.

FEATURES

- Master bedroom suite comes with a garden tub, walk-in closet and bay window

- Walk-through kitchen and breakfast room

- Front bay windows offer a deluxe touch

- Foyer with convenient coat closet opens into large vaulted living room with attractive fireplace

- 3 bedrooms, 2 baths, 2-car drive under garage

- Basement foundation

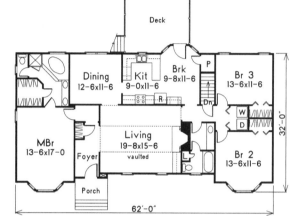

Plan 567-0119

Facade Combines Siding And Brick

Total Living Area:	**2,159 sq. ft.**
Blueprint Price Code:	**C**
Garage:	572 sq. ft.
Storage:	69 sq. ft.
Front porch:	35 sq. ft.

FEATURES

- Energy efficient home with 2" x 6" exterior walls

- Entry opens into large foyer with skylight and coat closet

- Master bedroom includes private bath with angled vanity, separate spa and shower and walk-in closet

- Family and living rooms feature vaulted ceilings and sunken floors for added openness

- 3 bedrooms, 2 baths, 2-car garage

- Basement foundation, drawings also include crawl space and

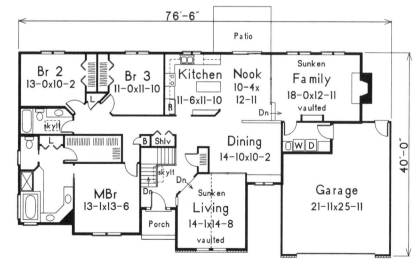

Plan 567-0261

Interior Angles Add Excitement

- Interior angles add a touch of excitement to this one-story home.
- A pleasantly charming exterior combines wood and stone to give the plan a solid, comfortable look for any neighborhood.
- Formal living and dining rooms flank the entry, which leads into the large family room, featuring a fireplace, a vaulted ceiling and built-in bookshelves. A covered porch and a sunny patio are just steps away.
- The adjoining eating area with a built-in china cabinet angles off the roomy kitchen. Note the pantry and the convenient utility room.
- The master bedroom suite is both spacious and private, and includes a dressing room, a large walk-in closet and a secluded bath.
- The three secondary bedrooms are also zoned for privacy, and share a compartmentalized bath.

Plan 567-E-1904

Bedrooms: 4	Baths: 2½
Living Area:	
Main floor	1,997 sq. ft.
Total Living Area:	**1,997 sq. ft.**
Garage	484 sq. ft.
Storage	104 sq. ft.
Exterior Wall Framing:	2x4

Foundation Options:
Crawlspace
Slab
(Please specify foundation type when ordering.)

BLUEPRINT PRICE CODE:	**B**

MAIN FLOOR

Plan 567-E-1904

Classic Country-Style

- At the center of this rustic country-style home is an enormous living room with a flat beamed ceiling and a massive stone fireplace. A sunny patio and a covered rear porch are just steps away.
- The adjoining eating area and kitchen provide plenty of room for casual dining and meal preparation. The eating

area is visually enhanced by a sloped ceiling with false beams. The kitchen includes a snack bar, a pantry closet and a built-in spice cabinet.
- The formal dining room gets plenty of pizzazz from a stone-faced wall and an arched planter facing the living room.
- The secluded master suite has it all, including a private bath, a separate dressing area and a large walk-in closet with built-in shelves.
- The two remaining bedrooms have big closets and easy access to a full bath.

Plan 567-E-1808

Bedrooms: 3	**Baths:** 2
Living Area:	
Main floor	1,800 sq. ft.
Total Living Area:	**1,800 sq. ft.**
Garage	506 sq. ft.
Storage	99 sq. ft.
Exterior Wall Framing:	2x4

Foundation Options:

Crawlspace
Slab
(Please specify foundation type when ordering.)

BLUEPRINT PRICE CODE:	**B**

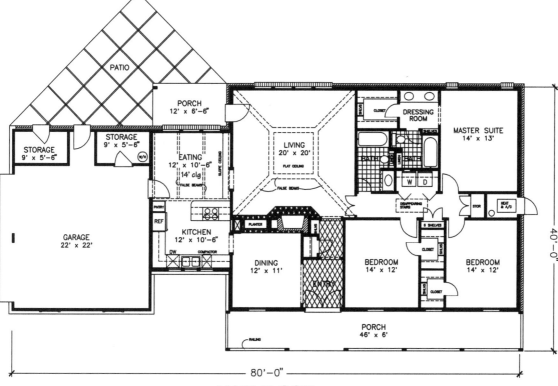

MAIN FLOOR

Plan 567-E-1808

Bold Windows
Enhance
Front Entry

Total Living Area:	**2,252 sq. ft.**
Blueprint Price Code:	**D**
Garage:	528 sq. ft.
Storage:	64 sq. ft.
Front porch:	64 sq. ft.
Rear porch:	148 sq. ft.

FEATURES

- Central living area

- Private master bedroom with large walk-in closet, dressing area and bath

- Energy efficient home with 2" x 6" exterior walls

- Secondary bedrooms are in a suite arrangement with plenty of closet space

- Sunny breakfast room looks out over the porch and patio

- Large entry area highlighted by circle-top transoms

- 4 bedrooms, 2 baths, 2-car garage

- Slab foundation, drawings also include basement and crawl space foundations

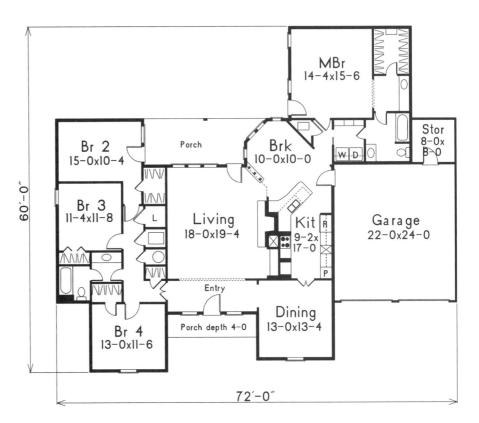

Plan 567-0193

Elegant Extras

- Ornate windows set off by stucco and stone give this home an Old World look. Inside, the modern floor plan features many elegant extras.
- The vaulted foyer, brightened by a window above, opens to the living room. This spectacular space is enhanced by a 16-ft. flat ceiling and a rear wall of glass topped by a half-round window.
- An arched opening over a half-wall separates the living room from the sunny breakfast room, which features a French door to the backyard. The fireplace in the adjoining family room is accentuated by tall windows topped by quarter-rounds.
- A serving bar lies between the family room and the gourmet kitchen, which offers a large walk-in pantry and a butler's pantry. An arched opening leads into the formal dining room.
- The bedroom wing is highlighted by a superb master suite with a tray ceiling. The vaulted bath hosts a corner spa tub set beneath an arched window.

Plan 567-HFB-5169-HEND

Bedrooms: 3	Baths: 2½
Living Area:	
Main floor	2,177 sq. ft.
Total Living Area:	**2,177 sq. ft.**
Daylight basement	2,177 sq. ft.
Garage and storage	550 sq. ft.
Exterior Wall Framing:	2x4
Foundation Options:	

Daylight basement
Crawlspace
(Please specify foundation type when ordering.)

BLUEPRINT PRICE CODE:	C

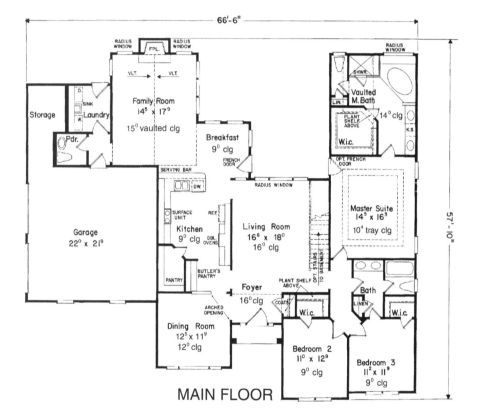

MAIN FLOOR

Plan 567-HFB-5169-HEND

Adobe Home, Something Different

Total Living Area:	2,350 sq. ft.
Blueprint Price Code:	D
Garage and Shop:	594 sq. ft.
Front entry:	51 sq. ft.

FEATURES

- Gourmet kitchen opens to family room with heavy rough sawn beams defining ceiling
- 8" x 8" exposed headers at architectural openings
- Stylish raised dining room ceiling
- Glass block at shower and whirlpool makes master bath bright and warm
- Skylights brighten up entry, master bath and hall
- Energy efficient home with 2" x 6" exterior walls
- 3 bedrooms, 2 baths, 2-car garage
- Slab foundation

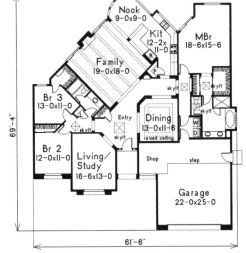

Plan 567-0423

High-Styled Master Bedroom Suite

Total Living Area:	2,255 sq. ft.
Blueprint Price Code:	D
Garage:	633 sq. ft.
Front porch:	63 sq. ft.

FEATURES

- Walk-in closets in all bedrooms
- Plant shelf graces hallway
- Family room adjoins kitchen and features fireplace and access outdoors
- Master bath comes complete with double vanities, enclosed toilet, separate tub and shower and cozy fireplace
- Living/dining rooms combine for large formal gathering room
- 4 bedrooms, 2 1/2 baths, 3-car garage
- Slab foundation

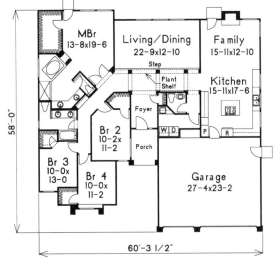

Plan 567-0443

Wonderful Windows

- This one-story's striking stucco and stone facade is enhanced by great gables and wonderful windows.
- A beautiful bay augments the living room/den, which can be closed off.
- A wall of windows lets sunbeams brighten the exquisite formal dining room, which is defined by decorative columns.
- The spacious family room offers a handsome fireplace flanked by glass.
- The kitchen boasts a large pantry, a corner sink and two convenient serving bars. A vaulted ceiling presides over the adjoining breakfast room.
- A lovely window seat highlights one of the two secondary bedrooms, which are serviced by a full bath.
- The magnificent master suite features a symmetrical tray ceiling that sets off an attractive round-top window. The elegant master bath offers a vaulted ceiling, a garden tub and dual vanities, one with knee space.
- Ceilings not specified are 9 ft. high.

Plan 567-HFB-5009-CHAD

Bedrooms: 3	Baths: 2
Living Area:	
Main floor	2,051 sq. ft.
Total Living Area:	**2,051 sq. ft.**
Daylight basement	2,064 sq. ft.
Garage and storage	535 sq. ft.
Exterior Wall Framing:	2x4

Foundation Options:
Daylight basement
Crawlspace
Slab
(Please specify foundation type when ordering.)

BLUEPRINT PRICE CODE:	C

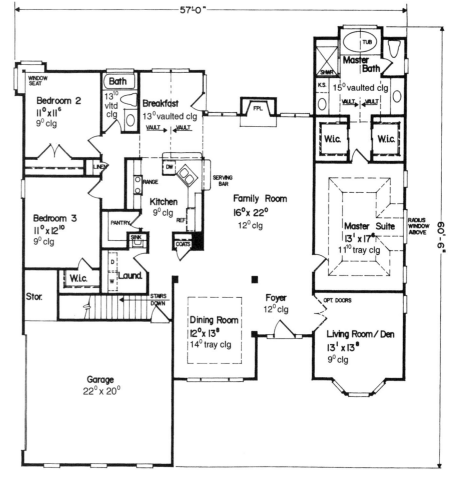

MAIN FLOOR

Plan 567-HFB-5009-CHAD

Upscale Ranch Boasts Both Formal And Casual Areas

Total Living Area:	1,950 sq. ft.
Blueprint Price Code:	C
Garage:	760 sq. ft.
Front porch:	146 sq. ft.

FEATURES

- Large corner kitchen with island cooktop opens to family room

- Master suite features double-door entry, raised ceiling, double-bowl vanities and walk-in closet

- Plant shelf accents hall

- 4 bedrooms, 2 baths, 3-car garage

- Crawl space foundation

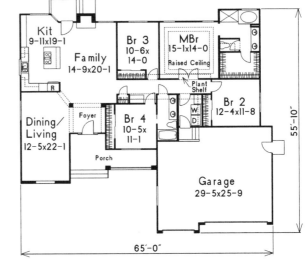

Plan 567-0442

Grand Entryway Adorns This Home

Total Living Area:	1,941 sq. ft.
Blueprint Price Code:	C
Garage:	540 sq. ft.
Front porch:	90 sq. ft.

FEATURES

- Kitchen incorporates a cooktop island, a handy pantry, and adjoins the dining and family rooms

- Formal living room to the left of the foyer lends a touch of privacy

- Raised ceiling in foyer, living, dining and kitchen areas

- Laundry room, half bath and closet located near the garage

- Both the dining and family rooms have access outdoors through sliding doors

- 3 bedrooms, 2 1/2 baths, 2-car garage

- Crawl space foundation

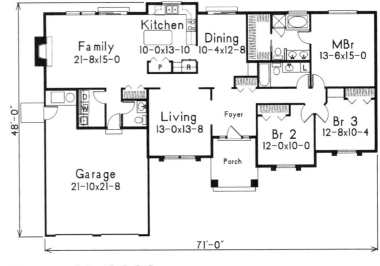

Plan 567-0682

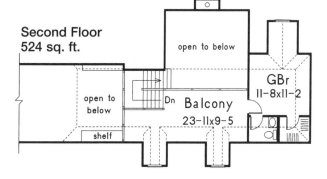

Striking Balcony Overlooks Great Room And Kitchen

Total Living Area:	**2,501 sq. ft.**
Blueprint Price Code:	**D**
Garage:	521 sq. ft.
Front porch:	24 sq. ft.
Back deck:	120 sq. ft.

FEATURES

- Oversized kitchen with work island, vaulted ceiling and plant shelves

- Open staircase overlooks kitchen

- Secluded second floor guest bedroom features private half bath

- Covered deck accessible from dining room and kitchen

- 4 bedrooms, 2 1/2 baths, 2-car side entry garage

- Basement foundation, drawings also include crawl space and slab foundations

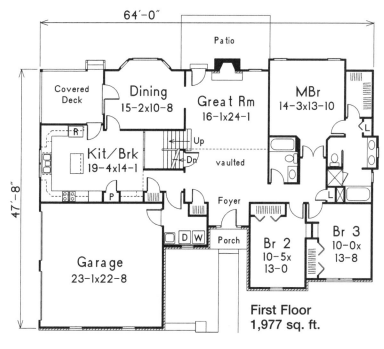

Plan 567-0235

Fully Columned Front Entrance

Total Living Area:	2,365 sq. ft.
Blueprint Price Code:	D
Carport:	485 sq. ft.
Front porch:	273 sq. ft.
Back porch:	184 sq. ft.

FEATURES

- 9' ceilings

- Expansive central living room complemented by corner fire-place

- Breakfast bay overlooks rear porch

- Master bedroom features bath with double walk-in closets and vanities, separate tub and shower and handy linen closet

- Peninsula keeps kitchen private

- 4 bedrooms, 2 baths, 2-car carport

- Slab foundation

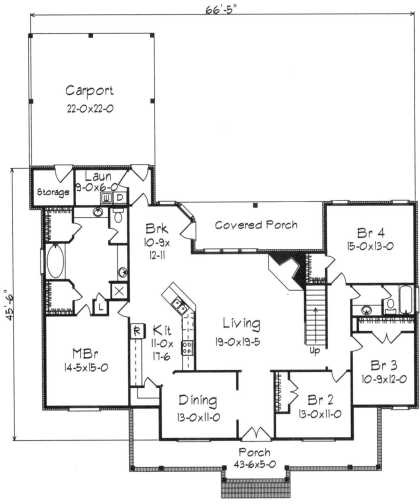

Plan 567-0440

TO ORDER BLUEPRINTS USE THE FORM ON PAGE 256 OR CALL **TOLL-FREE 1-800-367-7667**

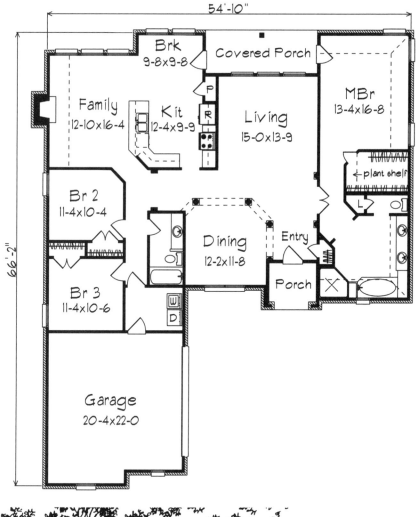

54'-10"

66'-2"

Brk
9-8x9-8

Covered Porch

Family
12-10x16-4

Kit
12-4x9-9

P
R

Living
15-0x13-9

MBr
13-4x16-8

plant shelf

Br 2
11-4x10-4

Dining
12-2x11-8

Entry

Br 3
11-4x10-6

Porch

W
D

Garage
20-4x22-0

Inviting Gabled And Arched Brick Entry

Total Living Area:	**2,109 sq. ft.**
Blueprint Price Code:	**C**
Garage:	447 sq. ft.
Front porch:	49 sq. ft.
Back porch:	125 sq. ft.

FEATURES

- 12' ceilings in living and dining rooms

- Kitchen designed as an integral part of the family and breakfast rooms

- Secluded and generous-sized master bedroom includes a plant shelf, walk-in closet and private bath with separate tub and shower

- Stately columns and circle-top window frame dining room

- 3 bedrooms, 2 baths, 2-car side entry garage

- Slab foundation, drawings also include crawl space foundation

Plan 567-0412

Soaring
Covered Portico

Total Living Area:	2,056 sq. ft.
Blueprint Price Code:	C
Garage:	413 sq. ft.
Front entry:	105 sq. ft.
Back porch:	229 sq. ft.

FEATURES

- Columned foyer projects past living and dining rooms into family room

- Kitchen conveniently accesses dining room and breakfast area

- Master bedroom features double-doors to patio and pocket door to master bath with walk-in closet, double-bowl vanity and tub

- 4 bedrooms, 2 baths, 2-car garage

- Slab foundation, drawings also include crawl space foundation

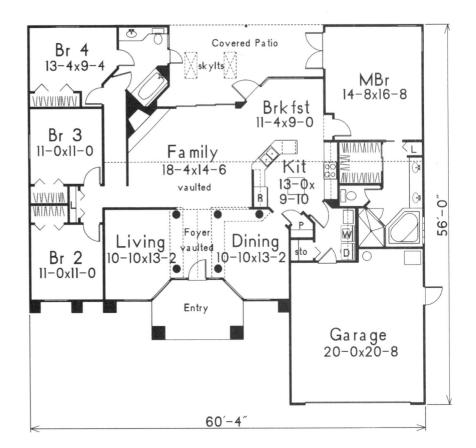

Plan 567-0343

Family Room Features Barrel Vaulted Ceiling

Total Living Area:	**2,153 sq. ft.**
Blueprint Price Code:	**C**
Garage:	354 sq. ft.
Front porch:	180 sq. ft.
Rear porch:	270 sq. ft.

FEATURES

- Master suite features wall of windows and also accesses porch

- Family room boasts twelve foot barrel vaulted ceiling and built-in bookshelves on each side of dramatic fireplace

- Varied ceiling heights throughout

- Three bedrooms, a bath and the utility room are located off of the family room

- 4 bedrooms, 2 baths, 2-car garage

- Slab foundation

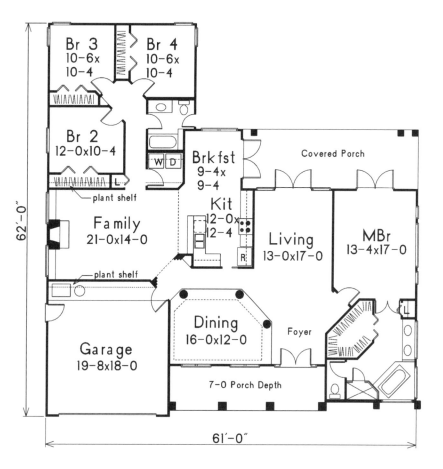

Plan 567-0340

Symmetry and Style

- This appealing one-story home boasts a striking facade with symmetrical rooflines, stately columns and gently curved transoms.
- The formal living spaces have a classic split design, perfect for quiet times and conversation.
- The unique layout of the bedroom wing gives each bedroom easy access to a full bath. The rear bedroom also enjoys pool and patio proximity.
- The huge family room opens up to the patio with 12-ft. pocket sliding doors, and boasts a handsome fireplace flanked by built-in shelves, perfect for your media equipment.
- The master suite just off the kitchen and nook is private, yet easily accessible. One unique feature is its bed wall with high glass above. The master bath offers a huge walk-in closet, a relaxing corner tub, a step-down shower, dual sinks and a private toilet.

Plan 567-HHDS-99-147	
Bedrooms: 4	**Baths:** 3
Living Area:	
Main floor	2,089 sq. ft.
Total Living Area:	**2,089 sq. ft.**
Garage	415 sq. ft.
Exterior Wall Framing:	2x4
Foundation Options:	
Slab	
(Please specify foundation type when ordering.)	
BLUEPRINT PRICE CODE:	C

MAIN FLOOR

Plan 567-HHDS-99-147

Garden Home

- A creative, angular design gives this traditional French garden home an exciting, open and airy floor plan.
- A covered, columned porch leads into the angled living and dining rooms, which feature 12-ft. ceilings, corner windows and a cozy fireplace.
- The large, angled kitchen is highlighted by a 12-ft. ceiling, a pantry closet and lots of work space. The informal eating nook faces a secluded courtyard.
- The private master suite features a luxurious bath and a walk-in closet.

Plan 567-E-2004

Bedrooms: 3	Baths: 2
Living Area:	
Main floor	2,023 sq. ft.
Total Living Area:	**2,023 sq. ft.**
Garage	484 sq. ft.
Storage	87 sq. ft.
Exterior Wall Framing:	2x6
Foundation Options:	
Crawlspace, slab	
(Please specify foundation type when ordering.)	
BLUEPRINT PRICE CODE:	C

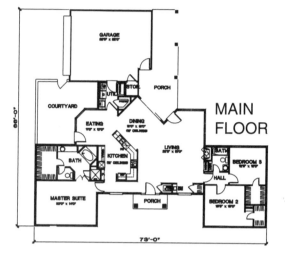

MAIN FLOOR

Plan 567-E-2004

Stunning Style

- The stunning detailing of this stucco home includes a stately roofline and an arched window above the entry door.
- The open floor plan begins at the foyer, where a column is all that separates the dining room from the living room. A 13½-ft. ceiling creates a dramatic effect in the living room.
- A sunny breakfast room and a great kitchen with a huge serving bar adjoin a 14½-ft.-high vaulted family room.
- The master suite has an 11-ft. tray ceiling in the sleeping area and a luxurious bath with a spa tub, a separate shower and a walk-in closet.

Plan 567-HFB-1802

Bedrooms: 3	Baths: 2
Living Area:	
Main floor	1,802 sq. ft.
Total Living Area:	**1,802 sq. ft.**
Garage and storage	492 sq. ft.
Exterior Wall Framing:	2x4
Foundation Options:	
Crawlspace, slab	
(Please specify foundation type when ordering.)	
BLUEPRINT PRICE CODE:	B

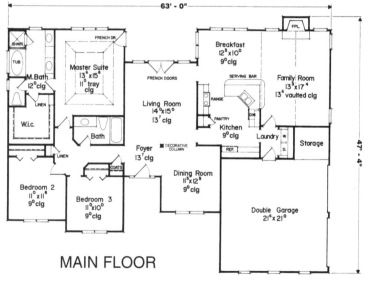

MAIN FLOOR

Plan 567-HFB-1802

Abounding in Natural Light

- Bright sunshine streams through the tall window wall of the beautiful formal dining room in this classic European-style home.
- The walk-through kitchen boasts a serving bar opening to the sunny breakfast nook, which offers access to the backyard through a French door.
- Nearby, two secondary bedrooms share a full bath.
- A toasty fireplace flanked by glorious windows warms the immense vaulted family room.
- The living room offers a bay window for quiet reading or gazing outdoors.
- A tray ceiling is the highlight of the master bedroom. Not to be outdone, the master bath flaunts a dual-sink vanity, a spacious walk-in closet, a garden tub and a separate shower.

Plan 567-HFB-1868

Bedrooms: 3	Baths: 2
Living Area:	
Main floor	1,875 sq. ft.
Total Living Area:	**1,875 sq. ft.**
Daylight basement	1,891 sq. ft.
Garage and storage	475 sq. ft.
Exterior Wall Framing:	2x4

Foundation Options:

Daylight basement

Crawlspace

Slab

(Please specify foundation type when ordering.)

BLUEPRINT PRICE CODE:	**B**

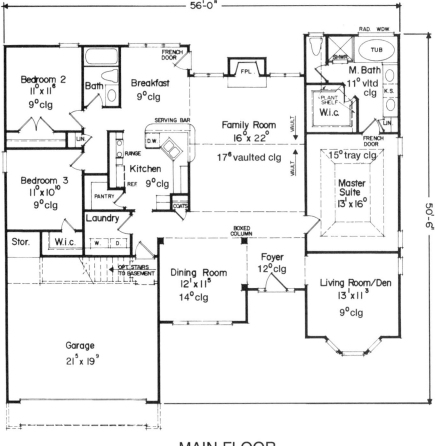

MAIN FLOOR

Plan 567-HFB-1868

Upscale Charm

- Country charm and the very latest in conveniences mark this upscale home. To add extra appeal, all of the living areas are housed on the main floor, while the upper floor offers plenty of space for future expansion.
- Set off from the foyer, the dining room is embraced by elegant columns. Arched windows in the dining room and in the bedroom across the hall echo the delicate detailing of the front porch.
- Straight ahead, the family room flaunts a wall of French doors overlooking a rear porch and a large deck.
- A curved island snack bar smoothly connects the gourmet kitchen to the sunny breakfast area, which features a dramatic vaulted ceiling brightened by skylights. Other amenities include a computer room and a laundry/utility room with a recycling center.
- The master bedroom's luxurious private bath includes a dual-sink vanity and a large storage unit with a built-in chest of drawers. Other extras are a step-up spa tub and a separate shower.

Plan 567-J-92100

Bedrooms: 3+	Baths: 2
Living Area:	
Main floor	1,877 sq. ft.
Total Living Area:	**1,877 sq. ft.**
Future upper floor	1,500 sq. ft.
Standard basement	1,877 sq. ft.
Garage and storage	551 sq. ft.
Exterior Wall Framing:	2x4
Foundation Options:	
Standard basement	
Crawlspace	
Slab	
(Please specify foundation type when ordering.)	
BLUEPRINT PRICE CODE:	**B**

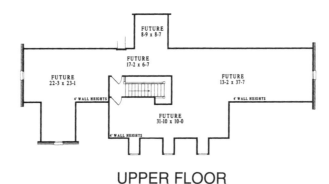

UPPER FLOOR

MAIN FLOOR

STAIRWAY AREA IN
NON-BASEMENT
VERSIONS

VIEW INTO FAMILY ROOM
AND BREAKFAST NOOK

Plan 567-J-92100

Front Entrance Flanked By Windows

Total Living Area:	**2,467 sq. ft.**
Blueprint Price Code:	**D**
Garage:	430 sq. ft.
Front entry:	80 sq. ft.
Back patio:	338 sq. ft.

FEATURES

- Tiled foyer leads into living room with vaulted ceiling and large bay window

- Kitchen features walk-in pantry and adjacent breakfast nook

- Master suite includes bay window and master bath with large walk-in closet

- Varied ceiling heights throughout

- 3 bedrooms, 3 baths, 2-car garage

- Slab foundation

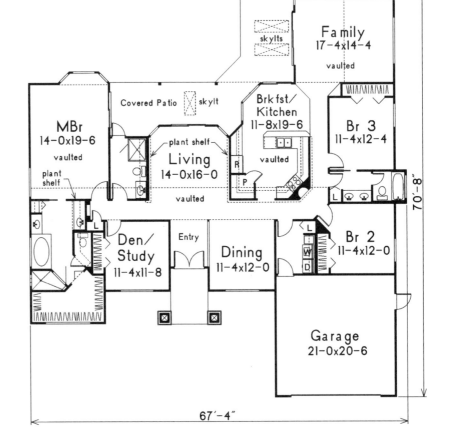

Plan 567-0336

Classic Three Bedroom

Total Living Area:	**2,228 sq. ft.**
Blueprint Price Code:	**D**
Garage:	397 sq. ft.
Front porch:	128 sq. ft.

FEATURES

- Convenient entrance from garage into home through laundry room
- Master bedroom features walk-in closet and double-door entrance into master bath with oversized tub
- Formal dining room with tray ceiling
- Kitchen features island cooktop and adjacent breakfast room
- 3 bedrooms, 2 baths, 2-car garage
- Basement foundation

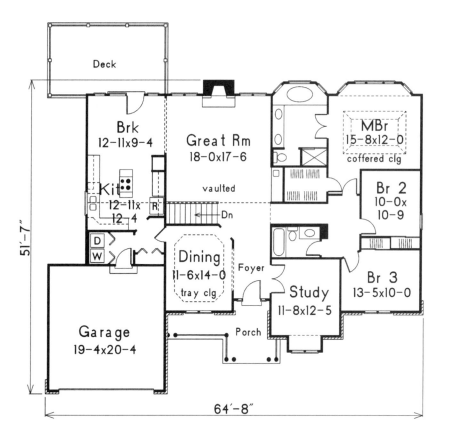

Plan 567-0320

Isolated Master Suite Has Grand Master Bath

Total Living Area:	**1,856 sq. ft.**
Blueprint Price Code:	**C**
Garage:	470 sq. ft.
Storage:	112 sq. ft.
Front porch:	80 sq. ft.

FEATURES

- Living room features include fireplace, 12' ceiling and sky-lights

- Energy efficient home with 2" x 6" exterior walls

- Common vaulted ceiling creates open atmosphere in kitchen and eating areas

- Garage with storage areas conveniently accesses home through handy utility room

- Private hall separates secondary bedrooms from living areas

- 3 bedrooms, 2 baths, 2-car side entry garage

- Slab foundation, drawings also include crawl space foundation

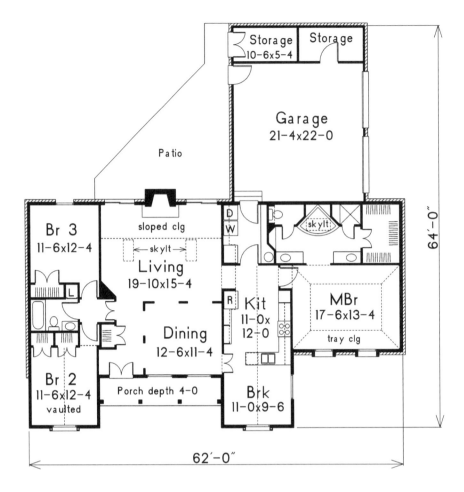

Plan 567-0286

Raised Foyer And Archways Create An Impressive Entry

Total Living Area:	**2,070 sq. ft.**
Blueprint Price Code:	**C**
Garage:	546 sq. ft.
Front entry:	26 sq. ft.

FEATURES

- Access to rear deck through kitchen/nook area

- Energy efficient home with 2" x 6" exterior walls

- Master bedroom features arched entrance into bath with separate shower and tub, dressing area and walk-in closet

- Sunken family room with fireplace

- 3 bedrooms, 2 baths, 2-car garage

- Basement foundation, drawings also include slab and crawl space foundations

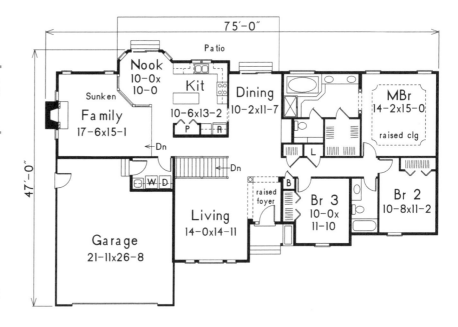

Plan 567-0262

Upscale Ranch With Formal And Informal Areas

Total Living Area:	**1,969 sq. ft.**
Blueprint Price Code:	**C**
Garage:	503 sq. ft.
Front porch:	240 sq. ft.
Back patio:	187 sq. ft.

FEATURES

- Master suite boasts luxurious bath with double sinks, two walk-in closets and an over-sized tub

- Corner fireplace warms a conveniently located family area

- Formal living and dining areas in the front of the home lend a touch of privacy when entertaining

- Spacious utility room has counter space and a sink

- 3 bedrooms, 2 baths, 2-car garage

- Crawl space foundation, drawings also include slab foundation

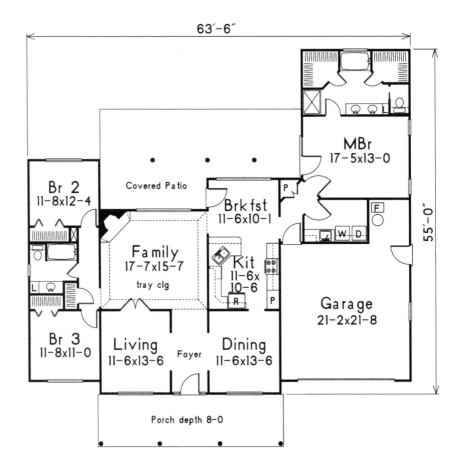

Plan 567-0724

Fireplaces Are Unique Focal Points

Total Living Area:	**2,481 sq. ft.**
Blueprint Price Code:	**D**
Garage:	630 sq. ft.
Front entry:	35 sq. ft.

FEATURES

- Varied ceiling heights throughout this home

- Master bedroom features built-in desk and pocket door entrance into large master bath

- Master bath includes corner vanity and garden tub

- Breakfast area accesses courtyard

- 3 bedrooms, 2 baths, 3-car side entry garage

- Slab foundation

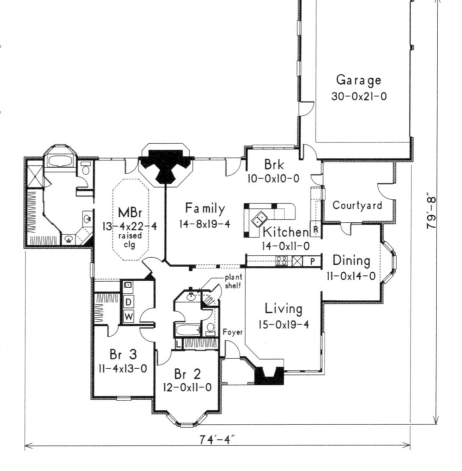

Plan 567-0315

Family Fun

- This home's spacious family room offers a high ceiling, a toasty fireplace and access to a large rear deck, making it the perfect spot for a dose of family fun.
- The central kitchen features a practical layout and a handy snack bar that serves the adjacent breakfast nook.
- The master suite boasts a private bath, a large walk-in closet and access to a rear deck and a cozy private morning porch.

Plan 567-APS-2018

Bedrooms: 3+	Baths: 2½
Living Area:	
Main floor	2,088 sq. ft.
Total Living Area:	**2,088 sq. ft.**
Bonus room	282 sq. ft.
Daylight basement	2,088 sq. ft.
Garage	460 sq. ft.
Storage	35 sq. ft.
Exterior Wall Framing:	2x4
Foundation Options:	
Daylight basement	
Crawlspace	
Slab	
(Please specify foundation type when ordering.)	
BLUEPRINT PRICE CODE:	C

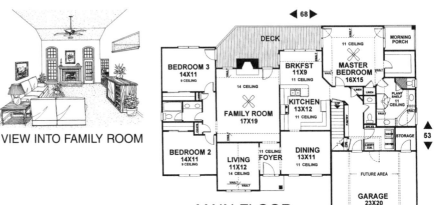

VIEW INTO FAMILY ROOM

MAIN FLOOR

Plan 567-APS-2018

Quiet Relaxation

- This one-story brick home features a stunning master bedroom with a sunny morning porch for quiet relaxation.
- A handsome fireplace warms the spacious family room, while a striking French door provides access to a deck also reached from the master bedroom.
- A few steps away, the open kitchen shares its high ceiling and handy snack bar with the bright breakfast nook.

Plan 567-APS-2117

Bedrooms: 4	Baths: 2½
Living Area:	
Main floor	2,187 sq. ft.
Total Living Area:	**2,187 sq. ft.**
Daylight basement	2,266 sq. ft.
Garage and storage	460 sq. ft.
Exterior Wall Framing:	2x4
Foundation Options:	
Daylight basement	
Crawlspace	
Slab	
(Please specify foundation type when ordering.)	
BLUEPRINT PRICE CODE:	C

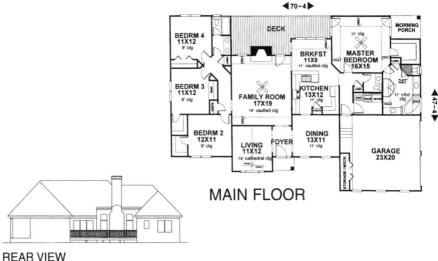

REAR VIEW

MAIN FLOOR

Plan 567-APS-2117

Elaborate Entry

- This home's important-looking covered entry greets guests with heavy, banded support columns, sunburst transom windows and dual sidelights.
- Inside, the foyer is flanked by the formal living and dining rooms, which both have vaulted ceilings. Straight ahead and beyond five decorative columns lies the spacious family room.
- The family room features a vaulted ceiling that soars over its 8-ft.-high walls, plus a fireplace and sliding doors to a covered patio. A neat plant shelf above the fireplace adds style.
- The bright and airy kitchen serves the family room and the breakfast area, which is enhanced by a corner window and a French door.
- The master suite enjoys a vaulted ceiling and features French-door patio access, a large walk-in closet and a private bath with a corner platform tub and a separate shower.
- Across the home, three secondary bedrooms share a hall bath, which boasts private access to the patio.

VIEW INTO
DINING AND
LIVING ROOMS

Plan 567-HHDS-90-806

Bedrooms: 4	Baths: 2
Living Area:	
Main floor	2,056 sq. ft.
Total Living Area:	**2,056 sq. ft.**
Garage	452 sq. ft.
Exterior Wall Framing:	2x4 or
	8-in. concrete block

Foundation Options:
Slab
(Please specify foundation type when ordering.)

BLUEPRINT PRICE CODE: C

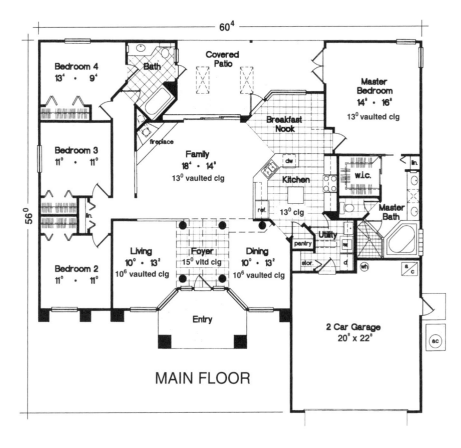

MAIN FLOOR

Plan 567-HHDS-90-806

Open Living Areas Separate Remote Bedrooms

Total Living Area:	1,868 sq. ft.
Blueprint Price Code:	D
Garage:	469 sq. ft.
Storage areas:	112 sq. ft.
Front porch:	68 sq. ft.

FEATURES

- Luxurious master bath is impressive with its angled, quarter-circle tub, separate vanities and large walk-in closet

- Energy efficient home with 2" x 6" exterior walls

- Dining room is surrounded by series of arched openings which complement the open feeling of this design

- Living room has a 12' ceiling accented by skylights and a large fireplace flanked by sliding doors

- Large storage areas

- 3 bedrooms, 2 baths, 2-car side entry garage

- Slab foundation, drawings also include crawl space foundation

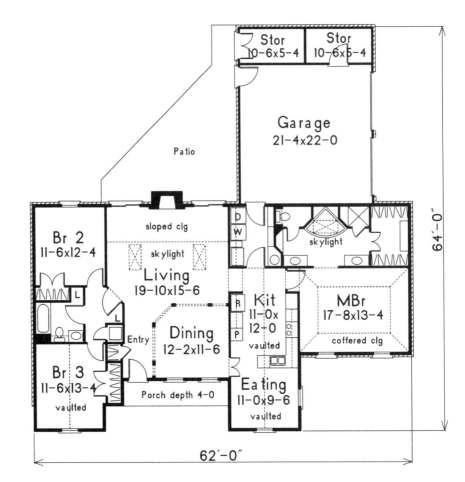

Plan 567-0191

Garden Courtyard Lends Distinction, Privacy

Total Living Area:	**1,996 sq. ft.**
Blueprint Price Code:	**D**
Garage:	392 sq. ft.
Front porch:	28 sq. ft.
Back porch:	250 sq. ft.

FEATURES

- Garden courtyard comes with large porch and direct access to master bedroom suite, breakfast room and garage

- Sculptured entrance has artful plant shelves and special niche in foyer

- Master bedroom boasts French doors, garden tub, desk with bookshelves and generous storage

- Plant ledges and high ceilings grace hallway

- 3 bedrooms, 2 baths, 2-car side entry garage

- Slab foundation, drawings also include crawl space foundation

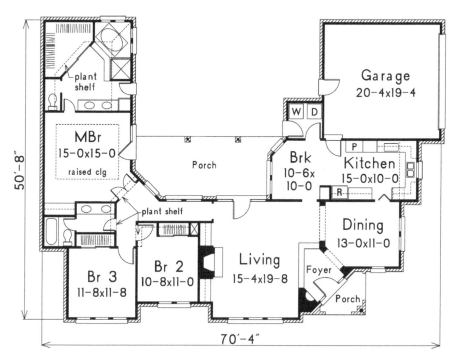

Plan 567-0127

Captivating Design

- This captivating and award-winning design is introduced by a unique entry landscape that includes striking columns, an exciting fountain courtyard and a private garden.
- The beautiful, open interior commands attention with expansive glass and ceilings at least 10 ft. high throughout.
- The foyer's 15-ft. ceiling extends into the adjoining dining room, which is set off by a decorative glass-block wall.
- A step-down soffit frames the spacious central living room with its dramatic entry columns and 13-ft. ceiling. A rear bay overlooks a large covered patio.
- The gourmet kitchen shows off an oversized island cooktop and snack bar. A pass-through above the sink provides easy service to the patio's summer kitchen, while indoor dining is offered in the sunny, open breakfast area.
- A warm fireplace and flanking storage shelves adorn an exciting media wall in the large adjacent family room.
- The secondary bedrooms share a full bath near the laundry room and garage.
- Behind double doors on the other side of the home, the romantic master suite is bathed in sunlight. A private garden embraces an elegant oval tub.

Plan 567-HHDS-99-185

Bedrooms: 3+	Baths: 2½
Living Area:	
Main floor	2,397 sq. ft.
Total Living Area:	**2,397 sq. ft.**
Garage	473 sq. ft.
Exterior Wall Framing:	2x4
Foundation Options:	
Slab	
(Please specify foundation type when ordering.)	
BLUEPRINT PRICE CODE:	C

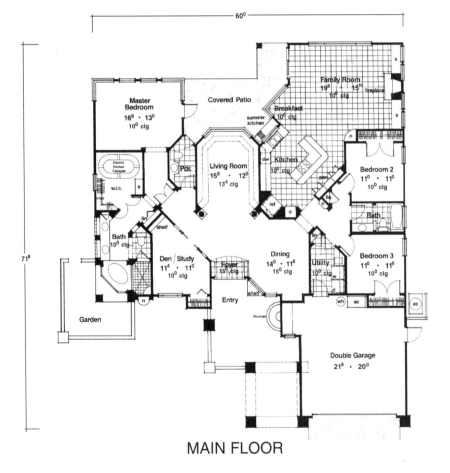

MAIN FLOOR

Plan 567-HHDS-99-185

Arched Entry

- A beautiful arched entry introduces this grand Mediterranean-style home. High ceilings and lots of windows create an atmosphere of space and relaxation.
- Elegant double doors open into a tiled foyer, which is flanked by the formal living and dining rooms. Both rooms boast volume ceilings, and the dining room offers a tray ceiling.
- In the huge family room, sliding glass doors open to a covered patio. A fireplace flanked by built-in cabinets sets the stage for fun evenings at home.

- An 8-ft. wall separates the family room from the kitchen, which shares an angled serving counter with the sunny bayed breakfast nook. A built-in desk nearby is a great spot to pay the bills.
- The secluded master suite includes a sprawling overhead plant shelf and sliding glass doors to the patio. A dramatic arch introduces the private bath, which includes a garden tub, a separate shower and a dual-sink vanity.
- Across the home, two more bedrooms share a hall bath. A quiet rear bedroom is serviced by another full bath. Each room boasts a neat plant shelf.

Plan 567-HHDS-99-233

Bedrooms: 4	**Baths:** 3

Living Area:	
Main floor	2,140 sq. ft.
Total Living Area:	**2,140 sq. ft.**
Garage	430 sq. ft.

Exterior Wall Framing: 8-in. concrete block

Foundation Options:

Slab
(Please specify foundation type when ordering.)

BLUEPRINT PRICE CODE:	**C**

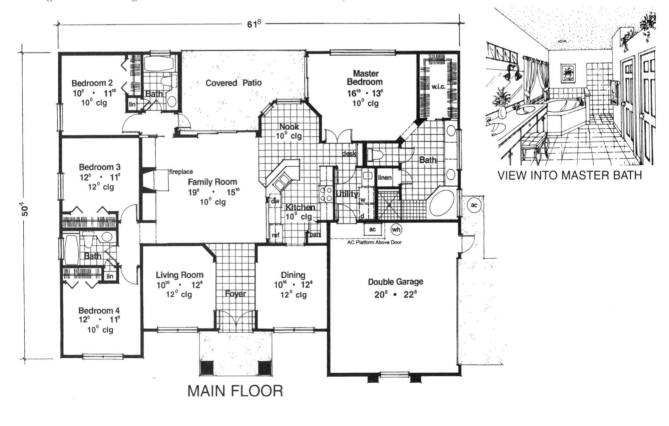

VIEW INTO MASTER BATH

MAIN FLOOR

Plan 567-HHDS-99-233

Double Gables
Frame Front Porch

Total Living Area:	**1,832 sq. ft.**
Blueprint Price Code:	**C**
Detached garage:	576 sq. ft.
Front porch:	336 sq. ft.
Back covered patio:	144 sq.ft.

FEATURES

- Distinctive master suite enhanced by skylights, garden tub, separate shower and walk-in closet

- U-shaped kitchen features convenient pantry, laundry area and full view to breakfast room

- Foyer opens into spacious living room

- Large front porch creates enjoyable outdoor living

- 3 bedrooms, 2 baths, 2-car detached garage

- Crawl space foundation, drawings also include basement and slab foundations

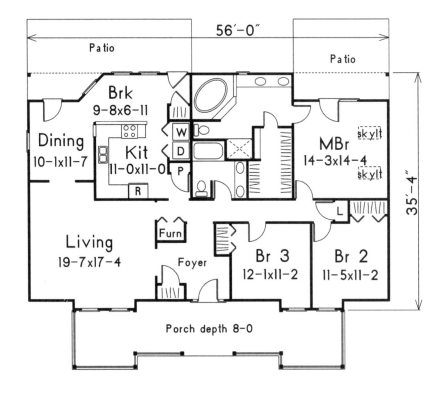

Plan 567-0542

Memories in the Making

- You will enjoy years of memories in this peaceful country home.
- A tranquil covered porch opens into the foyer, where regal columns introduce the formal dining room. Raised ceilings enhance the foyer, dining room, kitchen and breakfast nook.
- Past two closets, a cathedral ceiling adds glamour to the living room. A grand fireplace flanked by French doors under beautiful quarter-round transoms will wow your guests! The French doors

open to an inviting porch that is great for afternoon get-togethers.
- The sunny breakfast bay merges with the gourmet kitchen, which includes a large pantry and an island snack bar. Bi-fold doors above the sink create a handy pass-through to the living room.
- A neat computer room nearby allows the kids to do their homework under a parent's watchful eye.
- Across the home, a stylish tray ceiling crowns the master suite. The skylighted master bath features a refreshing whirlpool tub.
- A hall bath services two additional bedrooms. The larger bedroom is expanded by a vaulted ceiling.

Plan 567-J-9294

Bedrooms: 3	Baths: 2
Living Area:	
Main floor	2,018 sq. ft.
Total Living Area:	**2,018 sq. ft.**
Standard basement	2,018 sq. ft.
Garage and storage	556 sq. ft.
Exterior Wall Framing:	2x4

Foundation Options:
Standard basement
Crawlspace
Slab
(Please specify foundation type when ordering.)

BLUEPRINT PRICE CODE:	C

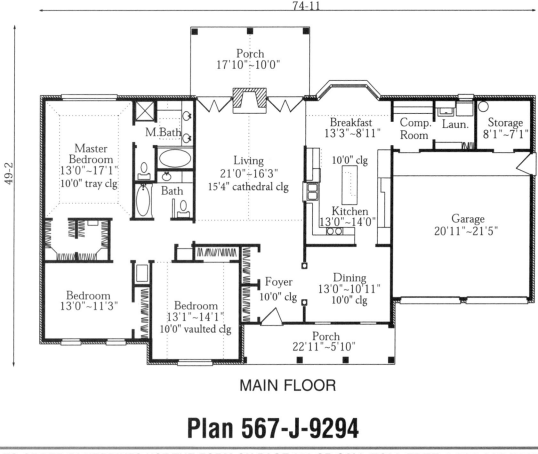

MAIN FLOOR

Plan 567-J-9294

Inviting And Cozy Covered Arched Entry

Total Living Area:	1,923 sq. ft.
Blueprint Price Code:	C
Garage:	454 sq. ft.
Front entry:	21 sq. ft.
Back patio:	216 sq. ft.

FEATURES

- Foyer opens into spacious living room with fireplace and splendid view of covered porch

- Kitchen with walk-in pantry adjacent to laundry area and breakfast rooms

- All bedrooms feature walk-in closets

- Secluded master bedroom includes unique angled bath with spacious walk-in closet

- 3 bedrooms, 2 baths, 2-car garage

- Slab foundation

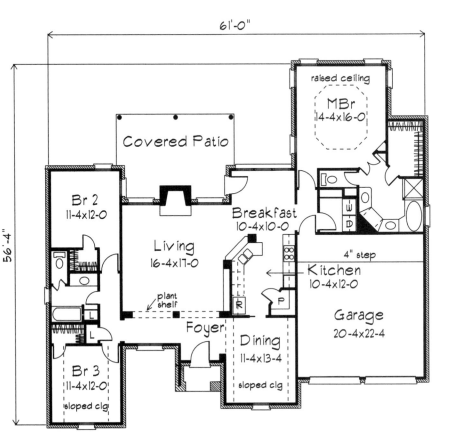

Plan 567-0400

Split Entry With Lots Of Room For Future Growth

Total Living Area: 1,803 sq. ft.
Blueprint Price Code: C
Drive-under garage: 899 sq. ft.

FEATURES

- Master bedroom features raised ceiling and private bath with walk-in closet, large double-bowl vanity and separate tub and shower

- U-shaped kitchen includes corner sink and convenient pantry

- Vaulted living room complete with fireplace and built-in cabinet

- 3 bedrooms, 2 baths, 3-car drive under garage

- Basement foundation

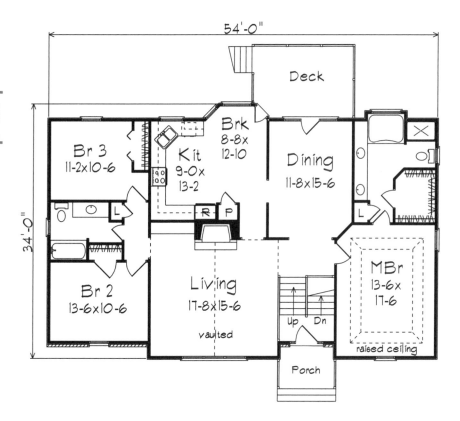

Plan 567-0395

Classic Combo

- This snappy home combines classic touches with thoughtful design.
- Eye-catching arches frame the front porch. Inside, you'll be stunned by the expansive family room, where a cathedral ceiling and a majestic fireplace enhance the space.
- Double doors lead into the living room, where a vaulted ceiling and a Palladian window create an ideal spot for entertaining visitors.
- Through a graceful archway, the efficient kitchen includes a handy pantry

and a serving bar overlooking the bayed breakfast nook.
- A screened porch with a vaulted ceiling opens to a deck for alfresco meals and relaxation.
- The dining room showcases a pair of tall windows and a tray ceiling.
- In the master suite, a cathedral ceiling, a separate sitting area, a lavish private bath and access to the deck create a wonderful retreat.
- Two more bedrooms share a bath on the other side of the home.
- The blueprints offer the choice of a two- or three-car garage.

Plan 567-APS-1911	
Bedrooms: 3	**Baths:** 2½
Living Area:	
Main floor	1,992 sq. ft.
Total Living Area:	**1,992 sq. ft.**
Screened porch	192 sq. ft.
Standard basement	1,992 sq. ft.
Garage	649 sq. ft.
Exterior Wall Framing:	2x4
Foundation Options:	
Standard basement	
Crawlspace	
Slab	
(Please specify foundation type when ordering.)	
BLUEPRINT PRICE CODE:	B

MAIN FLOOR

REAR VIEW

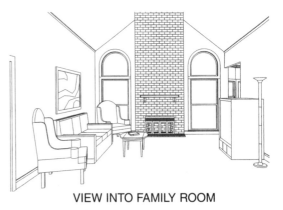

VIEW INTO FAMILY ROOM

Plan 567-APS-1911

Classic Styling

- Classic styling transcends the exterior and interior of this sprawling one-story.
- Outside, sweeping rooflines, arched windows and brick planters combine for an elegant curb appeal.
- The angled entry opens to a tiled foyer, which overlooks the spacious central living room. A handsome fireplace and a string of windows lend light and volume to this high-profile area.

- Unfolding to the right, the kitchen and dining room flow together, making the space seem even larger. A snack counter, bar sink and corner pantry are attractive kitchen efficiencies.
- The master suite is drenched in luxury with a romantic fireplace, a private porch and a grand Jacuzzi bath with lush surrounding plant shelves.
- Two good-sized secondary bedrooms share another full bath.
- Extra storage is offered in the garage.

Plan 567-L-824-EMB	
Bedrooms: 3	**Baths:** 2
Living Area:	
Main floor	1,826 sq. ft.
Total Living Area:	**1,826 sq. ft.**
Garage and storage	534 sq. ft.
Exterior Wall Framing:	2x4
Foundation Options:	
Slab	
(Please specify foundation type when ordering.)	
BLUEPRINT PRICE CODE:	**B**

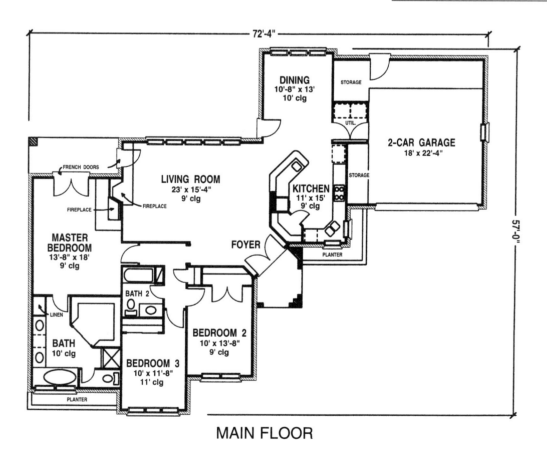

MAIN FLOOR

Plan 567-L-824-EMB

Dramatic Appeal, Inside And Out

Total Living Area:	**2,468 sq. ft.**
Blueprint Price Code:	**D**
Garage:	533 sq. ft.
Side porch:	34 sq. ft.
Back porch:	192 sq. ft.

FEATURES

- Open floor plan has family room with columns, fireplace, triple French doors and 12' ceiling

- Master bath features double walk-in closets and vanities

- Bonus room above garage with private stairway

- Bedrooms separate from main living space for privacy

- 3 bedrooms, 2 1/2 baths, 2-car side entry garage

- Slab foundation

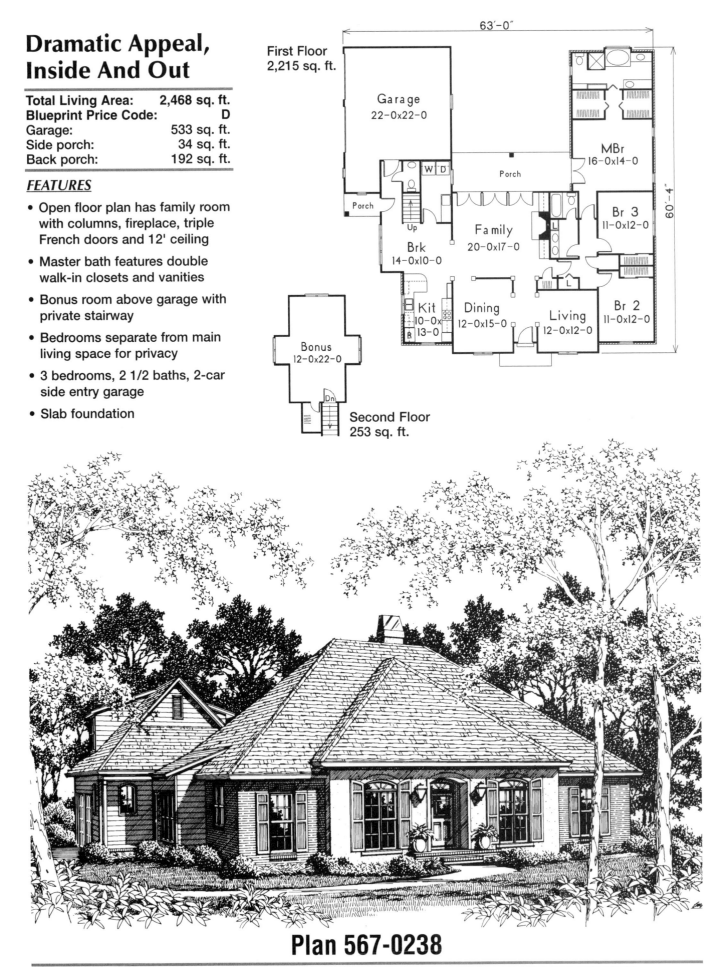

First Floor
2,215 sq. ft.

63'-0"

60'-4"

Garage
22-0x22-0

MBr
16-0x14-0

Br 3
11-0x12-0

Porch

Porch

Up

W D

Brk
14-0x10-0

Family
20-0x17-0

Kit
10-0x
13-0

Dining
12-0x15-0

Living
12-0x12-0

Br 2
11-0x12-0

Bonus
12-0x22-0

Dn

Second Floor
253 sq. ft.

Plan 567-0238

Stylish Features Enhance Open Living

Total Living Area:	1,846 sq. ft.
Blueprint Price Code:	C
Garage:	528 sq. ft.
Front porch:	38 sq. ft.

FEATURES

- Enormous living area combines with dining and breakfast rooms complemented by extensive windows and high ceilings

- Master bedroom has walk-in closet and display niche

- Secondary bedrooms share a bath and feature large closet space and a corner window

- Oversized two-car garage has plenty of storage and work space with handy access to the kitchen through the utility area

- Breakfast nook has wrap-around windows adding to eating enjoyment

- 3 bedrooms, 2 baths, 2-car garage

- Slab foundation

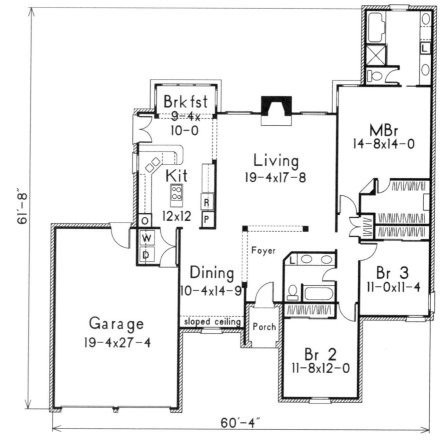

Plan 567-0215

Provides Family Living At Its Best

Total Living Area:	**1,993 sq. ft.**
Blueprint Price Code:	**D**
Garage:	484 sq. ft.
Front entry:	37 sq. ft.

FEATURES

- Spacious country kitchen with fireplace and plenty of natural light from windows

- Formal dining room features large bay window and steps down to sunken living room

- Master suite features corner windows, plant shelves and deluxe private bath

- Entry opens into vaulted living room with windows flanking the fireplace

- 3 bedrooms, 2 baths, 2-car garage

- Basement foundation

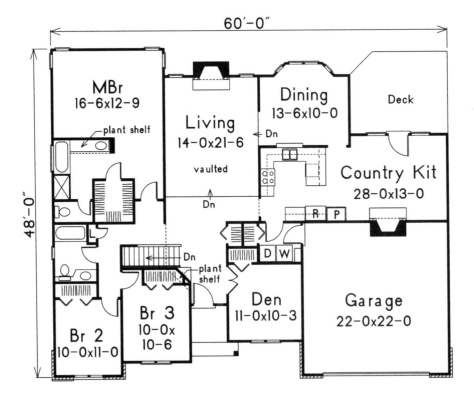

Plan 567-0279

Country Sun

- This home's inviting living room features a bright fireplace and proximity to the dining room, where French doors access a porch and a sunny patio.
- The island kitchen has plenty of counter space and a handy pass-through to the adjoining sun room, which is perfect for curling up with a good book.
- In a secluded corner of the home, the master suite enjoys privacy and a luxurious full bath.

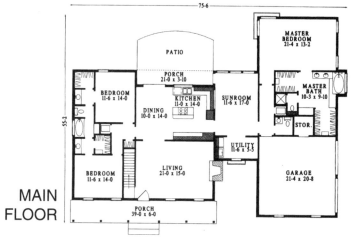

MAIN FLOOR

Plan 567-J-90014

Plan 567-J-90014

Bedrooms: 3	Baths: 2½
Living Area:	
Main floor	2,190 sq. ft.
Total Living Area:	**2,190 sq. ft.**
Standard basement	2,190 sq. ft.
Garage	465 sq. ft.
Storage	34 sq. ft.
Exterior Wall Framing:	2x4
Foundation Options:	
Standard basement	
Crawlspace	
Slab	
(Please specify foundation type when ordering.)	
BLUEPRINT PRICE CODE:	C

Deluxe Suite!

- Decorative corner quoins, arched windows and a sleek hip roofline give this charming home a European look.
- High half- and quarter-round windows brighten the living room; the dining room is enhanced by elegant columns.
- The island kitchen features a pantry and a sunny breakfast bay. A pass-through over the sink serves the family room.
- The deluxe master suite includes a private sitting room with a romantic two-sided fireplace. The master bath boasts a garden tub, a three-sided mirror and a dual-sink vanity.

MAIN FLOOR

Plan 567-HFB-5154-GEOR

Bedrooms: 3	Baths: 2½
Living Area:	
Main floor	2,236 sq. ft.
Total Living Area:	**2,236 sq. ft.**
Daylight basement	2,236 sq. ft.
Garage	483 sq. ft.
Exterior Wall Framing:	2x4
Foundation Options:	
Daylight basement	
Crawlspace	
(Please specify foundation type when ordering.)	
BLUEPRINT PRICE CODE:	C

Plan 567-HFB-5154-GEOR

Interesting Roof Lines And Appealing Use Of Brick

Total Living Area:	**2,520 sq. ft.**
Blueprint Price Code:	**D**
Garage:	480 sq. ft.
Front entry:	24 sq. ft.

FEATURES

- Open hearth fireplace warms family and breakfast rooms

- Master suite features private bath with deluxe tub, double-bowl vanity and large walk-in closet

- Vaulted living and dining rooms flank foyer

- Corner sink in kitchen overlooks family and breakfast rooms

- 4 bedrooms, 2 1/2 baths, 2-car side entry garage

- Basement foundation, drawings also include crawl space and slab foundations

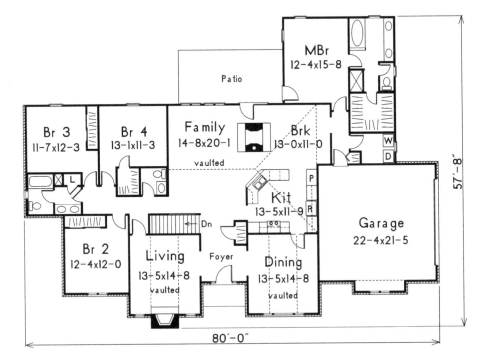

Plan 567-0250

Dramatic Roof Line Accents This Ranch

Total Living Area: 2,260 sq. ft.
Blueprint Price Code: D
Garage: 488 sq. ft.
Front porch: 38 sq. ft.

FEATURES

- Luxurious master suite includes raised ceiling, bath with oversized tub, separate shower and large walk-in closet

- Convenient kitchen and breakfast area with ample pantry storage

- Formal foyer leads into large living room with warming fireplace

- Convenient secondary entrance for everyday traffic

- 3 bedrooms, 2 baths, 2-car garage

- Slab foundation

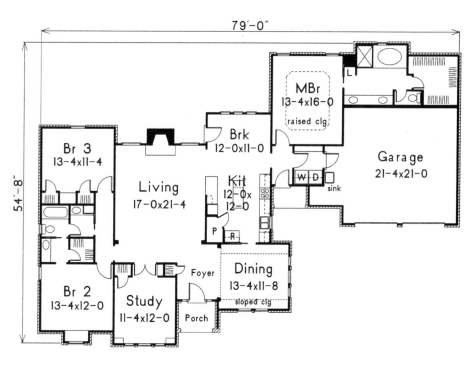

Plan 567-0245

Spacious Country-Style

- This distinctive country-style home is highlighted by a wide front porch and multi-paned windows with shutters.
- Inside, the dining room is to the left of the foyer and opens to the living room. It is defined by elegant columns and beams above.
- The central living room boasts a cathedral ceiling, a fireplace and French doors to the rear patio.
- Designed for both work and play, the delightful kitchen and breakfast nook enjoy natural light from two kitchen windows and a large bay in the nook.
- A handy utility room and a half-bath lie on either side of a short hallway leading to the carport.
- The master suite offers his-and-hers walk-in closets and an incredible bath that incorporates a plant shelf above the raised spa tub.
- The two remaining bedrooms share a hall bath that is compartmentalized to allow more than one user at a time.

Plan 567-J-86140

Bedrooms: 3	Baths: 2½
Living Area:	
Main floor	2,177 sq. ft.
Total Living Area:	**2,177 sq. ft.**
Standard basement	2,177 sq. ft.
Carport	440 sq. ft.
Storage	120 sq. ft.
Exterior Wall Framing:	2x4

Foundation Options:

Standard basement
Crawlspace
Slab
(Please specify foundation type when ordering.)

BLUEPRINT PRICE CODE: C

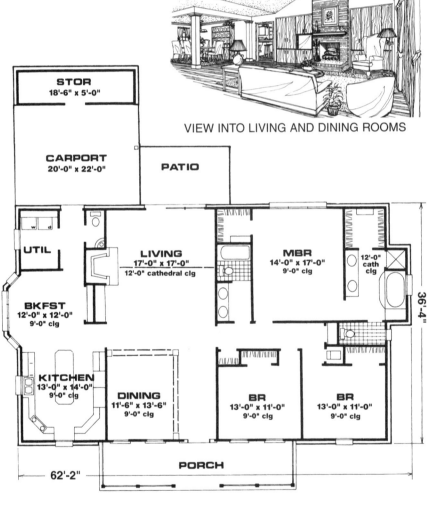

VIEW INTO LIVING AND DINING ROOMS

MAIN FLOOR

Plan 567-J-86140

Contagious Enthusiasm

- It will be difficult to contain your enthusiasm for this well-planned one-story home. The elegant foyer allows views of the formal dining room on the right and the living room on the left.
- The dining room is graced by a lovely bay window. The living room, with its high ceiling, features an impressive fireplace flanked by tall windows. Both of these spacious rooms nicely lend themselves to formal entertaining.

- The bright breakfast room—which has a pretty, built-in hutch—opens into the up-to-date kitchen. A handy utility room is nearby.
- The left wing of the home contains the bedrooms. Two front bedrooms have generous closet space and share a compartmentalized hall bath.
- The luxurious master bedroom boasts a built-in desk, bookshelves and fine French doors leading to a cozy, covered rear porch.
- The master bath is the picture of opulence, with its corner Jacuzzi tub, separate shower, big walk-in closet and dual-sink vanity.

Plan 567-L-91-FB	
Bedrooms: 3	**Baths:** 2
Living Area:	
Main floor	2,093 sq. ft.
Total Living Area:	**2,093 sq. ft.**
Garage	481 sq. ft.
Exterior Wall Framing:	2x4
Foundation Options:	
Slab	
(Please specify foundation type when ordering.)	
BLUEPRINT PRICE CODE:	C

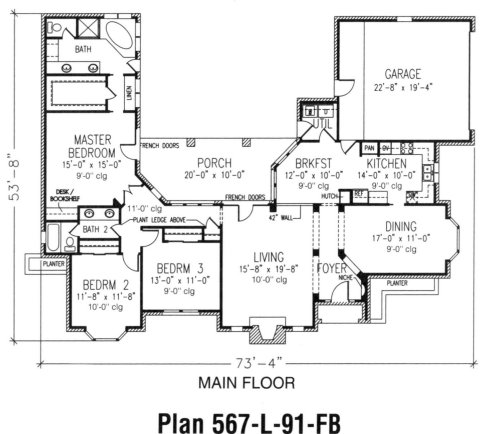

MAIN FLOOR

Plan 567-L-91-FB

A Real Charmer

- A tranquil railed porch makes this country one-story a real charmer.
- The main entry opens directly into the Great Room, which serves as the home's focal point. A cathedral ceiling soars above, while a fireplace and a built-in cabinet for games make the space a fun gathering spot.
- Beautiful French doors expand the Great Room to a peaceful covered porch at the rear of the home. Open the doors and let in the fresh summer air!
- A bayed breakfast nook unfolds from the kitchen, where the family cook will love the long island snack bar and the pantry. The carport is located nearby to save steps when you unload groceries.
- Across the home, the master bedroom features a walk-in closet with built-in shelves. A cathedral ceiling tops the master bath, which boasts a private toilet, a second walk-in closet and a separate tub and shower.
- A skylighted hall bath services the two secondary bedrooms.

Plan 567-J-9508

Bedrooms: 3	Baths: 2½
Living Area:	
Main floor	1,875 sq. ft.
Total Living Area:	**1,875 sq. ft.**
Standard basement	1,875 sq. ft.
Carport	418 sq. ft.
Storage	114 sq. ft.
Exterior Wall Framing:	2x4

Foundation Options:

Standard basement

Crawlspace

Slab

(Please specify foundation type when ordering.)

BLUEPRINT PRICE CODE:	**B**

MAIN FLOOR

Plan 567-J-9508

Genteel Luxury

- This extraordinary home offers count-less details and genteel luxury.
- In the foyer, an elegant marble floor and an 11-ft. ceiling define the sunny space.
- A fireplace serves as the focal point of the living room, which extends to the dining room to isolate formal affairs. The dining room features a bay window and a French door to a lush courtyard. Both rooms feature 11-ft. ceilings.
- A columned serving counter separates the kitchen from the breakfast nook and the family room. A convenient built-in desk to the right is a great place to jot down a grocery list.
- A 14-ft. ceiling soars over the versatile family room, where a corner fireplace and a French door to the backyard are great additions.
- A 10-ft. stepped ceiling, a romantic fire-place, a quiet desk and access to the backyard make the master bedroom an inviting retreat. A luxurious raised tub and a sit-down shower highlight the master bath, which also includes a neat dressing table between two sinks.
- Two more bedrooms, one with an 11-ft. ceiling and a bay window, share a bath.
- Unless otherwise mentioned, each room includes a 9-ft. ceiling.

Plan 567-L-483-HB

Bedrooms: 3	Baths: 2
Living Area:	
Main floor	2,481 sq. ft.
Total Living Area:	**2,481 sq. ft.**
Garage	706 sq. ft.
Exterior Wall Framing:	2 x 4

Foundation Options:

Slab
(Please specify foundation type when ordering.)

BLUEPRINT PRICE CODE: C

VIEW INTO KITCHEN

REAR VIEW

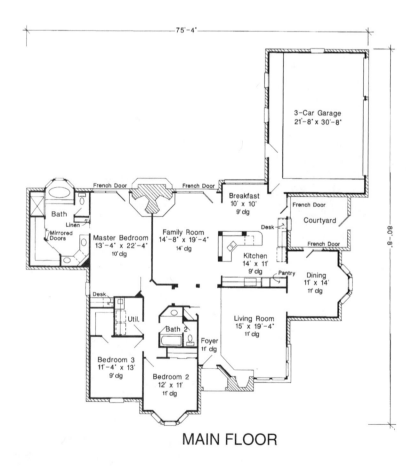

MAIN FLOOR

Plan 567-L-483-HB

Charming Design Features Home Office

Total Living Area:	**2,452 sq. ft.**
Blueprint Price Code:	**D**
Garage:	624 sq. ft.
Front porch:	72 sq. ft.

FEATURES

- Cheery and spacious room with private entrance, guest bath, two closets, vaulted ceiling, and transomed window perfect for home office or a 4th bedroom

- Delightful great room with vaulted ceiling, fireplace, storage closets and patio doors to deck

- Extra-large kitchen features walk-in pantry, cooktop island and bay window

- Vaulted master suite includes transomed windows, walk-in closet and luxurious bath

- 4 bedrooms, 2 1/2 baths, 3-car garage

- Basement foundation

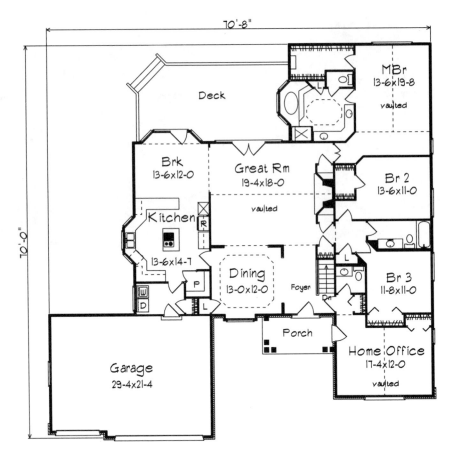

Plan 567-0368

Comfortable Family Living In This Ranch

Total Living Area:	**1,994 sq. ft.**
Blueprint Price Code:	**D**
Garage:	430 sq. ft.
Storage:	94 sq. ft.
Front entry:	40 sq. ft.

FEATURES

- Convenient entrance from the garage into the main living space through the utility room

- Standard 9' ceilings, bedroom #2 features a 12' vaulted ceiling and a 10' ceiling in the dining room

- Master bedroom offers a full bath with oversized tub, separate shower and walk-in closet

- Entry leads to formal dining room and attractive living room with double French doors and fireplace

- 3 bedrooms, 2 baths, 2-car garage

- Slab foundation

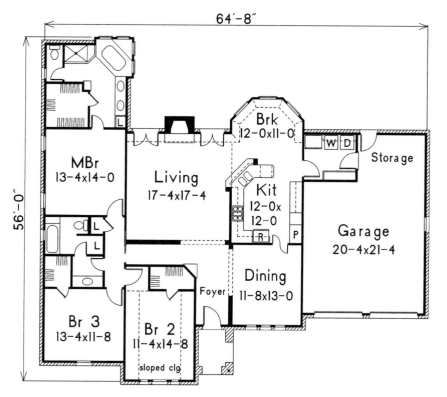

Plan 567-0244

Classic Elegance

Total Living Area:	2,483 sq. ft.
Blueprint Price Code:	**D**
Garage:	454 sq. ft.
Front porch:	135 sq. ft.

FEATURES

- A large entry porch with open brick arches and palladian door welcomes guests

- The vaulted great room features an entertainment center alcove and ideal layout for furniture placement

- Dining room is extra large with a stylish tray ceiling

- 4 bedrooms, 2 baths, 2-car side entry garage

- Basement foundation

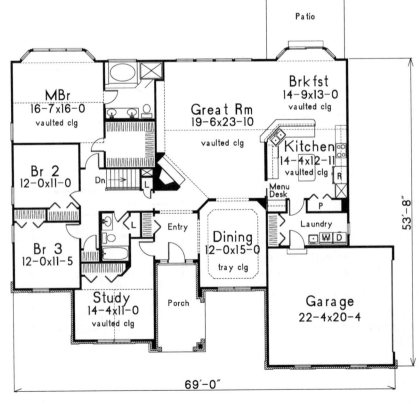

Plan 567-0719

Impressive Master Suite

Total Living Area:	**2,287 sq. ft.**
Blueprint Price Code:	**E**
Garage:	450 sq. ft.
Front porch:	48 sq. ft.
Back patio:	428 sq. ft.

FEATURES

- Double-doors lead into an impressive master suite which accesses covered porch and features deluxe bath with double closets and step-up tub

- Kitchen easily serves formal and informal areas of home

- The spacious foyer opens into formal dining and living rooms

- 4 bedrooms, 2 1/2 baths, 2-car side entry garage

- Slab foundation

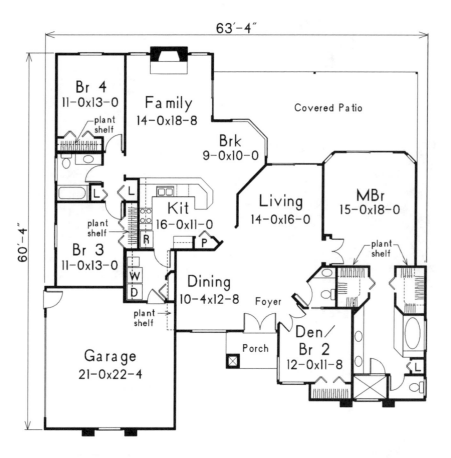

Plan 567-0339

Mark Englund/HomeStyles

Picture-Perfect!

- With stately columns and graceful arches, the wonderful front porch makes this home the picture of country charm. Quaint dormers and shutters add more style.
- Inside, the foyer shows off sidelights and a fantail transom. The dining room opens to the right of the foyer, and boasts elegant arched windows overlooking the porch.
- The central living room is enhanced by a fireplace and a pair of French doors to a skylighted porch.
- The spacious kitchen features an island cooktop, a snack bar and a sunny breakfast nook.
- A Palladian window arrangement brightens the sitting alcove in the master suite. Other highlights include private porch access and a fantastic bath with a garden tub, a separate shower and twin walk-in closets.
- The future upper floor presents a wealth of opportunities for expansion.

Plan 567-J-9401

Bedrooms: 3+	Baths: 2½
Living Area:	
Main floor	2,089 sq. ft.
Total Living Area:	**2,089 sq. ft.**
Future upper floor	878 sq. ft.
Standard basement	2,089 sq. ft.
Garage and storage	530 sq. ft.
Exterior Wall Framing:	2x4

Foundation Options:

Standard basement

Crawlspace

Slab

(Please specify foundation type when ordering.)

BLUEPRINT PRICE CODE:	C

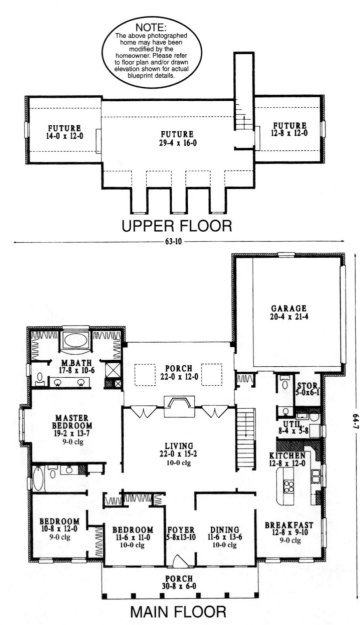

NOTE:
The above photographed home may have been modified by the homeowner. Please refer to floor plan and/or drawn elevation shown for actual blueprint details.

UPPER FLOOR

FUTURE 14-0 x 12-0

FUTURE 29-4 x 16-0

FUTURE 12-8 x 12-0

63-10

MAIN FLOOR

GARAGE 20-4 x 21-4

M.BATH 17-8 x 10-6

PORCH 22-0 x 12-0

STOR. 5-0x6-1

MASTER BEDROOM 19-2 x 13-7 9-0 clg

LIVING 22-0 x 15-2 10-0 clg

UTIL. 8-4 x 5-8

KITCHEN 12-8 x 12-0

BEDROOM 10-8 x 12-0 9-0 clg

BEDROOM 11-6 x 11-0 10-0 clg

FOYER 5-8x13-10

DINING 11-6 x 13-6 10-0 clg

BREAKFAST 12-8 x 9-10 9-0 clg

PORCH 30-8 x 6-0

64-7

Plan 567-J-9401

Strength of Character

- The solid, permanent feel of brick and the intelligent, efficient floor plan of this stately one-story home give it an obvious strength of character.

- Guests are welcomed inside by an attractive raised foyer, from which virtually any room can be reached with just a few steps.

- With a high ceiling, a built-in bookcase, a gorgeous fireplace and French doors that lead to the backyard, the centrally located living room is well equipped to serve as a hub of activity.

- Smartly designed and positioned, the galley-style kitchen easily serves the cozy breakfast nook and the formal dining room.

- The beautiful master bedroom provides a nice blend of elegance and seclusion, and features a striking stepped ceiling, a large walk-in closet, a private bath and its own access to the backyard.

- Two additional bedrooms feature walk-in closets and share a full-sized bath.

Plan 567-L-851-A

Bedrooms: 3	Baths: 2
Living Area:	
Main floor	1,849 sq. ft.
Total Living Area:	**1,849 sq. ft.**
Garage	437 sq. ft.
Exterior Wall Framing:	2x4
Foundation Options:	

Slab
(Please specify foundation type when ordering.)

BLUEPRINT PRICE CODE:	**B**

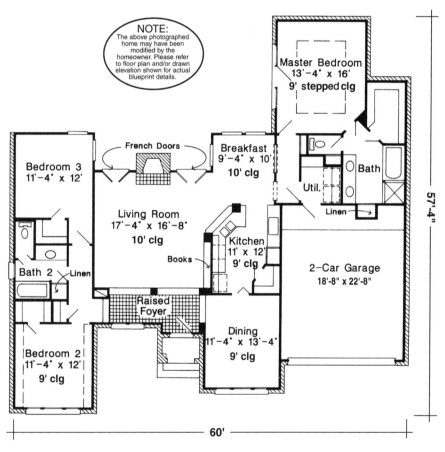

NOTE:
The above photographed home may have been modified by the homeowner. Please refer to floor plan and/or drawn elevation shown for actual blueprint details.

Mark Englund/HomeStyles

French Doors

Bedroom 3
11'-4" x 12'

Breakfast
9'-4" x 10'
10' clg

Master Bedroom
13'-4" x 16'
9' stepped clg

Bath

Util.

Linen

Living Room
17'-4" x 16'-8"
10' clg

Kitchen
11' x 12'
9' clg

Books

2-Car Garage
18'-8" x 22'-8"

Bath 2

Linen

Raised Foyer

Dining
11'-4" x 13'-4"
9' clg

Bedroom 2
11'-4" x 12'
9' clg

57'-4"

60'

MAIN FLOOR

Plan 567-L-851-A

LEFT VIEW

Mediterranean Splendor

- This splendid Mediterranean design has sunny living spaces both inside and out.
- Handsome double doors open to a huge covered porch/loggia. French doors beyond escort you into the tiled foyer. Windows along the left wall overlook a dramatic courtyard/arbor.
- Stately columns and overhead plant shelves accent the living and dining rooms, which are designed to view the courtyard. The living room features a built-in media center and a fireplace.
- The kitchen boasts a pantry, a Jenn-Air range, a serving counter and a sunny breakfast nook. A wet bar serves both the indoor and outdoor entertainment areas.
- The gorgeous master bedroom, crowned by a 9-ft. ceiling, shares a rotating entertainment cabinet and a see-through fireplace with the luxurious master bath. The bath includes a sunken bathing area and a huge walk-in closet.
- A second bedroom features a peaceful window seat, a walk-in closet and private bath access. The third bedroom also has a walk-in closet.
- For added spaciousness, all ceilings are 10 ft. high unless otherwise specified.

FRONT VIEW

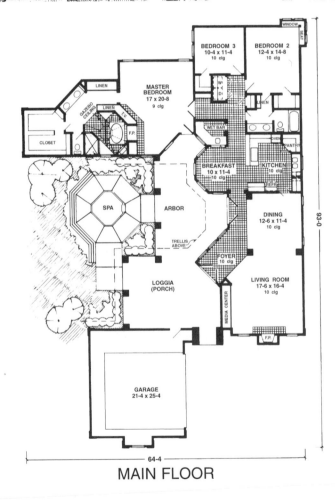

MAIN FLOOR

Plan 567-L-2176-MC

Bedrooms: 3	Baths: 2
Living Area:	
Main floor	2,176 sq. ft.
Total Living Area:	**2,176 sq. ft.**
Garage	549 sq. ft.
Exterior Wall Framing:	2x4

Foundation Options:

Slab
(Please specify foundation type when ordering.)

BLUEPRINT PRICE CODE:	C

Plan 567-L-2176-MC

Live the Dream

- Enjoy the home of your dreams with this beautiful yet practical design.
- Brick dominates the exterior to give it a look of noble permanence.
- At the heart of the interior is the huge living room, which is highlighted by a cozy corner fireplace and access to a brilliant screened porch in back. A serving counter shared with the kitchen holds hors d'oeuvres during parties.
- A big corner pantry and a center island give the kitchen an extra dash of efficiency. Centered between the formal dining room and the casual breakfast nook, it's ready for any culinary mood.
- Luxurious is the word for the stunning master suite, which features two large walk-in closets and a sumptuous private bath with a gorgeous garden tub.
- Each of the two secondary bedrooms boasts a walk-in closet and access to a full bath. The rearmost bedroom has French doors leading out to the porch.
- A secluded study easily converts to a fourth bedroom.

Plan 567-L-363-MSB

Bedrooms: 3+	Baths: 3
Living Area:	
Main floor	2,361 sq. ft.
Total Living Area:	**2,361 sq. ft.**
Screened porch	214 sq. ft.
Garage and storage	512 sq. ft.
Exterior Wall Framing:	2x4
Foundation Options:	
Slab	
(Please specify foundation type when ordering.)	
BLUEPRINT PRICE CODE:	C

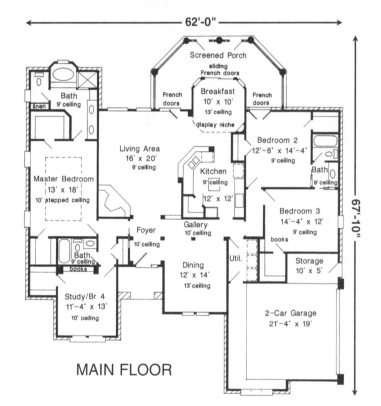

MAIN FLOOR

REAR VIEW

Plan 567-L-363-MSB

Secluded Kitchen, Center Of Activity

Total Living Area: 1,882 sq. ft.
Blueprint Price Code: C
Garage: 447 sq. ft.

FEATURES

- Handsome brick facade

- Spacious great room and dining room combination brightened by unique corner windows and patio access

- Well-designed kitchen incorporates breakfast bar peninsula, sweeping casement window above sink and walk-in pantry island

- Master suite features large walk-in closet and private bath with bay window

- 4 bedrooms, 2 baths, 2-car side entry garage

- Basement foundation

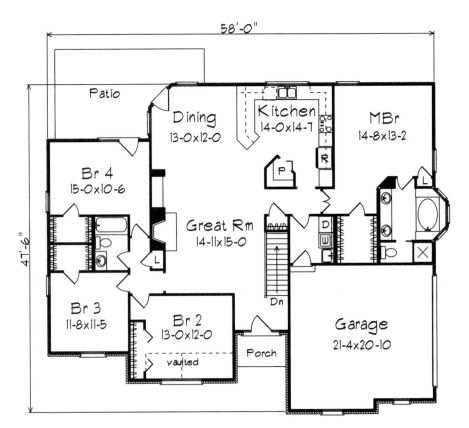

Plan 567-0419

Country Home With Front Orientation

Total Living Area: 2,029 sq. ft.
Blueprint Price Code: C
Garage: 460 sq. ft.
Front left porch: 74 sq. ft.
Front right porch: 330 sq. ft.

FEATURES

- Stonework, gables, roof dormer and double porches create a country flavor

- Kitchen enjoys extravagant cabinetry and counterspace in a bay, island snack bar, built-in pantry and cheery dining area with multiple tall windows

- Angled stair descends from large entry with wood columns and is open to vaulted great room with corner fireplace

- Master bedroom boasts walk-in closets, opulent master bath and private porch

- 4 bedrooms, 2 baths, 2-car side entry garage

- Basement foundation

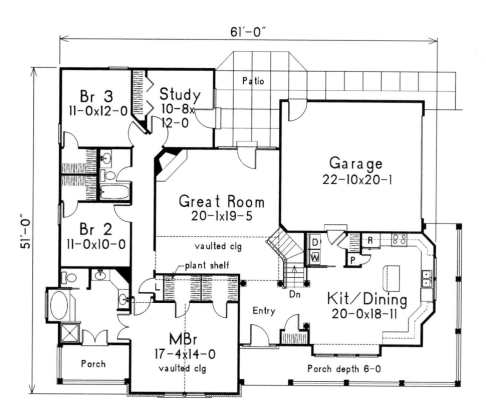

Plan 567-0712

Traditional Exterior, Handsome Accents

Total Living Area:	**1,882 sq. ft.**
Blueprint Price Code:	**D**
Garage:	430 sq. ft.
Front porch:	46 sq. ft.
Back porch:	72 sq. ft.

FEATURES

- Wide, handsome entrance opens to the vaulted great room with fireplace
- Living and dining areas are conveniently joined but still allow privacy
- Private covered porch extends breakfast area
- Practical passageway runs through laundry and mud room from garage to kitchen
- Vaulted ceiling in master bedroom
- 3 bedrooms, 2 baths, 2-car garage
- Basement foundation

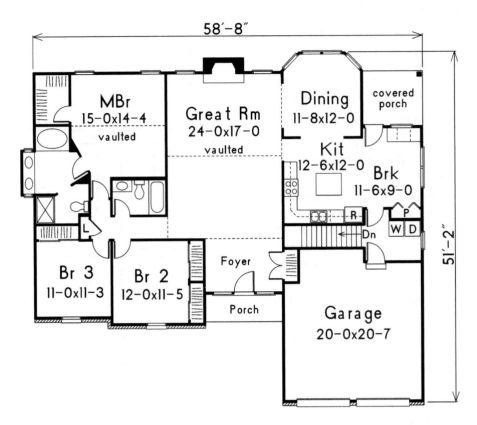

Plan 567-0162

High Luxury in One Story

VIEW INTO LIVING ROOM

- Beautiful arched windows lend a luxurious feeling to the exterior of this one-story home.
- Soaring, high ceilings add volume to both the wide entry area and the central living room, which boasts a large fireplace and access to a backyard porch and the patio beyond.
- Double doors separate the formal dining room from the corridor-style kitchen. Features of the kitchen include a pantry and an angled eating bar. The sunny, bayed eating area is perfect for casual family meals.
- The plush master suite has amazing amenities: a walk-in closet, a skylighted, angled whirlpool tub, a separate shower and private access to the laundry/utility room and the patio.
- Three good-sized bedrooms and a full bath are situated across the home.

Plan 567-E-2302

Bedrooms: 4	Baths: 2
Living Area:	
Main floor	2,396 sq. ft.
Total Living Area:	**2,396 sq. ft.**
Standard basement	2,396 sq. ft.
Garage	484 sq. ft.
Storage	84 sq. ft.
Exterior Wall Framing:	2x6

Foundation Options:
Standard basement
Crawlspace
Slab
(Please specify foundation type when ordering.)

BLUEPRINT PRICE CODE:	C

MAIN FLOOR

Plan 567-E-2302

HOME PLANS INDEX

HOME PLANS INDEX - *continued*

WHAT KIND OF PLAN PACKAGE DO YOU NEED?

Now that you've found the home plan you've been looking for, here are some suggestions on how to make your Dream Home a reality. To get started, order the type of plans that fit your particular situation.

YOUR CHOICES

The One-set package - This single set of blueprints is offered so you can study or review a home in greater detail. But a single set is never enough for construction and it's a copyright violation to reproduce blueprints.

The Minimum 5-set package - If you're ready to start the construction process, this 5-set package is the minimum number of blueprint sets you will need. It will require keeping close track of each set so they can be used by multiple subcontractors and tradespeople.

The Standard 8-set package - For best results in terms of cost, schedule and quality of construction, we recommend you order eight (or more) sets of blueprints. Besides one set for yourself, additional sets of blueprints will be required by your mortgage lender, local building department, general contractor and all subcontractors working on foundation, electrical, plumbing, heating/air conditioning, carpentry work, etc.

Reproducible Masters - If you wish to make some minor design changes, you'll want to order reproducible masters. These drawings contain the same information as the blueprints but are printed on erasable and reproducible paper. This will allow your builder or a local design professional to make the necessary drawing changes without the major expense of redrawing the plans. This package also allows you to print as many copies of the modified plans as you need.

Mirror Reverse Sets - Plans can be printed in mirror reverse. These plans are useful when the house would fit your site better if all the rooms were on the opposite side than shown. They are simply a mirror image of the original drawings causing the lettering and dimensions to read backwards. Therefore, when ordering mirror reverse drawings, you must purchase at least one set of right reading plans.

ORDER FORM

IMPORTANT INFORMATION TO KNOW
BEFORE YOU ORDER YOUR HOME PLANS

- **Building Codes & Requirements -** Our plans conform to most national building codes. However, they may not comply completely with your local building regulations. Some counties and municipalities have their own building codes, regulations and requirements. The assistance of a local builder, architect or other building professional may be necessary to modify the drawings to comply with your area's specific requirements. We recommend you consult with your local building officials prior to beginning construction.

- **Exchange Policies -** Since blueprints are printed in response to your order, we cannot honor requests for refunds. However, if for some reason you find that the plan you have purchased does not meet your requirements, you may exchange that plan for another plan in our collection. At the time of the exchange, you will be charged a processing fee of 25% of your original plan package price, plus the difference in price between the plan packages (if applicable) and the cost to ship the new plans to you.

  Please note: Reproducible drawings can only be exchanged if the package is unopened, and exchanges are allowed only within 90 days of purchase.

- **Remember To Order Your Material List -** You'll get faster and more accurate bids and you'll save money by paying for only the materials you need. *Please call for availability.*

Plan prices guaranteed through December 31, 2001

BLUEPRINT PRICE SCHEDULE

Price Code	One-Set	SAVE $75.00 Five-Sets	SAVE $150.00 Eight-Sets	Material List*	Reproducible Masters
AAA	$195	$260	$290	$40	$390
AA	245	310	340	45	440
A	295	360	390	45	490
B	345	410	440	45	540
C	395	460	490	50	590
D	445	510	540	50	640
E	495	560	590	50	690

OTHER OPTIONS
Additional Plan Set*........ $35.00
Print in Mirror Reverse*.......add $5.00 per set

Rush Charges............Next Day Air $38.00
Second Day Air..$25.00

Available only within 90 days after purchase of plan package or reproducible masters of same plan.

ORDER FORM

Please send me Plan Number: **567-**_____
Blueprint Price Code _____ *(See Home Plan Index)*

- ☐ Reproducible Masters — $_____
- ☐ Eight-Set Plan Package — $_____
- ☐ Five-Set Plan Package — $_____
- ☐ One-Set Plan Package (no mirror reverse) — $_____
- ☐ ___(Qty) Additional Plan Sets ($35.00each) — $_____
- ☐ Print___(Qty.) sets in Mirror Reverse (add $5.00/set) $_____
- ☐ Material List (call for availability) — $_____
- SUBTOTAL — $_____
- Sales Tax (MO residents add 7%) — $_____
- ☐ Rush Charges — $_____
- Shipping & Handling — $ **12.50**
- Total Enclosed (US funds only) — $_____

☐ Enclosed is my check or money order payable to HDA, Inc.
  (Sorry, no COD's) Please note that plans are not returnable

Mail To: Sunset/HDA, Inc.
4390 Green Ash Drive
St. Louis, MO 63045

I hereby authorize HDA, Inc. to charge this purchase to my credit card account (check one):

☐ MasterCard ☐ VISA ☐ DISCOVER NOVUS ☐ AMERICAN EXPRESS Cards

My card number is_____
The expiration date is _____
Signature_____
Name_____
  Print or type
Street Address_____
  Do not use PO Box
City, State, Zip_____
My daytime phone number (_____) - ____ - _____
I am a ☐Builder/Contractor ☐Homeowner ☐Renter
I ☐have ☐have not selected my general contractor.
Thank you for your order!